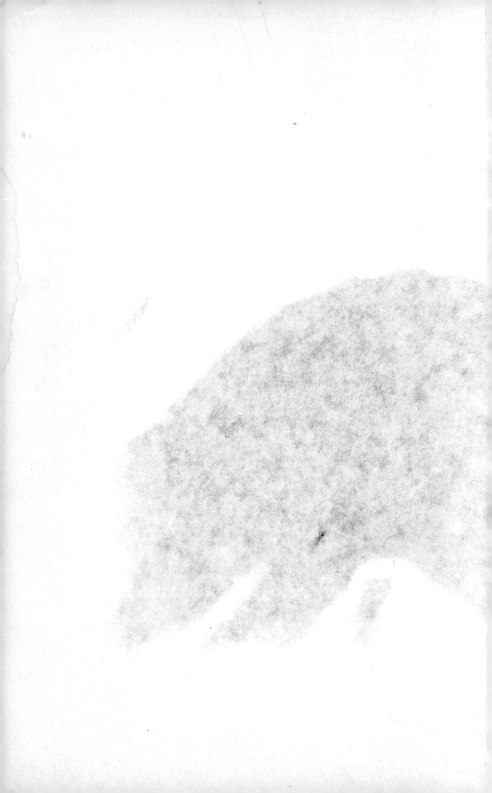

The Pound in Your Pocket 1870–1970

THE POUND IN YOUR POCKET 1870-1970

Peter Wilsher

CASSELL · LONDON

CASSELL & COMPANY LTD
35 Red Lion Square, London, WC1
Melbourne, Sydney, Toronto
Johannesburg, Auckland

First published 1970

I.S.B.N. 0 304 93661 8

Printed by
The Camelot Press Ltd,
London and Southampton

F. 870

Contents

Acknowledgements

A book like this is essentially a patchwork, put together from books, magazines, newspapers, old railway time-tables, reminiscences, memoirs and the kind of conversation that begins, 'Ah, when I was a lad, you could buy four pints of beer and a corn-cob pipe for a shilling, and still have enough change left for a seven-course meal at the Savoy. . . .' It would be impossible to list all the people who have contributed, one way and another, to the magpie hoard of facts, figures and prices which are now collected in my notebooks, but several names must be mentioned. I should like to thank the Editor of the *Sunday Times*, Harold Evans, for not only providing me with time to work on the project, but for his encouragement and his kindness in letting me reproduce several charts which made their first appearance in his pages. My colleagues on the *Sunday Times Business News* and the staff of the *Sunday Times* Library have been endlessly free with help, ideas and forbearance, and George Schwartz, in particular, has been a mine of esoteric information. Rex Clifford prepared material for the graphs on pages 125 and 156, and my father, H. S. Wilsher, performed prodigies of research in the British Museum Newspaper Library. The Army & Navy Stores were kind enough to let me consult their unique run of catalogues, stretching from 1871 to 1939. Mr Rob Robinson, of Distillers Company Ltd, kindly provided the whisky prices on p. 131. And my wife, Phoebe, bore manfully with an orgy of comparison shopping, such as no housewife should be asked to undertake.

I would like to thank the various companies, government departments and museums who have given me permission to reproduce photographs and advertisements (or parts of advertisements) still in copyright, to illustrate this book. I should stress that the advertisements have not always been reproduced to their original size, and that they do not necessarily represent any part of the present policies of the advertisers. Similarly, my captions are not, and are not intended to be, a commentary on the advertisers themselves, their policies or products: my concern has been simply to illustrate in a varied and I hope entertaining way some of the yardsticks by which we, our parents and our grandparents, might have measured the value of our pound during the past hundred years. I therefore acknowledge with gratitude the interest and co-operation of the following:

Cardin dress—Selfridges Ltd; various advertisements from *Yesterday's Shopping* (David & Charles, 1969)—Army & Navy Stores; Rover car—The Rover Company Ltd; Cruises to Norway—Furness, Withy & Co. Ltd; Broads holiday—British Railways, Eastern Region; New Sweater Suit—Harvey Nichols & Co. Ltd; Morris-Cowley car—British Leyland (Austin-Morris) Limited; A.M.C. typewriter—Harrods Limited; The Gamage Roller—A. W. Gamage Ltd; Kendals Sale—Kendal Milne & Co.; Player's—John Player and Sons; Aristoc—W. L. Arber Ltd; An umbrella (1931) and Sports jackets (1949)—Lewis's Ltd; Whisky—Matthew Gloag & Son Limited; Grosvenor House—Grosvenor House and Partnerplan Ltd; Galeries Lafayette—Galeries Lafayette Ltd; Portable Battery Receiver—The Ever Ready Company Ltd; H.M.V. Radiogram— E.M.I. Ltd; Aer Lingus—Aer Lingus, Irish Air Lines; Spangles— Mars Limited; Postal charges—Post Office; Murphy TV—The Rank Organization; Fry's Crunch—Cadbury Schweppes Ltd; Vidor Vagabond—Crompton Parkinson Limited; Switzerland—Swiss National Tourist Office and Rex, Stewart & Associates (London) Ltd; Babycham—Showerings Ltd; Green Shield stamps—Green Shield Trading Stamp Co. Ltd; Graduating 1967?—Department of Education and Science; Oceanic Unit Trust—First Finsbury Trust Limited and Derek Dale & Co.; Half-crown—Decimal Currency Board. I would also like to acknowledge the assistance of those newspapers in whose pages many of these advertisements appeared.

I would like also to thank the following for their help in finding, producing, and giving me permission to reproduce illustrations; Peter Clayton; The British Museum and the British Museum Newspaper Library; Peter Jackson; Dorothy Hartley; William Heinemann Ltd; Press Association; Derek Roberts, The Southern Veteran-Cycle Club; Cunard Line; Duncan Haws; Abbot's Hall Museum of Rural Life of East Anglia; University of Reading, Museum of English Rural Life; Birmingham Public Libraries; the *Guardian*; the *Daily Mail*; Hereford City Library; *Farmer's Weekly*; Camera Press Ltd; George G. Harrap & Co. Ltd.

Photography at the British Museum and the British Museum Newspaper Library by John Freeman & Co. (Photographers) Ltd; copy photography by Morgan-Wells Ltd; other photographs by W. G. Belcher, A.R.P.S., and Kershaw Studios.

The poem by Professor Kenneth Boulding on page 9 is reprinted by kind permission from the March 1969 issue of the *Michigan Business Review*, published by Michigan University's Graduate School of Business Studies. William Whiteley's Christmas Gift List 1957 on page 202 is reprinted by kind permission of William Whiteley Ltd.

P. W.

The Pound in Your Pocket

Money does not make the world go round but,
at least, it greases the axis.

Professor A. A. Walters:
Money in Boom and Slump
(Institute of Economic Affairs, 1969)

This is a book about money. In particular, it concerns itself with the recent history of the Pound Sterling, a token of considerable potency and charisma which has acted continuously as a symbol and index of British power, sovereignty, wealth and ability to make a noise in the world for over nine hundred years. William the Conqueror laid it down as our national standard of value in AD 1067—building on the foundations laid by King Offa of Mercia, who first caused a pound weight of silver to be minted into 240 pennies around the year AD 760—and it has been inextricably woven into the political, social and economic life of these islands ever since.

In February 1971, with the advent of Decimalization, the £1/240 penny finally disappears, along with the farthing, the groat, the noble, the royal, the angel, the ora, the teston, the half-crown, the golden guinea, and all the other bits and pieces which have fallen along our monetary wayside. But the pound goes on—depreciated, devalued, occasionally floating, subject to speculation, hot money flows, balance-of-payments weaknesses, inflation, deflation and every other ailment that a currency can suffer, and yet still the best yardstick, lubricant and repository that we have with which to conduct our infinitely complicated day-to-day affairs, both among ourselves and between us and the rest of the world.

The general feeling, both here and abroad, is, quite understandably, that the pound is not what it was. Domestically, as the somewhat depressing graph on page 3 demonstrates, its purchasing power has slumped dramatically—by four-fifths since Britain reached the peak of her nineteenth-century power in 1870; by six-sevenths since prices touched their Victorian low point in 1892; and by a full three-quarters just in the thirty-five years since the slump of the 1930s. Internationally, the endemic series of sterling crises in the 1950s and 1960s, the rising burden of foreign debt incurred to 'support the pound' and the vulnerability of our economic policies to every little flurry of trouble in the world mark only too clearly the distance we have moved since the Navy ruled the waves and the Bank of England dominated the exchanges. The full, and somewhat unhappy, story of the changing relationship between the pound and the dollar is vividly brought out in the chart on page 5.

To many observers the message is only too obvious—moral decay has set in, the national backbone has collapsed, and the whole place has been given over to the work-shy, the feather-bedded beneficiaries of the Welfare State, and the agents of the international conspiracy whose evil objective is to disrupt our honourable export drive. But such judgments—like 'The World is Going to the Dogs' and 'When *I* was a lad, I *helped* my parents. . . !'—are part of the perennial vocabulary of nostalgic grouch. It is much more interesting

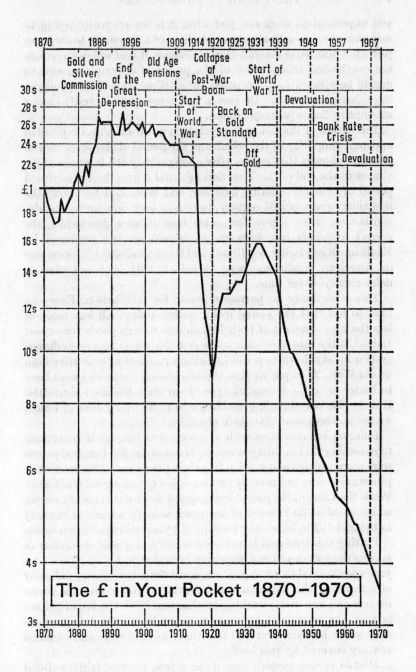

The £ in Your Pocket 1870–1970

and important to work out just what it is we are really trying to measure when we talk about the 'decline' of a currency; to diagnose just what disease, or combination of diseases, it is of which we reckon the overheated temperature of the pound is a symptom; and to decide how far we are prepared to go (Operation? Hot poultice? Psychiatric treatment? Or just a few more days in bed?) in our attempt to find a permanent cure.

The nature of the illness is anything but self-evident, despite the apparent simplicity of the pound and the pound–dollar fever charts. All these show is that prices, after a long steady fall from the 1870s almost to the end of the Victorian age, and a long, highly confused period of recovery, soaring inflation, and boom and bust over the first thirty years of this century, have now been on a pretty steady, continuous, rising course for nearly four decades. Meanwhile, the correct exchange rate between goods and services produced by Englishmen in English conditions and those produced by Americans in American conditions have varied—usually, but not always, deleteriously—over time.

This is certainly no particular cause for satisfaction. Everyone likes to feel that the pound in his pocket today will buy more or less the same amount of both British and foreign goods tomorrow. Indeed, if the rate of erosion is too fast the whole money-exchange system breaks down as it did in Germany and elsewhere after both World Wars. Then people virtually abandoned marks and went back to barter or to a cowrie-shell type of currency based on cigarettes. But despite our chronic grumbling about the rising cost of living, we are nowhere near that state of affairs.

Inflation has now been with us a long time (though it is salutary to remember that in thirty-seven years out of the last hundred people were more worried about price falls than price rises). But even while prices have risen, incomes, by and large, have risen a good deal faster. While the value of the pound has dropped like a stone, money wages, which stood at an average of not much over £2 a week as recently as the mid-1920s, have since multiplied by something over ten times.

Putting this into real terms—the amount of goods or services or satisfactions that you can purchase in exchange for an hour's or a year's work—and forgetting for a moment the extraordinary difficulty of comparing the horse-and-candle world of 1870 with the moon rockets and automatic washing-machines of 1970, the broad picture is that the return on an average person's labours has gone up somewhere between four and five times in the hectic and troubled century covered by this book.

Hostile critics abroad, and quite a few, usually fairly well-fed moralists at home have sometimes suggested that this is partly what

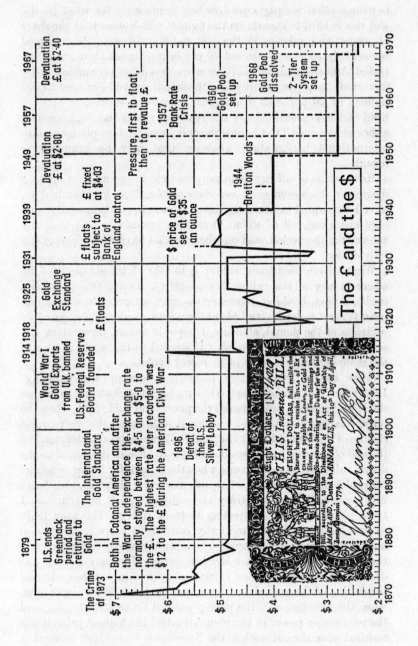

The £ and the $

1967 — Devaluation £ at $2·40

1968 Gold Pool dissolved
2-Tier System set up

1960 Gold Pool set up

1957 Bank Rate Crisis

Pressure, first to float, then to revalue £

1949 — Devaluation £ at $2·80

1944 Bretton Woods

£ fixed at $4·03

$ price of Gold set at $35 an ounce

£ floats subject to Bank of England control

1931 — Gold Exchange Standard

£ floats

1925 Gold Standard

1914 1918 — World War I
Gold Exports from U.K. banned
U.S. Federal Reserve Board founded

The International Gold Standard

Both in Colonial America and after the War of Independence the exchange rate normally stayed between $4·5 and $5·0 to the £. The highest rate ever recorded was $12 to the £ during the American Civil War

1896 — Defeat of the U.S. Silver Lobby

1879 — U.S. ends Greenback period and returns to Gold

The Crime of 1873

is wrong—that we pay ourselves too handsomely for what we do. But this is hard to sustain on the figures, which show that the share of wages and salaries in the real national income has remained remarkably constant—around 40 per cent—almost throughout the period. And although our short-term overseas debts have undoubtedly increased sharply in recent years, the sums involved—around £4,000 million, or 10 per cent of one year's national income, or £80 per head of the population—are not really anything like high enough, either to keep us all in Champagne and Jaguars, or to plunge us into international bankruptcy (whatever that may be supposed to mean).

However, it is not my main purpose here to produce yet another diagnostic discussion of *la maladie anglaise*. Nor, for that matter, have I attempted to usurp the job of the social, economic and monetary historians, all of whom have been intensively and fruitfully active over the period, and on whose work I have widely and gratefully drawn.

What I have tried to do, rather, is to take all those aspects of life where money is the ruling factor—prices, wages, taxes, welfare, credit, saving, banking, economic thought, attitudes to wealth and poverty, and so forth—and blend them into a series of photographic portraits of the pound, showing, I hope, in colour, perspective and several dimensions, the face that it showed to the world in nine of the more climacteric years of its recent evolution.

Some of the years chose themselves, almost automatically: 1925, when Churchill attempted to turn back the clock and to restore the High Victorian link between the pound and gold; 1931, when the project failed, just in time to save Britain from the very worst rigours of the Great Slump; 1949 and 1967, when devaluation marked the end of more or less misguided efforts to 'defend the pound to the death'; all these were moments when the pound, for better or worse, suffered a decisive change of course. For other chapters, the choice was necessarily more arbitrary and subjective, but in each case, I trust, significant and interesting features emerge. The year 1870, as well as being an arithmetically convenient place to start, also marks in many ways a watershed between the wholly unfettered and the increasingly conscience-stricken forms of money-making endeavour in Britain; 1886 and 1896 stood respectively at the nadir and the ending of the now-almost-forgotten Victorian Great Depression, when the rich groaned, the poor prospered (in relative terms), and the purchasing power of the pound reached the highest point it has touched since the outbreak of the Napoleonic Wars; 1909 ushered in Lloyd George's Old Age Pensions, and the real beginnings of the Welfare State; and 1957 was the year in which we were told that we

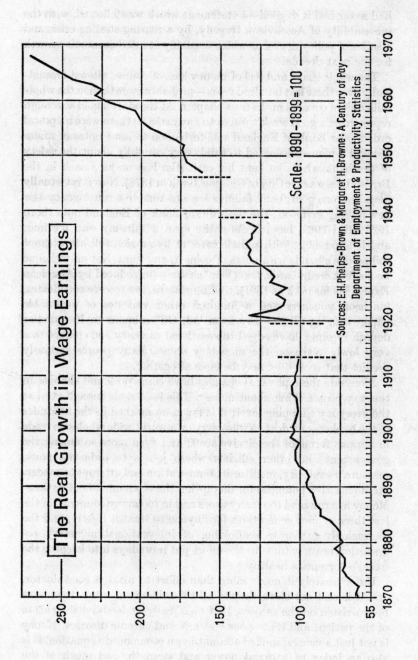

The Real Growth in Wage Earnings

Scale: 1890-1899 = 100

Sources: E.H.Phelps-Brown & Margaret H.Browne: A Century of Pay
Department of Employment & Productivity Statistics

had never had it so good—a statement which was followed, with the inevitability of Aeschylean tragedy, by a roaring sterling crisis and a series of policy decisions which arguably stunted economic growth for the next decade.

The whole shape and feel of money has, of course, altered dramatically over these last hundred years—probably more than in the whole millennium covered in the next chapter. At the start a gold sovereign represented a good week's wages to any artisan; there were no postal orders; the Bank of England was forbidden to issue notes of under £5; and a man still needed to think very carefully about the safety of the bank where he kept his cash (the last major smash in the British Isles was the City of Glasgow Bank in 1878). Now it is virtually illegal to own gold; bank failures are as a remote a contingency as a new Viking invasion; the ten-shilling Bank of England note (born 1928; died 1969) has run its entire span within my own lifetime; and it is possible, with a little care, to live a rich full life without soiling one's hands with notes or coins in any form. Not only cheque books, but credit cards, travellers' cheques (introduced by American Express as far back as 1891), trading stamps, tax reserve certificates, luncheon vouchers and a hundred other varieties of negotiable paper, ranging all the way from '3d. Off' coupons to Euro-dollar deposit receipts, have edged conventional currency and coinage to a very lowly place on the monetary scene. Many people seriously predict that soon they may be gone altogether.

Alongside these physical changes have come profound changes in the way people think about money. This is obvious enough even at the everyday shopping level; it is far more marked in the attitudes of the bankers and dealers who carry on a world-wide wholesale trade in various forms of the elusive stuff; and even more so among the government and other officials whose job is to order its flows, measure its velocity, monitor its temperature and attempt to moderate its massive potential for disrupting the economic life of nations. Money has run mad too many times and in too many countries in the last three or four generations for anyone to treat it lightly, and the increasingly elaborate scaffolding of international monetary co-operation bears witness to the effort put nowadays into keeping the world's currencies healthy.

Unfortunately it needs more than effort to make a good doctor, and it is still not clear, despite all the millions of words that have been written on the subject, that men really understand the nature of the patient and its various endemic and chronic diseases. Money is not just a neutral unit of account in an econometric equation, it is also an index of national power and strength, and much of the history of the last century can be read as part of the continuing conflict between the two concepts. One way and another that struggle enters into every chapter in this book, and there is little reason, as I write in 1970, to feel that it has finally been resolved. Not only has monetary nationalism by no means disappeared from the scene, but there is now a deep intellectual rift—commonly, though not wholly accurately, described as being between the disciples of Keynes, and the school headed by Milton Friedman and the staff of the International Monetary Fund—over both the importance and the best method of controlling the expansion of the world's (and the individual nation's) money supply. And more fundamentally, there is still widespread disagreement even about the basic question, 'What is Money?'

This is not new. A hundred and fifty years ago most men would have said money was gold but not banknotes. A hundred years ago they would have accepted notes but rejected bank-deposits. Forty years ago they would have agreed that current bank-deposits counted as money, but would have been doubtful (as some still are) about the inclusion of items like investments in building societies and trustee savings banks. And now there are all sorts of new problems. Is gold to be regarded as money nowadays, as it is progressively fenced off from day-to-day transactions? What about the Special Deposit Receipts recently introduced, after gargantuan diplomatic effort, to bolster the liquidity of the international banking system? And most controversial of all, what is the status of the $30,000 million worth of Euro-dollars created, at a stroke of the pen, by a world-wide regiment of anonymous bank cashiers over the last few years? Is this an augmentation of the world's money supply, or just a transformation of something that already existed? And does it matter? To such questions current theory offers only the most tentative and confusing answers. As Professor Kenneth Boulding neatly put it in a recent issue of the *University of Michigan Business Review*:

> We must have a good definition of Money,
> For if we do not, then what have we got,
> But a Quantity Theory of no-one-knows what,
> And this would be almost too true to be funny.

In its absence, one cannot help feel that claims to have achieved final mastery over the world's currency problems must be regarded as premature. The pound—if it survives as an independent entity, and is not absorbed into some all-embracing new Euro-Unit—can look forward to quite a few more vicissitudes yet to round off its long history.

A NOTE ON PRICES

The first question that people ask when they discuss the changing value of money is 'What was it worth x years ago?' It is a question almost impossible to answer, over periods of more than a decade or so—quality, design, legal standards, tastes, fashions and the patterns of people's spending change so much that no comparison will stand up to anything like scientific standards of rigour. For the purposes of this book, however, I have taken what all economists will regard as an unforgivably brutal grab at this nettle. I am well aware of the subtle pitfalls involved; of the divergences between the Paasch and Lespeyre approaches to index-making; of the ever-changing basis of the British civil service's cost-of-living statistics; of the inadequacy and wholesale-price bias of the earlier data; and all the rest. Here they are all ignored, in the interests of giving a broad-brush, order-of-magnitude indication of the kind of changes that have taken place. And to compound the methodological sin, I have placed at the head of each chapter a single, unqualified figure by which readers can convert the money of the year concerned into something like 1970 values. I apologize for this intolerably crude approach, and some of its deficiencies are referred to in the text when they really seem to affect the issue. But in general I feel that people will find an uncluttered conversion figure, however inadequate, better than a lot of semi-mystical economic double-talk. Just so long as no one takes it as gospel truth.

The Pound in 760

can be taken very approximately to represent something over £300 in 1970 money

Money, like certain other essential elements in civilization, is a far more ancient institution than we were taught to believe some few years ago. Its origins are lost in the mists when the ice was melting, and may well stretch back into the paradisaic intervals in human history of the interglacial periods, when the weather was delightful and the mind free to be fertile of new ideas—in the Islands of the Hesperides or Atlantis or some Eden of Central Asia.

J. M. Keynes: *A Treatise on Money*
(Macmillan, 1930)

The one obvious instrument of measurement available in social life is money. Hence the range of our enquiry becomes restricted to that part of social welfare that can be brought directly or indirectly into relation with the measuring rod of money.

A. C. Pigou: *Economics of Welfare*
(Macmillan, 1920)

Money of some kind had circulated in Britain long before the Romans came. The Angles, Jutes and Saxons were familiar with coins and with payments when they sailed up the east-coast estuaries to pillage and colonize. The Kentish kings fixed money-fines for murder in the sixth century, and failure to deliver up the necessary church-tribute carried a cash penalty probably as early as the seventh. But the continuous history of the English currency began with Offa, king of Mercia, in about AD 760. It was he who laid it down that two hundred and forty pennies were to be struck from a pound of silver. Soon afterwards Anglo-Saxon texts like the *Liber Eliensis* were explicitly referring to a shilling made up of twelve such silver pence, and describing specific deals, like the lump sum payment of 1,000 shillings for a West Midland estate, in or before the year 800.

The value of such sums is almost impossible to relate to modern conditions, but they were clearly by no means negligible. The legal compensation payable if you accidentally killed a neighbour's ox was set at thirty silver pennies, while a sheep cost four or five pence and the going price for a male slave was £1. Even a single penny was thus a distinctly significant piece of property; certainly worth travelling quite a long distance to change on those not infrequent occasions when the local ruler called them in to his central mint for recoinage. H. R. Loyn suggests in his recent *Anglo-Saxon England and the Norman Conquest* that the Offa penny should be thought of as roughly equivalent, in esteem if not in precise purchasing power, to the pre-1914 half-sovereign. On that scale the single person's old age pension in 1970 would come out at round about 1½d. a week in Mercian money.

No such welfare payments were of course available in Offa's day (though by the early tenth century the thanes' guilds of Cambridge and Canterbury were already offering their members a rudimentary fire and burial insurance scheme), but the silver penny formed the basis for all sorts of other fiscal and contractual payments—hidage, cornage, sheriff-silver, wardpenny, to the king; heddornwerch woodpenny, shernsilver, hedingsilver, bedripsilver, averpenny and many others to the church and the manor. By the time that William the Conqueror arrived in 1066, the foundations for an elaborate and generally accepted monetary system had been well and truly laid.

William's first decision in this area set a precedent only too frequently to be followed by later kings and governments—he nibbled away at the standard of value. After founding the Tower Mint in 1067 he changed the legally acceptable weight of silver from the troy pound to the Tower pound, which was 6½ per cent lighter, and laid down that the silver itself need be pure only to the extent of 925 parts in a thousand. In the best tradition of party political broadcasts, this modest debasement was described as defining 'the ancient right standard of England'. And such was the force of William's authority that it did indeed remain the standard for Britain's 'Sterling Silver' coinage—despite multifarious state and regal backslidings—until as recently as 1920, when the last attempt to regulate value by metallic content was formally abandoned.

At this time, of course, the country was entirely on a silver standard, and the amount of goods and services that coins would buy varied in fairly close relationship to the availability of silver. That alone made it fairly difficult to keep the value of money stable. But that was only the start of the problem. Coins were defined by weight, but used by number—an ox cost thirty pennies, not two Tower ounces—so that until Charles II finally persuaded the Mint to accept milled edges in 1663 there was every incentive to clip, file, wash and sweat the maximum amount of silver off each coin, and sell the difference in the open market. Between them, the battle with the clippers, and its obverse, the struggle by the Royal Exchequer to make a profit out of providing a clean coinage, form the main thread in British monetary history till the end of the seventeenth century.

By the time of King John, at the beginning of the thirteenth century, these factors had combined to depreciate values sharply. It appears that the Magna Carta penny was probably worth only somewhere between a sixth and an eighth as much as its equivalent in Offa's day, which would put it (in so far as such comparisons have any real value) roughly in the 3s. 6d. to 5s. range at 1970 prices. Normally such a rate of inflation would no doubt have caused grave unrest, but the economy of the early Middle Ages was still too bound up with the near-self-sufficient life of the manors for the cost of living to become a major issue. That only happened after the Black Death and the Peasants' Revolt, when money wages started to take over on a large scale from payment in keep and in kind. But even in 1300 the use of currency was becoming widespread in the towns and the upper reaches of society—not only for the occasional tax payment or legal fine, but for court and professional services, and all sorts of day-to-day transactions. Many of the sums recorded—like the 5d. a day with food, which was the normal pay of a royal huntsman—look quite reasonable even by modern standards (especially when it was regarded as perfectly possible to live a simple, healthy life on 1d. a day, and the qualification for knighthood was only £20 a year). And the 5s. a day and all found, which was the going rate for a Royal Chancellor, works out at a figure very closely comparable with the £8,500 a year (before tax) which the occupant of No. 11 Downing Street receives today.

Gold came in to complicate the picture when, in 1257, Henry III decided to issue a gold penny, mainly for use in overseas trade. It was to weigh as much as two silver pennies, and to pass current at a value of 20d. This slightly undervalued it (the figure was later revised to 24d.) and there were howls of protest—shades of 1969's equilateral curve heptagons—from London merchants who claimed that they could not persuade anyone to give them change for the new coins. This first issue was a failure—the authorities reluctantly agreed after three months to make acceptance voluntary—but the yellow stuff, once it had entered the currency, proved impossible to dislodge. The florin of Florence became an international trading medium (any handful of change in medieval and Renaissance times was liable to contain coins of half a dozen nationalities) and the foreign exchange complexities involved in the sale of English wool to Flemish weavers for French écus and Italian florins created almost as much trouble as the post-1945 dollar shortage. Despite manful efforts to swing matters in a more favourable direction by issuing first an English florin and then a gold noble, this merely made confusion worse, until the arrival of the Black Death sent both gold and silver pouring out to safer and more profitable havens abroad. There is very little new about flights from sterling and runs on the pound.

Meanwhile, the clippers and sweaters, undiscouraged by wholesale use of the death penalty against them, were hard at work on the silver front. Good coins vanished into hoards or were melted down, so it was no good attempting to issue new ones at full weight, and the only remedy the Mint could think of was to have a recoinage every few years, with the new pennies reformulated to weigh approximately as much as the average of the battered and mutilated variety still in circulation. The first serious reduction in William's 'right standard' came in 1343–4, when the penny-weight dropped from 22 grains of silver to 20·3. A year later it was 20·15, in 1346 exactly 20, and in 1351, as the plague receded, leaving Britain's population reduced by between a third and half, Edward III brought it down to 18 grains, at which point 25s. instead of William's 20s. were being produced from every pound weight. The idea was that this would make the coins so light that no one would want to export them. But the effort was only partially successful: prices soared, thanks to a combination of poor money and the acute shortage of labour and goods; and by 1382 it was found necessary to conduct Britain's first full-scale public inquiry into the state of the national currency.

The experts, in this case five leading City goldsmiths and

merchants, produced no very useful answers, but they brought into the open the fundamental quarrel between the 'bullionist' believers in the primacy of sound domestic money, and the overseas traders, who wanted the minimum restriction on the export of goods and capital. The argument is with us to this day, and so are most of the devices that the men of 1382 thought up to protect the pound. They clamped down particularly on imports, insisting that a 50 per cent deposit be placed with the customs officials before any goods were brought into the country. In addition, for every pound's worth of cloth-of-gold, silk, jewels or other luxury goods imported, and wool and hides exported, a shilling's worth of gold had to be paid in to the Tower. And as a final gesture, which no recent Chancellor has had the wit, or the courage, to emulate, they forbade the wearing of any of these items of imported finery to anyone with an income of less than £40 a year.

Shortly after the imposition of these measures, an almost un-paralleled period of monetary peace descended on the English econ-omic scene. The quantity of silver in the currency was almost halved again over the 150 years between Edward III and the start of Henry VIII's Great Debasement. But the rise in the price of the metal so exactly compensated for the fall in its amount that, as Adam Smith shows in *The Wealth of Nations** the accepted fair price of wheat hardly varied from 6s. 8d. a quarter throughout the period. Indeed, this fundamental item survived all the violent downs and ups of financial policy, and remained pretty well unaltered until the death of Elizabeth.

Henry VII, who set the seal on Britain's growing commercial power by issuing the first £1 gold piece, called the 'souveraigne', just in time for the great Spanish bullion discoveries of 1494, was a sound man, in currency as well as in more general political affairs, and so was his son for the first sixteen years of his somewhat tem-pestuous reign. But in 1542, Henry VIII's needs for funds to pay the mounting costs of the French wars finally overcame his monetary scruples; and when he succumbed he succumbed in a really spectacu-lar way.

Unlike his predecessors, who had been content merely to squeeze more and more coins out of a pound of full-standard gold (23 carats 3½ grains) or silver, Henry proceeded to tamper with the standard itself. After a cautious trial run among the Irish, the mints were told that from now on they were to use an alloy with only 10 oz. of sterling silver to the lb., and to cut the gold fineness to 23 carats. This was only the beginning, too. As the royal cash drain grew, so the precious metal content of the coinage shrank—to 9 oz., then to

* Everyman Edition, p. 164.

6 oz., then to 4 oz., and then, in the final financial agonies of Edward VI, to a mere 3 oz. in the lb. There was so little silver and so much copper in one coin, the teston, that the men marching in Ket's Rebellion (triggered off in 1549 by the soaring cost of living) sang a bitter rhyme:

> These testons look red; how like you the same?
> 'Tis a token of grace; they blush for shame!

By the end of Henry's reign, in 1547, some £500,000 worth of bad coin had been substituted for £400,000 worth of good. This in turn set off a slide in the foreign exchanges, which brought the pound down from 32 Flemish shillings in Antwerp to 13s. 4d. in 1551. That summer inflation reached its peak. Prices were reckoned to have doubled in the past ten years. And a proclamation that from now on the shilling would only pass current for 9d., and the 4d. groat for 3d., set off a full-scale monetary panic.

The ending of this Great Inflation has always counted as one of Elizabeth's crowning achievements. As Sir Roy Harrod has said in the course of lambasting a modern government's recent performance: 'The citizen body . . . do not wish that the currency should be debased. It is the positive duty of the Government to implement the general will in this regard. One of the greatest claims to fame of Queen Elizabeth I was that she finally terminated the progressive debasement of the currency that had been proceeding for a long time and which culminated in her father's measures. In that she both laid the foundation of the subsequent prosperity of Britain and implemented the will of the people.'

What Elizabeth did, in fact, was to call in all the dud coins, on pain of the most frightful penalties, refine out the copper, and re-issue them in full-standard sterling silver. However, the effects of this feat, though remarkable, should not be exaggerated. All the Queen really succeeded in doing was to stabilize the money at its existing value—she did not restore any part of the value which had been lost. Even that achievement turned out to be fairly fragile—prices went up by about a third again in the disastrous harvests and general unrest of the 1590s. But after that relative calm did set in. The perennial financial embarrassments of the Stuarts (James I even managed to find a new way of cashing in on the coinage, by selling the monopoly of farthing-making to Lord Harington) and the upheavals of the Civil War and the Protectorate only raised the cost of living by about 40 per cent. And the Restoration of Charles II ushered in an Age of Stability as well as of Enlightenment. If you take the purchasing power of the pound as 100 in 1913, then you can say that values did not vary by more than 20 points on either side of this mark in the 140 years from the death of Cromwell to the storming of the Bastille. And apart from an occasional outbreak, as there was during Marlborough's French wars, the old disease of price-inflation appeared at last to have been brought under control.

This did not mean, of course, that nothing was happening in the world of money all this time. The air was rent with drama and fury of every kind, from the South Sea Bubble to the chronic eighteenth-century shortage of small change, and from this period date all the main developments in credit, banking and paper currency which underpin the monetary structure of our own time.

Two crucial developments took place, which helped both to power the industrial revolution and to set Britain far ahead of her financial competitors overseas. The country moved decisively (though for mixed and somewhat accidental reasons) on to a unified internal Gold Standard. And the Bank of England, which had been founded in 1696 to relieve some of William III's more pressing war-finance problems, started learning to control and direct the burgeoning new trade of large-scale money-lending.

Ever since Edward III's florins, gold and silver had circulated together in England. But the relationship was always uneasy—even the arrival of one Spanish treasure ship in Cadiz, or the departure of a single silver-laden trader for the East, could shift the value-ratio between them by several points. A bi-metallic standard, even when not disrupted by official regulation and interference, was always an awkward drag on commerce. And although Charles II, by raising the age-old ban on exporting bullion, by introducing the milled edge and by ending the practice of charging a fee for turning people's gold and silver into money, had removed several of the worst distortions, there was now a major new problem: gold, at the prices prevailing at the opening of the eighteenth century, was flowing into the country at an embarrassing rate; while silver, the important metal for everyday dealing, was getting scarcer every day, as people rushed to export it to high-demand markets like India.

Getting rid of such a double standard, however, was by no means a simple matter. All sorts of vested interests were tied up with the traditional ways of doing business, and other countries, like France, Germany and the United States, were stuck with the double standard till late in the nineteenth century. Even then they only succeeded in moving to gold after major legal and political upheavals. But Britain was lucky enough to drift on to the Gold Standard, with all its certainty and simplicity, at precisely the right time. A little earlier, and silver, a much less satisfactory commodity, might have won the day; a little later and the chance would probably have been missed for a hundred years. As it was, Sir Isaac Newton, when asked (in his capacity as Master of the Mint, rather than in his better-known role of Astronomer Royal) to solve the dilemma, chose a price—£3 17s. 10½d. per ounce—for gold which effectively, if unintentionally, established the 21s. gold guinea as the coin to which all other British currency was related. Silver virtually disappeared from the scene for the next ninety years (to the great distress of people needing small change, who had to make do with all sorts of counterfeit, light-weight and semi-illegal copper substitutes). And trade and society flourished as never before.

Gold, however, was not the only—or even the main—factor in the eighteenth-century success story. It was the development of entirely new kinds of money—the Bank of England note, the private-bank note, the cheque, the inland bill of exchange, the Exchequer bill, the Excise tally, and even such exotic bits of paper as malt tickets and State lottery tickets, which, when suitably endorsed, passed freely for currency—that really set the wheels of industry moving. Enterprise was no longer limited by the amount of coin men could assemble and transport, but only by the amount of credit which the banks and financiers could be persuaded to give. The proper way to dam and channel this flood of 'fairy gold'—and avoid being overwhelmed on those occasions when it breaks loose, or unaccountably dries up—has occupied most of the best financial and economic minds for the past three centuries.

The first attempts did not augur particularly well. Almost as soon as it opened its doors, the Bank of England, with its free-handed issue of 'Speed's notes' (named after its first cashier), had triggered off a full-blown credit explosion, with all the classic symptoms—roaring boom on the Stock Exchange, company frauds galore, the pound down by almost one-third (from 37s. to 27s.) on the Amsterdam exchange, and a quite extraordinary speculation in golden guineas. This was well before Newton took them in hand, and the gamblers had pushed the price up from 21s. 2d. to 30s. before the tax authorities spoilt the game by refusing to accept them at any such ridiculous figure. But even these hectic beginnings could not halt the march of the bankers and the bill-brokers. They had found the way to tap the stagnant wealth of Britain's agricultural counties and to funnel it into the future—coal mines, canals, roads, iron works, salt and sugar refineries, wool and cotton spindles, glass foundries and paper mills, all were ready to swallow whatever capital could be made available. And the banks throve on providing it—first in London and then in the provinces, where the number jumped from a mere dozen in 1750 to almost four hundred by 1793.

That year marked the first great test for the new structure. Till then the growth of the credit base had been controlled by the fact

that all paper—notes, bills and everything—was ultimately convertible, on demand, into gold, so that the volume of outstanding
loans could not get too far out of touch with the actual amount of
bullion in the vaults. But now, with the outbreak of war with revolutionary France, serious weaknesses started to show. A bank in
Newcastle stopped payment when its panicky customers asked for
their deposits in gold, and dozens more collapsed as the panic spread
and the big London and Scottish banks, fearful for their own
reserves, refused to help. The Bank of England kept things going for
a time, with a big issue of Exchequer bills which saved some 238
private bankers from bankruptcy. But pressure continued, the Bank's
own reserves dropped from a peak of £13 million to only £2·5 million,
and rumours of a Christmas invasion in 1796 added the final straw.
In February 1797, after the Newcastle farmers had again closed
the local bank by demanding gold for all their outstanding notes,
the price of government securities crashed, and it was agreed that
the Bank of England itself must stop payment. Britain for the
first time was on an inconvertible paper currency standard—a
situation which was to last, against mounting opposition, for almost
a quarter of a century.

Paper money itself was familiar enough by this time, of course—
first scores and then hundreds of little local banks had been printing
their own notes for years, and there had already been several Acts of
Parliament prohibiting the issue of notes for small amounts like
1s. and 18d., or notes with fancy conditions written in small print.
Even in far away Pennsylvania, and as early as 1729, the enterprising Mr Benjamin Franklin had conceived the idea of writing and
printing a pamphlet entitled *A Modest Enquiry into the Nature and
Necessity of a Paper Currency* to urge the issue of a more copious
colonial money supply. Parliament rewarded him not only with
approval, but also with the contract, which netted him altogether
£2,762 in Pennsylvanian 15s. notes between 1739 and 1750, and
produced a suitably self-congratulatory item in his journal. 'My
friends there (in the House) who conceived I had been of some service,
thought fit to reward me by employing me in printing the money; a
very profitable job and a great help to me. This was another advantage gain'd by me in being able to write.'

All that was a long way, however, from the conditions brought in
by the Bank Restriction Act of 1797. Unfettered by any need to
relate the amount of cash and credit outstanding to the quantity of
gold in the vaults, the Bank of England saw its job as providing as
much currency as those members of the trading and spending public
were prepared to match with suitable securities. This view, known
to the text-books and the pamphleteers as 'The Doctrine of Real

Bills' was utterly opposed by most of the more acute economic critics of the time, who grouped themselves under the banner of 'the Bullionists' and finally, in 1844, brought the Bank permanently to heel. But in the meantime, as the Bank of England's own notes passed for the first time into general use, prices leapt and the value of the pound on the exchanges started to drop like a stone.

How far the Bank's activities were really responsible for the great Napoleonic inflation, and how far it was just the normal by-product of a major war, remains fairly unclear. The cost of living roughly doubled between 1797 and 1812, and the note issue increased in more or less the same proportion, neither of which developments looks particularly sensational by recent standards. But Englishmen at the time were acutely aware of the fate of the French Revolutionary currency, the *assignats*, whose value had crumpled virtually to nothing, like the German mark in 1923, and any sign of monetary laxness scared them to death.

Signs of such laxness were not far to seek. In both the great wheat gamble of 1799 and the mad 1809 rush to get into the newly opened Brazil trade, the Bank had freely poured out funds to any speculator capable of carrying the money away (including one optimistic group who wanted to export a shipload of ice-skates to Rio de Janeiro). Symptoms of currency disorder sprouted on all sides, and David Ricardo was only the most articulate of an army of attackers when he said later, during the Commons' Resumption of Convertibility debates in 1819: 'The House did not withdraw its confidence from the Bank from any doubt as to its wealth, or integrity, but from a conviction of its total ignorance of the principles of political economy.'

This was not the only reason for the Bank's unpopularity, either. The introduction of its notes into everyday business had produced a fine crop of forgers, and throughout the whole Restriction time they were hanging them regularly by half-dozens. Altogether 307 people went to the gallows for counterfeiting and another 521 were gaoled or transported for having forged notes in their possession. This activity generated a vitriolic wave of protest. Cobbett, in the *Political Register*, trumpeted that 'this villainous Bank has slaughtered more people than would people a *State*. With the rope, the prison, the hulk and the transport ship, this Bank has destroyed, perhaps, fifty thousand persons, including the widows and orphans of the victims.' The *Black Dwarf* magazine thundered that: 'The "Old Hag of Threadneedle Street" must have no repose, until she consents to abandon her infernal traffic in the blood of those who are tempted to imitate her ragged wealth.' George Cruikshank produced one of his most savage cartoons, in the shape of a Bank Restriction Note signed by 'Jack Ketch', the Hangman. And even the relatively gentle Leigh Hunt, in *The Examiner*, quoted with approval a correspondent who suggested that all hangings for forgery should be personally performed by one of the Bank's directors, and added pensively: 'Our Correspondent professes to have been some time debating with himself, whether it would not be still more effective if the Forger were to hang the Director.'

The directors survived to table their considered opposition to the resumption of convertibility in 1821, but they were overridden. The country, by and large, was eager to get back to gold coins and eighteenth-century stability, and the authorities, after some initial indecision, almost fell over themselves to gratify the wish. Advocates of a more cautious approach, like Ricardo and Francis Baring, the banker, were ignored, and the Bank expressed its willingness to resume payment in gold guineas and the new gold sovereigns, at the full Newtonian value, for all its notes as from 1 May 1821.

The immediate results of this precipitate return to the gold standard were predictably disastrous. The sudden leap in the value of money sent prices plunging; the equally sharp contraction in credit, as the Government for no very good reason decided to repay the Bank a huge slice of its wartime loans, had a savagely deflationary effect on industry; and the only gainers were the holders of the vastly swollen National Debt, who had invested nearly £500 million in depreciated paper pounds and were now collecting their interest in full-value gold. Farmers and manufacturers joined in a furious outcry against the excesses and unfairnesses of the new sound currency regime, and for a moment there was a serious move to get the gold-price of the pound devalued to 14s. But the country was now too wary, and weary, of monetary experiments to try another. Reluctantly, it was agreed to soldier on.

The Bullionists had won, and the pound was now as firmly fixed on its gold pedestal as it was ever destined to be. Metal poured freely in and out of the country, according to the relative price levels in London and the key overseas markets, and supposedly the volume and value of money was automatically regulated thereby. But nobody saw it as being their business to regulate the towering and frequently tottering two-tier wedding cake of credit which had been erected on this golden base. Not the privately owned Bank of England, whose lending policies were primarily directed to making a profit for the shareholders, rather than managing the state of the currency. And certainly not the 750-odd commercial banks which had now sprung into existence, whose only concern was with their own local advantage. Trouble was only too quick to develop.

The first bout came in 1825, just four years after Resumption.

Deflation had run its course, prices had started to rise, and the whole country had gone off on one of those mad bouts of speculative investment to which the nineteenth century was prone. This time it was the idea of putting English steam engines to work in South American gold mines that caught the public imagination, and in late December, when the bubble burst, prospectuses had been concocted calling for over £150 million of capital. The banks were stuffed with mortgages and dud shares which they had taken as loan security; small merchants who had pawned their businesses to get into the gamble started to fail; several financial groups crashed spectacularly; everyone scrambled to swap their notes for gold; and just before Christmas it was said that 'the country was within twenty-four hours of barter'. One of the richest men in the Midlands, Sir Charles Knightley, had to ride twenty miles to borrow a few sovereigns from his small daughter's money-box before he could afford to proceed to London. 'He told us', wrote Mrs Arbuthnot, the wife of the joint-secretary of the Treasury, who was in a good position to observe the panic, 'that at the moment he had not the means of getting a shilling. The banks he deals with have suspended their payments and tho' he feels sure they are perfectly solvent, yet the monetary embarrassment is as great as if they were bankrupt.' At the height of the run, the Bank of England itself was down to a cash reserve of £18,000. Nathan Rothschild, then personally worth £2·5 million, had twenty-five couriers out buying sovereigns wherever they could be got. And the situation was only saved with an emergency outpouring of £1 and £2 banknotes (providentially found by a clerk in an old forgotten deed box, according to one hallowed story) after the government had agreed to the suspension of the legal issue limit.

A succession of similar, though slightly less traumatic upheavals—notably involving investment in North America, at a time when, as one American said, 'there were few regions in the world whose public treasuries and private enterprises had as little credit as those of the United States'—started men thinking once more about better ways to dam and civilize the dangerous, roaring flood of early-Victorian money. They already had a metallic standard, eliminating any discretion in the price of gold. After 1829, they had laws outlawing the issue of any notes with a face value of under £5.* And now in a further attempt to eliminate the vagaries of human discretion from

* These laws stopped short, though, north of Berwick. The Scots liked notes, had a well-organized and sophisticated banking system and refused to change their ways. As one Glasgow pamphleteer wrote: 'Any southern fool who has the temerity to ask for a hundred sovereigns might, if his nerve supported him through the cross examination at the bank counter, think himself in luck to be hunted only to the border.'

the system, Sir Robert Peel prepared to introduce the 1844 Bank Act, which still remains one of the cornerstones of British monetary management.

The Bank Act essentially split the Bank of England into two more or less watertight compartments—the Issuing Department, which concerned itself with the currency, and the Banking Department, which remained in business to make profits. Note issues, from now on, were to exceed the Bank's holding of gold coin and gold and silver bullion by no more than £14 million, plus any note issue rights taken over from private banks, who were now forbidden to extend their present activities in this line. This followed the reasoning of the Currency school of thought, which held that control of the notes and coins in circulation was all that really mattered. As it was almost impossible under the new rules for a note-conversion run to exhaust the gold reserves, this part of the system was now virtually crisis-proof. But the same, unfortunately, did not apply on the credit side of the picture, where the Banking Department soon came under pressure even more catastrophic than in 1825.

The trouble was, as Peel had been warned in 1844 by the rejected advisers of the Banking school, that the largest part of the country's business now involved cheques and bills rather than cash in people's pockets, and every upsurge in commercial demand, whether it took the form of rising prices, increased trade, or higher activity among the bullion dealers, all impinged directly on the reserves of the Banking Department. But there was nothing whatever in the Act to ensure that these would be strong enough to take the strain. When they inevitably failed, as Peel had also been warned, the only recourse was to suspend the Act entirely. This happened three times, in conditions of acute panic—in 1847, in 1857, and in 1866 —before the Bank, reluctantly, pragmatically, but ultimately triumphantly, got on top of the situation. From then on, Britain enjoyed the stablest and safest financial climate in the world for almost fifty years. And much of its resulting prestige, despite all the more recent vicissitudes, still miraculously survives.

There was little prestige, however, to be extracted in the early days. Once the Act was passed the Bank directors assumed the Currency principle would take care of everything, and settled down to the straightforward pursuit of profits, to which end they pushed up their commercial lending from £21 million to £35 million, largely in highly speculative railway ventures. It was all part of what *The Economist* called 'the folly, the avarice, the insufferable arrogance, the headlong, desperate and unprincipled gambling and jobbing, which disgraced nobility and aristocracy, polluted senators and senate houses, contaminated merchants, manufacturers, and traders

c

of all kinds, and threw a chilling blight for a time over honest plod
and fair industry'. And it led directly to the 'prostration and
dejection' of 1847, when the private firms of the Governor, a former
governor and another prominent director went under. There were
open suggestions that the Bank's interest rates had been kept far
too low for far too long for the sole purpose of keeping these shaky
concerns afloat.

These allegations were never proved, or even seriously probed, and
they were all forgotten by 1857, when a parliamentary committee
was set up to assess how well the Bank Act had worked. The current
Governor, Mr T. M. Weguelin, gave some extraordinarily complacent
evidence that 'on the whole, I think, there has been no anxiety in the
public mind with regard to the state of our reserves'. No one could
have been more surprised when, a few weeks later, news reached
London that no fewer than 1,400 banks had closed their doors on the
East Coast of the United States (they too being now in the grip of a
railway panic), or by the subsequent overnight evaporation of the
Bank's famous reserve, which went down to a mere £581,000. The
troops were out in Glasgow, where the Western Bank and the City of
Glasgow Bank, which had deliberately set out to encourage working-
class depositors, were among the worst hit. But despite the surprise
and the complacency, the Bank managed to come fairly effectively
to the rescue, and after this panic, it was noted, more defaulters
than ever before ended up by paying in full.

In the last real banking crisis of the century, the Overend Gurney
affair of 1866, matters were even more adroitly handled. Furious
mobs were parading the City, stunned by the collapse of what had
been probably the best-known and most highly respected financial
house in England only ten years before, and there were minor runs
on banks all over the country. But the basic strength of the economy,
reinforced by the burgeoning power of the great London joint-stock
banks, was now sufficient to shrug off such localized strains. The
Bank Act was suspended, as usual, but it was not in fact necessary
to issue a single extra note. And although there was furious controversy every time the subject was publicly mentioned, it was now
clear that the Bank of England was prepared to drop its pretence of
being 'just another competing bank' and step in as genuine lender-
of-last-resort whenever the system appeared in danger. The day of
Britain's financial maturity had finally arrived.

Not everyone was happy. Even in the mid-1870s, lone voices like
George Anderson MP were still inveighing against the workings of
Peel's Act: 'We have set up gold for our idol—we worship it with a
senseless superstition . . . and at last, when our commerce is in
collapse, when one half of our merchants are ruined and the other

half on the brink of it, we give the Bank leave to issue a few more
credit notes, as the only refuge from universal bankruptcy.' But
Anderson was now a voice in the wilderness.

The true tone of the Victorian booster is heard rather in John
Culmer's 1869 pamphlet, *A Defence of the British Currency,* which
admits of no doubts or reservations at all. In round terms he states:
'If a committee of twelve or twenty good businessmen (I don't
mean philosophers or professors) could be selected, and were to study
the subject closely for a twelve-month, and could find a plan that
would compare with our British coinage and currency (or, in comparison, to come within a hundred miles of it) the writer would be
willing to submit to any forfeiture of penalty or liberty.' And on that
heady note—coupled with the information that, for a brief moment
in 1864, the going rate of exchange between Britain and America
had attained an all-time peak of \$12 to the pound—we commence
our more detailed study of the last hundred years.

The Pound in 1870

was worth £5 10s. in 1970 money

How blest the youth, the maiden pure,
Whose income is both ample and secure;
Invested in Consolidated Three
Per Cent Annuities, paid quarterly.

Victorian Credo

On 1 January 1870—when few people either in England or abroad would have questioned Bagehot's description* of the City of London as 'by far the greatest combination of economical power and economical delicacy that the world has ever known'—an inquest was opened by the Coroner of St Mary-le-Bone into the death of an elderly woman who had died from lack of food. Her husband, a cab-driver, was referred to as an honest, hard-working man who had always maintained his home in good order. Unfortunately, six weeks before, his cab had been involved in an accident and he had been taken to hospital with fairly extensive injuries. This meant that his livelihood ceased and there was no income or savings on which his wife could call. Accordingly, she applied for relief from the Parish, and, after a delay of two weeks, she was duly granted assistance—to the hardly generous extent of 2s. 6d., plus one loaf of bread, then costing retail 7d. a quartern, per week.

On his release from hospital the husband, being without work or money, also applied for relief. After some further delay he was granted no cash, but an additional half a loaf per week. Despite further application no more could be prised out of the authorities. This was partly because the Relief Officer had forgotten, or omitted, to note the fact that there were now two people dependent on his help instead of one. Not unnaturally the wife fell seriously ill on the meagre sustenance available, and although the doctor was eventually called and prescribed beef tea and wine (though without specifying where these were to come from) it was too late, and she shortly expired. In evidence the husband stated that with the 2s. 6d. his wife had bought tea (of which the normal working-class quality then cost 3s. 4d. a lb.), sugar (at around 9d. a lb.) butter (very expensive, at up to 2s. a lb.) and a few other necessities. He also mentioned that the rent they paid was 2s. a week.

The jury, it is hardly surprising to hear, were deeply incensed by the case and strongly in favour of impeaching the Relief Officer for neglect. This was, with some difficulty, overruled by the Coroner. But the really interesting thing about the affair is the amount of space and the degree of indignation which *The Times* (then published at 4½d.) was prepared to devote to its report. It was one among a thousand tiny signs that year that the Age of Laissez-faire—and with it the golden age of Britain's financial and political power—was about to enter into its long, slow, reluctant and strife-punctuated decline.

Very few people, however, were thinking of decline in any shape or form at the opening of the 1870s. The rich were richer than ever

* *Lombard Street* (1873).

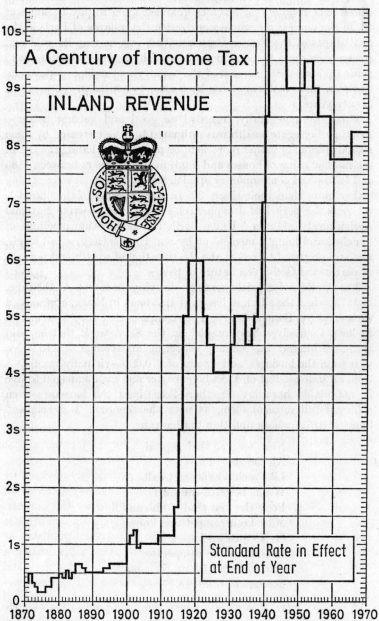

A Century of Income Tax

INLAND REVENUE

Standard Rate in Effect at End of Year

before; income tax, for those 200,000 fortunates or unfortunates
whose over £300 a year incomes qualified them to pay it, stood at
4d. in the pound; the whole world, with the collapse of Paris in the
final stages of the Franco-Prussian War, was moving its gold and
currency reserves to London; and even the manual labourers, who
made up almost 80 per cent of the country's 24 million population,
had seen their real wages rise by a clear two-fifths in the previous
twenty years.

Times were generally regarded as good and getting better—
Britain's aggregate wealth was estimated to have increased by some
£2,400 million, or rather more than 50 per cent (excluding the rise in
the market value of houses and land) in the ten years between 1865
and 1875—and contemporary opinion felt that the poor were getting
rather more than their share. There were pockets of discontent—
this was the period of Joseph Arch's angry but abortive National
Agricultural Labourers' Union, with its countrywide meetings of
'pinched and hungry men'—but by and large society, at all levels,
was still prepared to accept the stratification of wealth and poverty
as part of the God-given nature of things.

The stratification produced some dizzying contrasts. At the time,
in 1873, when the silk mill hands of Halstead, in Essex, approached
their employer Samuel Courtauld to complain that they were unable
to keep themselves 'respectable' on the 8s. a week that he paid
them, he himself was already collecting an average of £46,000 a
year from the business, and a total of £70,000—virtually tax-free—
from all sources. But on the whole master and man managed to live
in reasonable harmony together. Sometimes the harmony even
achieved full musical form, as with the sonorous 'Boilermakers'
Song' of 1872, whose uplifting burden ran:

> Now 'tis true that capital
> All the risk must run,
> Like a ship exposed to all
> Winds beneath the sun;
> Feels the first trades' ebb and flow,
> Must keen competition know;
> So 'tis just and meet
> Labour should co-operate,
> And to help with all their might
> Masters to compete.

A century later, in a society where the mere publication of such
a ditty would be enough to bring the Clyde to a standstill for a
month, it is hard to imagine sentiments like this being sung seriously
and without irony, but apparently they were. And the likely explana-

tion is twofold. First, although it was clear by 1870 that the machine
had conquered society, the actual scale of operation was still tiny
by any twentieth-century standard—the average 'dark, satanic'
cotton mill still had less than 180 people in it, and there was only
one ironworks in the country with more than 600. And second it was
still relatively easy for a sufficiently clever, hard-working, ruthless
and lucky working man to claw himself right up into the new
'aristocracy of stocks and bonds' in a single generation. As that
sturdy 1867 compendium *Songs for English Workmen to Sing* put it:

> Work, boys, work and be contented
> So long as you've enough to buy a meal;
> The man you may rely
> Will be wealthy by and by
> If he'll only put his shoulder to the wheel.

To the great, ill-educated, malnourished mass of urban society,
living at or near Marx's subsistence level, it was as big a fraud then
as it looks now.* But Marx worked on, unknown and unrecognized,
in the British Museum Library, failing then, as later, to ignite any
real spark in the British working man. And in the meantime there
were just enough spectacular successes—just as nowadays there are
just enough £250,000 pools winners—to keep the myth alive.

Behind the myth, building it, underpinning it, and to a large
extent giving it life, lay two layers of reality—first, and best known,
of course, the quite staggering growth of British trade, in iron and
coal and cotton and ships, which at this time eclipsed that of France,
Germany, Italy and the USA put together; and second, less widely
appreciated, but inextricably entwined with the first, the un-
paralleled brilliance, virtuosity and frequent unscrupulousness with
which the British bankers and financiers manipulated the nation's
burgeoning capital savings.

To quote Bagehot again: 'Money is economical power. Everyone is
aware that England is the greatest moneyed country in the world;
everyone is aware that it has much more immediately disposable and
ready cash than any other country. But very few persons are aware
how much greater the ready balance—the floating loan fund which
can be lent to any body for any purpose—is in England than it is
anywhere else in the world.' And the discrepancy was every bit as
startling as he suggested—the published deposits of London banks

---

* As Dickens wrote slightly earlier in *Hard Times*: 'Any capitalist who
had made sixty thousand pounds out of sixpence, always professed to
wonder why the sixty nearest Hands didn't each make sixty thousand
pounds out of sixpence, and more or less reproached them every one for
not performing this little feat.'

in the early 1870s stood at £120 million, against £13 million in Paris, £8 million in Germany and only £40 million even in New York, where the post-Civil-War recovery boom was in full swing.

The point about Britain's wealth, though, was not its sheer quantity—plenty of other nations had people as individually rich as the richest Englishmen, and careful peasants with substantial stores of cash squirrelled away—but the fact that it was 'borrowable'. Britons came to believe in banks, and the virtues of depositing money in them, earlier and much more thoroughly than other people. And on this basis they constructed, with all its blemishes and evils and self-contradictions, the first industrial society, and a network of world-wide investments which by 1875 had reached a total of £1,200 million.

It was not only that Englishmen were bolder than the rest of the world in deploying their money—though this boldness, even excluding the two manic periods of mid-Victorian railway building, often ran well beyond the normal frontiers of foolhardiness*—but the fact that the savings of even the most cautious were concentrated in easily obtainable forms. 'A million in the hands of a single banker is a great power; he can at once lend it where he will and borrowers can come to him, because they know or believe that he has it. But the same sum scattered in tens and fifties through a whole nation has no power at all; no one knows where to find it or who to ask for it.' In 1870 the whole world, from Santo Domingo to the Sublime Porte, knew that the place to ask was in London.

The five continents were on the move together. Japan had been opened up by the Meiji restoration two years before; news of the Kimberley diamond discoveries reached London that very spring; America was back into top gear, riding the crest of the great 'greenback' inflation; the railways were pumping new life through the steppes, the pampas, the prairies and the Indian plains; Bismarck was forging a new German nation in the flames of the French defeat at Sedan; and the company-promoters, the politicians and the civil servants who had come to believe that the greatest world powers

---

* The archetypical story of misplaced nineteenth-century investment concerns a splendid concept called the Churning Company, formed in the 1820s to manufacture butter in Buenos Aires. The capital was subscribed, a shipload of Scottish milkmaids sent out, and 'the wild cattle of the River Plate led captive to the milking stools'. The Latin American shops were filled with butter. But unfortunately no one had performed the obvious piece of market research: asking the Argentinians whether they actually liked the stuff. Unaccountably they preferred oil and the whole enterprise foundered in debts and recrimination. There must be a book to be written tracing the contribution made by those sturdy, stranded milkmaids to the future development of South America.

were those who had incurred the greatest international debts were embarked on an explosion of enterprise whose successes and failures were destined, in many cases, to scar and shape history for the next hundred years.

Few people at the time glimpsed more than a tiny fraction of what was going on. It is very easy to forget just how self-sufficient the British Isles still were a century ago. They pumped out iron rails and capital and lengths of calico for the rest of the world in enormous quantities, and in the process acquired claims of varying strength to vast areas of the earth's surface. But in a very real sense, this was peripheral—the basic nineteenth-century achievement, of defeating the Malthusian threat, and not only feeding and clothing, but actually enriching a population which had virtually doubled (and grown by 150 per cent if you exclude Ireland) since 1800, was an almost entirely domestic affair.

In 1868 Britain still produced four-fifths of her own wheat, meat, wool, dairy produce and the bulk of her own fuel and raw materials. Apart from cotton, which had inevitably created close economic links with the USA and India (causing great panic and disruption during the Civil War 'cotton famine') it was still possible, at a pinch, to go it alone. The 'great commerce' which kept British ships (still tiny, and still predominantly wooden) plying so busily across the seven seas was largely in the nature of jam on the bread; or, as Leland Jenks put it:* 'An adventure—the fruit of the super-abundant energy of Great Britain rather than the essential root of her economic existence.'

All this was about to change drastically, as we shall see in the next chapter, and indeed throughout the rest of the book. But for the moment the jam was to be had for the taking. And the most profitable forms of adventure required little in the way of direct and arduous contact with the world's jungles or cannibal tribes; they were conducted with sharp wits, alluring prospectuses and other people's money in the teeming, top-hat-filled alleys off Lombard Street and Throgmorton Street, where the foreign government loan boom, which eclipsed even the bouts of railway, gas company, mineral and finance house mania which had punctuated earlier Victorian decades, was just working itself up into the first stages of frenzy.

The immediate agents of this frenzy—which helped to boost Britain's overseas investments by almost £400 million between 1869 and the time the boom definitively collapsed in 1875—were houses of essentially foreign or cosmopolitan origin: Bischoff-heims, Rothschilds, Erlangers, Raphaels and the rest of the list

* In his brilliant and often caustic account, *The Emigration of British Capital to 1875* (Nelson, 1927).

xenophobically cited later, on page 87. The traditional City was still busy either unravelling itself from the knotty tangle of railway finance, following the Overend Gurney smash of 1866, or else re-deploying the proceeds of past operations (some of which, like the loan which Barings organized for Russia at the height of the Crimean War, offer hair-raising testimony to the independence then arrogated by the London money market). But the fructifying flow of capital and profit touched everyone—the old land-owning aristocracy, who had now fully come to terms with the new joint-stock-company ethos; the big manufacturers, of Manchester and Birmingham and Leeds, who were happy to switch some of their Consols, then yielding $3\frac{1}{2}$ per cent, into Columbian and Honduran bonds at anything up to 8 or 10 per cent; the small manufacturers, who found finance as easy as it had ever been; the growing professional middle class, who were beginning to found modest fortunes of their own; and even the great mass of the population below the 28s. a week mark, who at last were beginning to reap the benefits of the 1846 Repeal of the Corn Laws, and get a bit more food to eat.

In some ways it was already a surprisingly modern world—the first successful transatlantic cable, for instance, had been laid in 1866, and within a few months 'London and Wall Street talked to each other as two neighbours across the way'—but in many others the country was only just emerging from the dark ages. The last public execution in England had taken place only two years before, in 1868, and that very January ninety-four people were released from Whitecross Street Prison under the Act which had recently abolished imprisonment for debt, that well-known hazard of the eighteenth century and Dickensian life. One old man among this particular batch had been in gaol since 1843—a little matter of twenty-six years.

Disraeli's great 'leap in the dark'—the Tory Reform Act of 1867, which gave votes to the urban working man and first seriously started to break down the political barriers between the men of property and the rest of society—was firmly on the Statute Book. And Gladstone's newly elected Liberal Cabinet was in process of introducing a whole series of supporting reforms, which in time would release new forces and change the whole pattern of Britain's policies and desires. Forster's Education Act, which at last made it compulsory for English children to get at least some rudimentary schooling, went through in 1870. The civil service—then costing the taxpayers the huge sum of £12 million a year (against today's £400 million)—conducted its first competitive entry examinations. And a year later the Army, reluctantly accepting the lessons of Sebastopol, abandoned its pernicious system of selling commissions and opened its ranks, at least to some extent, to non-moneyed talent.*

But these, like the indignation of the St Mary-le-Bone jury, were little more than portents of things to come. To an overwhelming extent the Britain of 1870 was still the country of Disraeli's 'Two Nations': the rich and the comfortable, with their cheque books and their servants (of which the number grew by half a million, to 1·4 million, between the censuses of 1851 and 1871) and their holdings in the Funds; and the rest, who were lucky to see a gold sovereign from one year's end to another. To get any useful picture of the value and nature of money at this time it is necessary to treat these as virtually different worlds.

The structure of wealth and power in Britain had changed out of all recognition in the fifty-odd years since Waterloo. When Wellington marched home in triumph, England had been a landholding aristocracy, making only tentative contact with business and commerce. Coal and iron and railways and canals helped to push up the value of land, and banks and the Stock Exchange were useful for keeping and investing the proceeds, but land itself was still the only real source of influence and social esteem.

All that had now been changed. As W. S. Gilbert happily wrote, on the passing of the definitive Limited Liability Act of 1862:

> Seven men form an association
> (If possible all peers and baronets)
> They start with a public declaration
> To what extent they mean to pay their debts.
> That's called their capital.

And indeed this was what was happening. The more alert of the old dukes and earls and their sons were shrewdly allying their names with the new commercial enterprise (though this became much more prevalent in the 1890s). But much more important, the new men were beginning to rise and take their own place. The wealthiest of the recently ennobled bankers (no one in active trade or industry reached the peerage till 1885) were reckoned to be Alexander Baring, now Lord Ashburton, and Samuel Jones Loyd, of the two firms which had united to form the London & Westminster Bank, second only in prestige to the Bank of England. Loyd was said to be worth £5 million in the seventies and left £2,118,804 in stocks and shares and £1,670,000 in estates when he died in 1883. But they were only the leaders among many.

* Gladstone himself, however, seems to have been less interested in educational reform than in the Post Office's 1870 introduction of the ½d. postcard—an innovation of which, according to Sir Philip Magnus, he was immensely proud, and made quite immoderate use.

Of course, the fiction was kept up that it was all still based on broad acres. When Edward Strutt, the first of the great cotton magnates, became Lord Belper in 1856, it was observed that his origins had been 'mellowed' by generations of landowning, and Bruce and Guest, who became Lords Aberdare and Wimborne in the seventies, had both taken the precaution of converting their stakes in the Dowlais Ironworks of South Wales into substantial estates. But by this time there was little doubt that, in Jenks's words: 'England was now a stock-and-bond holding aristocracy, measuring income in dividends and wealth in the quotations of the Stock Exchange. It owned land and exploited it, and apportioned social esteem by its scale. Land was the conspicuous visible sign of the visibly accumulating grace of successful business. But the real interests of the Forsytes and other men of property now lay in stocks and bonds.'

The visible badges of prosperity were fairly narrowly held at this time. Lord Derby's *Return of the Owners of Land* in 1873 showed that four-fifths of the land area of the United Kingdom was in the hands of under 7,000 people. Of these 363 persons—186 peers, 58 baronets and 119 commoners—had estates of over 10,000 acres, which was roughly calculated at the time to be the equivalent of an income of £10,000 a year. As *The Economist* oracularly intoned in 1870: 'It would "pay" a millionaire in England to sink half his fortune in buying 10,000 acres of land to return a shilling per cent and live upon the remainder, rather than live upon the whole without land. He would be a greater person in the eyes of more people.'

Slightly below this level of eminence came what was then known as the 'Greater Gentry'—1,000 of them, with estates and/or incomes in the £3,000 to £10,000 a year range, and some 2,000 'squires' with between £1,000 and £3,000. And the income-tax-paying classes were made up, first by a heterogeneous group of 'greater yeomen' with farms or land yielding between £300 and £1,000 a year; then by the growing group of professional men—15,000 doctors, 12,000 solicitors, 3,500 barristers, 7,000 architects, 5,000 civil engineers and 2,148 'authors, editors and journalists'—some of whom must presumably have been landowners on a substantial scale; and finally by a proportion of what the 1871 census described as '170,000 persons of rank and property without visible occupation'. Almost all of these were women—or rather 'ladies'—and many of them unmarried: victims of the Victorian tendency for girls to outlive (or more accurately, outsurvive) their high-mortality brothers.

Ten years earlier J. B. Burke, editor of the famous *Peerage*, had fixed on £500 a year for a baronet and £2,000 a year for a peer, as the absolute minimum below which anyone of aristocratic pretensions would find himself in disgracefully reduced circumstances, and the figures probably remained roughly applicable. At the other end of the scale, W. Bruce Jones, in his key Victorian treatise, *Landowning as a Business* (1882), laid it down that 'a man who only wanted all the conveniences and comforts that London and the country could give, could have them for 10,000*l*. a year. To spend more than this he must go into horse-racing or illegitimate pleasures.'

Not all, by any means, succeeded in avoiding these pitfalls. In 1870 the Duke of Newcastle, the Earl of Winchilsea and Lord de Manley were all before the bankruptcy courts with sagas of personal extravagance. Some 'stately homes' were already open to the public —like Wilton House, where the records for 1870 show an annual income of £50 from 'show days'. And the Earl of Verulam, whose family finances are particularly well documented, seems to have been in continual nagging difficulty, trying to fit his £19,000 a year expenditure (including a most worrying and inexplicable item of £1,000 for 'incidentals') within the rigid confines of his £17,000 a year income. This was made up of £13,500 a year in rents, £1,000 from timber and some £2,500 in dividends on one King's Share and one-sixth of an Adventurer's Share in the New River Company (which now owns large areas of property between Gray's Inn Road and Islington, but was at that time supplying the City with most of its water, under a charter dating back to Charles I). In his case there were no windfall profits from the changing face of the country, like the compensation paid by the Metropolitan Board of Works to the Duke of Northumberland, when they acquired Northumberland House in the Strand for demolition and street widening. They paid over the handsome sum of £497,000—more than enough to meet the £320,000 bill for rebuilding Alnwick Castle, which had been finished in 1866, to the wonder of all, and to the comment of the local paper, the *Newcastle Journal*: 'It surprises the beholder that so grand a piece of architecture could be designed in this degenerate age.'

Even at Alnwick Castle, though, it was impossible to insulate oneself totally from the inconveniences of Victorian life—the inadequate light, from gas or oil lamps (electric power and, even more important, reliable electric light bulbs only arrived in the 1880s); the unreliability of the water supply, which forced people to instal porcelain filters, filled with charcoal, in all their main living-rooms and bedrooms (price between 14s. 6d. and 70s. a time); the still incredibly primitive sewage arrangements—Birmingham alone had 14,000 open middens and ash-pits in the city in 1870, though Joseph Chamberlain had abolished them all five years later; the continued heavy adulteration of food, even after the 1862 Public Health Acts; and the universal sharp stench of horses.

These, apart from rents and servants, represented the prime cost in setting up a respectable Victorian household. And to cut any kind of dash was an extremely expensive business—every bit as costly as running a Rolls-Royce in the twentieth century.

Ross Murray, in his encyclopaedic *The Modern Householder* (1870), sets out the basic essentials for the various possible kinds of equine establishments. An ordinary riding horse cost £35–£40 for 'a light blood hack with low action'; £70–£80 for a 'good, useful' specimen; and £150–£200 or more for 'first-class style and manners and a grand action'. A 'good ladies' horse' would always cost between £100 and £150. Hunters came at £80–£200 in close plough counties, and £100–£300 in grass counties. And a well-matched pair of carriage horses, with style and 'grand action', could easily set you back as much as £600–£700—though it was possible to pick up a 'good average' pair for as little as £270. Alternatively, of course, you could hire a pair— at £21–£22 a month in the Season (May, June and July) and £12–£16 for the rest of the year; or at the bargain price of £90–£100 for the whole twelvemonth. And then of course there were the other members of the family to worry about—ponies, at £15–£30 for the children; cobs for odd messages, at £30–£120 'according to shoulder action', and so on down the line.

The horse-flesh itself was only the beginning. There were the vehicles, at anything from £60 for a dog cart, or an out-of-fashion buggy, or a dashing 'skeleton phaeton', up to £200 for a double brougham. Then there was the harness (£12–£16 single; £25–£35 double) and the saddles (straight, 6 guineas; side, 10 guineas) and the hay (£4–£5 10s. a ton) and the oats (at 20s.–30s. a quarter). Even if you managed to dispense with a full-scale coachman, at £2 a week, including livery, stable dress, coals, candles and a room over the stables—and as there were only 16,000 coachmen listed at the 1871 census, quite a few families must have made this sacrifice—there was still the necessity in most cases of employing an experienced groom, at between 30s. and 35s. a week, and probably also a helper or two, at 15s. to £1.

As a final burden, the whole lot was taxed—10s. 6d. duty on every horse; 2 guineas on every four-wheeled carriage; 15s. for the two-wheelers; and another 15s. for every man-servant. No wonder that Mrs Beeton a little earlier had seen fit to remark that 'to employ anything masculine, however diminutive, is the first sign of affluence'.

With females, however, it was a different matter. Anyone with £500 a year in the 1870s, it was reckoned, could afford to employ both a cook and a well-turned-out parlour-maid. Indeed, domestic service, during the late Victorian and Edwardian period was, apart from farming, the biggest single British industry in terms of people employed. And its economics, its fragmentation, its relative affluence, and its peculiarly hierarchical career structure made it a conservative, non-radical social force of some considerable, if rather negative, magnitude.

Some of the economic sidelights are fascinating. Ross Murray, for instance, reports that, in grand households, the dripping which arises from the endless nineteenth-century joints of beef and pork is to be regarded as the cook's perquisite. She is then free to sell it in the open market, and use butter or lard instead. But if the mistress wishes her to use the dripping for cooking, then the cost of buying out this privilege should be taken as something between £10 and £15 a year.

It was worth keeping cook sweet, especially if she was responsible for the marketing. For the pitfalls of 1870 shopping were many and profound. 'Butter', said one contemporary housewives' guide, 'has been frightfully expensive in London of late years; the best cannot be bought under 2s. a lb. This rate has caused great adulteration, of which the most frightful stories are told: the suet or fat of dead dogs melted down with oils and chemically prepared is said to be sent to Holland and from thence imported back as Dutch butter: nay, by a chemical preparation the slimy sewage of the Thames is said to be convertible into butter. It is wise therefore for a housewife to have her butter sent up from a dairy she knows, if possible.'

Butter was not the only hazardous commodity. Even tea had its hidden dangers. At this time 85 per cent of it still came from China— the India-Ceylon trade only really got going in 1878—and high duty, though it had come down from 2s. 2½d. a lb. in the 1840s to 1s., made it worth while for unscrupulous grocers to get to work. 'Tea', as the same handbook observes, 'is either green or black. As it is now well known that the green teas are painted with Prussian-blue or indigo, black tea is now the general choice of the nation . . . English adulterations are sloe-leaves, blackthorn leaves dried, broken up in pieces and mixed up with a paste made of gum and catechu, or Japan earth; ash and plum leaves, silkworm dung, dung of pigs and dogs, or exhausted tea-leaves bought from hotels, mixed with gum and faced with rose-pink, or black-lead, or copper for green tea.' Far better, one would have thought, to stick to coffee, which could be bought wholesale (28 lb. minimum) for the equivalent of 1s. a lb. Or even one of those 'numerous hocks sold in England of inferior quality, varying in price from 18s. to 54s. or even higher'. A dozen, of course.

This was the golden age of the self-employed. For anyone with common sense and drive, setting up in trade was as easy as it has ever been, before or since. Expanding markets, improved and cheaper

D

distribution, ready access to finance from the aggressively competitive banking system, and minimal opposition from established businesses, all went together to produce buoyant profits. Although low wages, in general, were thought to be an essential factor in this prosperity, it was by no means unheard of to pay £1,000 a year to keep a good man in a top management job. Courtaulds, then busy making their first fortune out of the extraordinary Victorian passion for mourning crêpe, paid that, plus 3 per cent of the profits, to the manager of their Essex steam factory (he averaged £3,500 a year from 1870-75), and William Whiteley, whose great Bayswater department store was about to blossom out with the title 'Universal Provider', offered the same sum to a bright young man called John Barker in 1870, in an attempt to dissuade him from going off to colonize the retailing wastes of Kensington.

Initially this sort of money accrued mostly, as William Ashworth says in his *Economic History of England 1870-1939*, to 'families accustomed to modest standards and not confronted by the temptation of a wide variety of consumer goods and services', so that the first effect was a staggering build-up in savings and investment. But the period of temptation—and spending—was about to begin.

Barker himself set up 'on the new system of supplying goods direct from the manufacturers at a small rate of profit for cash payment, thus saving the profit of the middleman', and joined a growing group which already included Whiteleys, Harrods (started as a grocer in 1849) and the Civil Service Stores, recently founded by some clerks in the Post Office, who found they could save 9d. a lb. by buying a chest of tea wholesale. And in 1871 a number of military officers followed their example with a cask of wine, and started the Army & Navy Stores.

To begin with the goods sold were mostly clothes, fabrics and household linens (very good 'extra super' blankets 30s.-50s. a pair; Aldershot blankets suitable for servants, 6s. a pair). But even in 1870 the *Modern Householder* found it necessary to mention 'the washing and wringing machines of recent invention' which 'make household washing, where there is no drying ground, both cheap and easy'. These in fact seem to have been rather cumbrous devices, of American origin, more akin to flax-breakers than to a modern twin-tub or automatic; but there is no mistaking the authentic siren call of the consumer-durable salesman, about to enter into his inheritance.

Laundry, naturally, was a major preoccupation of the Victorians. The well-off wore an inordinate number of clothes, and changed them frequently, which entailed a great deal of skilled, intricate work with starch, goffering irons and the like. This was either done at home, which normally meant hiring a woman specially to help

the servants ('Her wages are in London 2s. per day and she expects
beer three times a day and gin-and-water at night.') or sent out to the
laundry, which generally collected on Monday and delivered on
Saturday. In London it was possible to get this done for 1s. a dozen,
including everything, 'but this is not the price of good washing'.
For that you paid 2d. for each large article of underclothing,
except petticoats which varied from 4d. to 8d. according to
trimming; 1d. a pair for stockings; 4d. a pair for sheets; 1d. each
for counterpanes, and 2s. each for curtains. 'Servants are usually
allowed 1s. 3d. a week each for their own washing.'

This, in fact, appears to have been one of the main things that put
domestic servants a distinct cut above the great mass of the urban
poor. However appalling their living conditions, hours of work, and
general treatment, they ate regularly, had a watertight roof over
their heads, and received a rate of pay which, however inadequate,
tended to look distinctly attractive against the various unskilled
and semi-skilled alternatives. Courtaulds' factory reports in the
1870s are full of complaints about the difficulty of keeping girls in
the silk trade when they are tempted off to London with offers of
£14-£18 a year to go into service. The going rate on the silk frames
was slightly more than this, in fact—6s. 11d. to 12s. 2d. a week, and
25s. for foremen weavers—but with no board and lodging, of course.
And the weaving girls had no particular security of tenure either—
they were thrown out after having their second illegitimate child
just as surely as they would be sacked in Mayfair after having their
first.

Courtaulds appear to have been fairly representative employers—
Leone Levi calculated in 1867 that the average family income of the
working classes was 31s. a week in England and Wales, 28s. in
Scotland and 23s. 6d. in Ireland, with an all-UK figure (somewhat
depressed by the low Irish wage levels) of 19s. a week for adult men,
11s. for women, 7s. 3d. for youths under twenty, and 7s. 10d. for
girls (boosted by earnings in Lancashire cotton). And like a number of
other Victorian manufacturers at this time they had their occasional
imaginative touch. For instance, in the early 1870s they sent twenty-
three of their senior skilled men to Paris for a week at a cost per
head of £6 1s. 8½d.—£3 19s. for the Cook's ticket, £1 8s. 0½d. for a
week's wages, 7s. 8d. for railway fares and 7s. pocket money.

This kind of thing was slowly becoming more frequent. Colmans,
the mustard people, had started a works kitchen in 1868 to provide a
pint of coffee for 1d. when the men gathered for work at 5.45 a.m.,
and a hot meat dinner for 3d. or 4d. The Prudential Insurance Co.,
which had introduced pensions for the widows of men who died in its
service in 1866, followed this in 1872 with a general retirement

scheme. The Gas Light & Coke Company, which supplied most of London's inadequate lighting at the price of 4s. 6d. per thousand cubic feet, had given its clerks contributory pensions since 1842, and in 1870 took the pioneering step of extending this to manual workers. Siemens, in Woolwich, adopted its German parent's pension ideas, complete with widows' and orphans' endowment fund, in 1872. But these were still the rarest of exceptions in a generally howling wilderness.

In some ways it was in the countryside that it howled most brutally. The nadir of conditions for Britain's nineteenth-century agricultural labourers had probably been passed in the late 1840s. But even in 1870, after two decades which had seen both the golden flowering of Victorian 'high farming' and the shuffling, hopeless departure of some 250,000 men—22 per cent of the whole workforce —from the land, they were still almost unspeakably frightful. The tied cottages were still as likely as not to have no privy; in Wales or Devon they frequently had mud walls and fermenting thatch; in Dorset and Somerset the more normal hazards were floors of clay or broken stone which 'heaved' or turned into quagmires with the rain. If the family were unfortunate they might still find themselves paid very largely in kind—over-priced sacks of corn and potatoes, cider unfit for the market, and even the carcasses of diseased stock. And even when the pay was in money, its adequacy can be judged from the typical budget quoted by the *Daily News* when the Warwickshire labourers (by no means the worst off) went on strike in 1872: 'Wages, father 12s.; son 3s.;—15s. per week. The week's bread and flour, 9s. 4d.; one cwt. of coal, 1s. 1d.; schooling for children, 2d.; rent of allotment (1 chain) 1d.; total 10s. 8d. Leaves for butcher's meat, tea, sugar, lights, pepper and salt, clothes for seven persons, beer, medicine and pocket money, per week 4s. 4d.'

As another account at that time put it: 'Let anyone picture to himself a partly-fed, half-clad and wholly ignorant family of eight or nine, including say two grown young women and two grown young men, who habitually slept in one room and in not a few instances in one bed. Let him think of all this and imagine what the worst consequences must be, and his imagination will probably have fallen far short of the fearful reality.'

But fearful realities were not confined to the countryside, where at least there was fresh air and occasional fresh food (which presumably explains why farm labourers, despite their hardships, always came out well ahead in all the Victorian statistics on death rates, infant mortality and expectation of life). Many of the emigrants who set off from the depths of places like North Devon with 'full and plain directions given to the simple travellers . . . written on a piece

of paper in a large and legible hand' took one look at the cities, with
their high prices and stinking, rat-warren streets, and crept thank-
fully back to their rural bread-and-cheese.

In the early 1870s, just before Chamberlain set about clearing the
centre of Birmingham to build Corporation Street, William White,
the chairman of the City's Improvement Committee, who had been
in France at the height of the Franco-Prussian War, wrote: 'The
rubbish and dilapidation in whole quarters have reminded me of
Strasbourg, which I saw soon after the bombardment. In passing
through such streets as Thomas Street, the back of Lichfield Street
and other parts indicated in the plan before the council, little else is
to be seen but bowing roofs, tottering chimneys, tumbledown and
often disused shopping, heaps of bricks, broken windows and coarse,
rough pavements, damp and sloppy. It is not easy to describe or
imagine the dreary desolation which acre after acre in the very heart
of the town presents to anyone who will take the trouble to visit it.'

Out of such stews, which accommodated millions of people in the
bursting, bustling, survival-of-the-fittest society which characterized mid-Victorian Britain, there occasionally erupted strange
phenomena, like the army of ragged, furious, screaming viragoes
from the East End of London, who invaded Westminster in 1871 to
protest against Chancellor Robert Lowe's proposed Match Tax,
which threatened to take away their pitiful livelihood. But on the
whole it was quite possible to forget their existence. Their inter-
mittent, casual and often quasi-criminal earnings were too minute
to affect the trade of more than a few marginal grocers and second-
hand rag merchants; even the shops which William Booth, in the
early 1870 days of the Salvation Army, opened to supply 'Food for
the Millions' failed by 1874; and the church at large, both established
and dissenting, preferred to deplore the whole problem from a safe
distance.*

For such marginal members of society—and in 1867 it was
estimated that half the working population was still scratching the
barest of bare livings at around the 10s.–12s. a week mark—the value
of the pound in your pocket was a pretty theoretical affair. The
quality of life tended to centre more round such matters as
the precise honesty of one's friendly neighbourhood beerhouse

* The Rev. Dr Clark summed it up briskly in 1866 in *The Church as
Established in its Relations with Dissent*—dissent, he said angrily, was
'mercantile' in spirit; it preached the gospel 'only to those who can pay
for it' and 'the lower strata of society' were 'left to rot in their vice and
squalor'. Many Victorians shared the views of Robert William Dale,
the Congregational pastor of Carr's Lane Church, Birmingham, who
believed that: 'The eleventh commandment is thou shalt keep a balance
sheet.'

proprietor, and the degree of access to those forms of personal charity which the 1870 middle classes happened to favour.

Household companions, such as Warne's *Model Cookery Books*, ranged from the first-class volume, price 7s. 6d., to the 'poor house-mother's guide' at 1d.; and the more expensive versions rarely failed to include the necessary instructions for preparing charitable soup. 'We subjoin a capital recipe for a pea soup which may be made weekly at a small expense for poor neighbours: peas 16 oz., meat 16 oz., pot barley 1½ oz., salt 1½ oz.; black pepper, 40 grains; water, 4 quarts. Add water to make up one gallon.'

In 1870 the only meat the really poor were likely to buy for themselves was bacon, at 5d. a lb. Butcher's meat, at 8d. or 9d. a lb., or even 1s. for rump steak in the cattle plague years of the 1860s, was quite beyond their reach, and the first attempt to bring in cheap imports, in the form of sun-dried 'chaqui' from Mexico, which was designed to enable 'our poorer classes' to 'indulge in animal food' at a mere 3d. a lb., had met with universal derision from the English worker, however undernourished (it finally had to be sold to the very poorest families, in the further reaches of Northern Ireland). But in 1870, the first arrivals of tinned corned beef from the USA, selling at 4d. a lb., heralded the era when food technology could really start to build up standards of nutrition in the British urban slums.

Margarine, or 'butterine' as the Victorians tended to call it, had been invented in 1869; Sainsbury's opened its first grocery shop in London's Drury Lane the same year; 1870 saw the opening in Oldham of that unique culinary phenomenon, the first English fish-and-chip shop. And although not all the early innovations were by any means wholly benign—condensed milk, which also first appeared in 1870, at 4d. a tin, lasting five or six people for a week, after suitable dilution, at a time when real milk was 4d. a quart, was probably responsible for more rickety legs, vitamin deficiency, and generally poor health than any other single product, except possibly roller-ground bread—the general trend began to move slowly but steadily upward.

Beer-drinking itself reached its all-time peak in 1876, at 34 gallons per head, but it tended to present a pretty hazardous road out of Manchester. Since the Beerhouse Act of 1830, the trade was open to anyone with 2 guineas for an Excise licence, and some very funny practices emerged in the effort to keep prices down to the 3½d. or even 3d. a quart which the rougher customers were prepared to pay. Three barrels were frequently diluted into four, and anything from quassia and coriander seed to the highly dangerous *cocculus indicus* or *nux vomica* were used to cover up the taste of the water.

High-class brewers like Whitbread charged 5d. on the premises and
4½d. to take away, against the 'standard' price of 4d. But there were
few places where an unfussy thirst could not be quenched for 1½d.
a pint—and that lasted right up to 1914.

Gradually, sometimes almost imperceptibly, the standard of life
of the mass of the population was beginning to rise in 1870. But at
the broad bottom of the heap, where the concepts of 'cheap' and
'nasty' had become inextricably interwoven, it was still largely a
matter of rags, filth and adulteration. Only workers with substantial
resources—chiefly those 830,000 or so members of the 'labour aristocracy' whose incomes were above 28s. a week, and whose skills were
sufficiently scarce to keep their pay moving significantly ahead of
prices—were able, either individually, or through the growing
'co-operative' movement, to get access to the range and quality of
Victorian consumer goods available to the middle classes. As Cole
& Postgate say in their *The Common People*: 'The Co-ops had no more
reason to poison than they had to cheat their members, and the
difference between good and bad bacon, flour, cheese, tea, bread,
sugar and butter, and faked or stale substitutes, was something of
immediately understood importance to every working class woman,
though it cannot be evaluated in wage tables.'

But the gulf between those workers able to afford such elementary
excellences of life, and the rest, had by now grown almost as wide as
that between the working and middle classes. Twenty years of relative prosperity had driven deep wedges. And as one eloquently
nostalgic survivor* from the Hungry Forties wrote: 'My sorrowful
impressions are confirmed. In our old Chartist time, it is true,
Lancashire working men were in rags by the thousands, and many of
them often lacked food. But their intelligence was demonstrated
wherever you went. You would see them in groups discussing the
great doctrine of political practice. . . . *Now* you will see no such
groups in Lancashire. But you will see well-dressed working men
talking, as they walk with their hands in their pockets, of 'co-ops'
and their shares in them, or in building societies. And you will see
others, like idiots, leading small greyhound dogs.'

It was an interregnum—a watershed. It saw Britain at the height
of her unique political, financial and mercantile power. And at the
same time it was a Britain largely ignorant, squalid and brutal,
impoverished in everything except capital resources and the more
unfettered forms of business enterprise. Even by 1891, only 23 per
cent of Londoners between twenty-five and fifty-five were reckoned
to have passed through anything that could conceivably be reckoned
as an efficient school; and it was not until the great Health Act of

* *The Life of Thomas Cooper, written by Himself* (1872).

1875 that the people of England, who, at this time, as the biographer
of one of the Victorian sanitary reformers wrote, 'appeared for the
first time to have acquired a sense of sight and smell, and realized
that they were living on a dung-heap', actually buckled down to
doing anything serious about it.

To make any dent in these vast social problems—education,
housing, health, poverty—was going to take large amounts of
money. And although private enterprise had provided the country
with a railway system, at the cost of a fantastic amount of waste,
overlapping, skulduggery and unplanned disruption, it was becoming clear that it was not equipped to construct an acceptable social
system at large. Slowly, reluctantly, people began to recognize that
the bulk of the money would have to come out of the public purse,
and the taxpayer's pocket.

In 1870, however, the process had scarcely started. Public
spending that year, by both central government and local authorities
combined, came to £93 million—just over 9·4 per cent of the national
income, and virtually the smallest proportion for the whole century.
Of that money, £24 million went in interest on the National Debt, in
the form of gilt-edged stock almost all held by the already rich;
£15 million in Poor Law relief payments, such as those to the unfortunate cab-driver's wife at the beginning of this chapter (and the
Poor Law rules were sharply tightened up in 1869–71, owing to
suspicion of extravagance); around £20 million on defence; and the
rest—£34 million or about 28s. per head of the population—on
roads, sewers, and the first beginnings of medical services and school
grants. Gladstone's administration, with its careful concern for
saving candle-ends, was still a very long way from abandoning the
John Stuart Mill maxim that 'the business of life is better performed
when those who have an immediate interest in it are left to take
their own course, uncontrolled either by the mandate of the law or
by the meddling of any public functionary'.

Meanwhile, on the Stock Exchange, the process of transmitting
Britain's wealth to fructify the further reaches of the outer world
was accelerating handsomely. Some £60 million went out in 1870—
to Alabama, Massachusetts, Russia, Chile, Japan, Honduras, Rou-
mania and Spain—including £10 million raised by J. S. Morgan &
Co., the ancestors of today's Morgan, Grenfell & Co., for the provision-
al French government, while the Prussian armies were actively engaged in besieging Paris. This was the kind of deal which helped to
make the City's international reputation—the agreement was made
on a single sheet of note-paper between Morgan's and Gambetta,
the French finance minister, and the government in Paris knew
nothing about it for weeks, because the pigeon carrying the message

was shot down and eaten by the starving populace. But there does appear to have been some serious imbalance between social spending at home, and the amounts that were now pouring overseas, which rose to £75 million in 1871, and £108 million in 1872, before the cracks in the international credit structure started to yawn.

This does not, however, seem to have had any serious braking effect on British businessmen, whose easy access to capital, and whose reputation for enterprise, reached a simultaneous peak in these years of the early seventies. It is almost creepy in the light of more recent views on British commercial enterprise, to read Bagehot's encomium on 'the dirty crowd of little men' who trade with borrowed capital and 'want business at once . . . and produce an inferior article to get it'. As he wrote in 1873: 'These defects and others in the democratic structure of commerce are compensated by one great excellence. No country of great hereditary trade, no European country at least, was ever so little "sleepy", to use the only fit word, as England; no other was ever so prompt at once to seize new advantages.'

And this marvellous mechanism of easy credit, he thought, would carry its own built-in guarantee. For the borrowed capital would bring in 'an income which will be ample recompense to the small man, but which would starve the rich man out of the trade. All the common notions about the new competition of foreign countries with England . . . require to be reconsidered in relation to this aspect. England has a special machinery for getting into trade new men who will be content with low prices and this machinery will probably ensure her success, for no other country is soon likely to rival it effectually.'

Alas for prophecy. Already Germany (under a Bismarck who later said he admired Britain, not for her trade, but for the fact that you could buy oranges for 1d. each in London) and the newly re-United States were beginning to show just how fragile England's industrial leadership might turn out to be. And all over the world countries irrigated by the almost casual mid-Victorian outflow of British capital, British machines and British engineers were about to demonstrate that, where Manchester and Birmingham had led, they too could follow.

At home, too, new forces were stirring. The towns, which had huddled grimly round the factories, were beginning to open up. The horse-drawn tram, which had been introduced to Birkenhead in 1860 (by an American, of course), was now establishing itself, and making possible both the first suburban building developments, and the first serious attempts at slum clearance. And in 1870 James Stanley and William Hillman patented the 'Ariel' penny-farthing bicycle, launched the following year at £8 for the standard model, and £12 with gears. This turned out to be one of those modest innovations with virtually endless repercussions—it fostered a whole school of political thought, via George Bernard Shaw and the 'Clarion' cycle clubs; it put the final *coup de grâce* to working-class 'Sunday Observance'; it opened people's minds and lungs and eyes to the open country beyond the factory smoke; and by putting the virtually immobilized Victorian wife on wheels it went a long way (together with the Aerated Bread Company's Tea Shops, which later became the only places in London where respectable ladies could sit talking unaccompanied and unmolested) towards fostering the whole women's suffrage movement.

But this, like the triumph of the Gold Standard, and the heyday of the British Empire, was still in the future. Only Free Trade, of the great Victorian economic triptych, was fully established in the early 1870s. On that basis alone *The Times*, in 1871, was prepared to announce, with sonorous certainty: 'We can . . . look on the present with undisturbed satisfaction. Our commerce is extending and multiplying its world-wide ramifications without much regard for the croaking of any political or scientific Cassandras. . . . Turn where we may, we find . . . no traces of decadence.' And that world, whatever hidden 'decadences' were to be found beneath its surface by more persistent searchers than *The Times*, was a fine place to be rich, or enterprising, and English in. It was a world where the sunlight, as reflected in the polished face of the golden sovereign, never set, and was only rarely dimmed.

The Pound in 1886

was worth £7 10s. in 1970 money

Capitalists would welcome any commercial re-organization which would give them a calmer life. It is, we believe, not as a remedy for the miseries of the poor, but as an alleviation of the cares of the rich, that socialism is coming upon us.

Archdeacon Cunningham:
Contemporary Review (1879)

Sixteen years later the economic sun was hidden in dank, lowering cloud. A million men were unemployed.* The Clyde, where shipbuilding had collapsed by 60 per cent since the boom of three years before, was prostrate. The 'Bloody Monday' riots in Trafalgar Square caused Queen Victoria to deplore 'a momentary triumph of Socialism, and a disgrace to the Capital'. Farming was at such a low ebb that the current Duke of Marlborough felt inspired to growl that: 'Half the land in England would be for sale tomorrow if only there was any effective demand for its purchase.' And the Royal Commission, appointed to inquire into the Depression of Trade and Industry, reported glumly and accurately that: 'Our position as the chief manufacturing nation of the world is not as undisputed as formerly.'

The raw wind of retrenchment blew particularly sharp along London's Cheapside on New Year's Day where three cockney girls, Kate Moore, Julia Moore, and Ann Smith, were engaged in the heinous practice of 'exposing flowers for sale'. The next morning, at the Mansion House Court, the Deputy Lord Mayor, Sir Andrew Lusk, who, according to the *Penny Illustrated Paper* which reported the matter, had 'a reputation for a kind heart' told the defendants: 'You think you make a nice bunch of flowers, I suppose? This time you will pay 2s. costs each; but the next time it will be 2s. 6d. and costs, and the next time 5s. and costs.' The girls said they had no money, not having earned 2s. between them all the week, to which Sir Andrew answered: 'Pay the money or go to prison for three days.' The editor of the paper suggested crisply that the Home Secretary should 'call this civic task-master to order' and investigate the disparity between the Lord Mayor's calls for contributions to the Mansion House poor-box, and the activities of his right-hand man upon the mayoral bench. But there is no hint in later issues that he received any response.

This was the deep heart of the Victorian 'Great Depression', which stretched its course from about 1873 to 1896. That spring, angry workmen were throwing rocks at the directors of Messrs Nettlefold's Birmingham screw factories, in protest at a suggested 10 per cent wage cut (on their basic average of about 30s. a week) imposed 'in consequence of the competition of the German screw makers'. It was no coincidence that the newspapers were widely advertising Kensington Secret Sword-Canes—Invaluable for Self-Defence. 1s. 9d., 2s. 3d., 2s. 9d., 3s. 6d. and Very Superior with Secret Spring from 5s. 6d. to 21s.

But in many ways it was a very odd and patchy depression. Its

* Significantly, the actual word 'unemployment' first entered the *Oxford Dictionary* in 1888.

main characteristic was a steady, inexorable fall in prices, from the peaks reached in the boom of the early seventies. Although this made life more difficult for many businessmen, and particularly difficult for the farmers, its effect on most ordinary working and middle-class people was nothing but good. At this time the benefits of the industrial revolution, with its fantastic multiplication of investment and invention, really began to percolate down to the roots of society. Between 1886 and 1896, which marked the official end of the 'Depression', the value of the individual pound in people's pockets reached its nineteenth-century peak—buying more of the basic necessities of life than at any time since 1793, and a greater number of new things, from electric light to safety bicycles, than had ever been available before.

Percolation had been, in many ways, a long, slow process. It took some sixty years to progress from Stephenson's 'Rocket' to the passing of the 1883 Cheap Trains Act, which finally forced the railways to introduce low-priced workmen's fares on a large scale. It took ten years of experiment before the ss *Strathleven* was able to bring the first successful cargo of frozen meat from Melbourne to London in 1880. (Bought at 1½d. a lb. in Australia, sold in Smithfield at only 5¼d., it opened up a vast new market for US pork, Argentine beef and New Zealand lamb which put *per capita* meat consumption up by almost 50 per cent between 1870 and 1900.) And it was well into the 1880s before the first mass, popular forms of entertainment (apart from the beerhouse) began to lighten the misery of urban life. Professional football was only legalized in 1885. And the music hall, 'purged of lewdness' by people like the group of reformers who took over London's notorious Old Vic and renamed it the Victoria Temperance Music Hall, enjoyed its first major boom.

But however slow in coming, these were genuine advances. And behind them lay a continuing improvement in the economic substructure of most people's lives. Real wages, for men who remained in full-time employment, rose by over a quarter between 1870 and 1886, and even allowing for unemployment, which was very heavy in the four years 1883–7, there was a rise of over a fifth. As Alfred Marshall, the leading late-Victorian economist, told one of the interminable Commissions on the State of Trade: 'It is doubtful whether the last ten years, which are regarded as years of depression . . . have not, on the whole, contributed more to solid progress and true happiness than the alternatives of feverish activity and painful retrogression which have characterized every previous decade of this century.' And when the chairman of a similar inquiry asked whether he thought that the depression of prices, interest rates and profits visible on every side was really compatible with such a condition of popular prosperity, Marshall replied without hesitation: 'Certainly; the employer gets less and the employee more.'

This change, it is important to notice, was almost entirely a matter of prices. Money wages, overall, were exactly the same in 1886 as they had been ten years before, and as there had been over the period a substantial movement into more skilled and relatively better-paid jobs, this probably concealed a small actual fall. But as the average cost of a 'typical' working-class food budget dropped by almost a third during these ten years, life, on the whole, tended to be considerably less of a struggle than it had been before.

Not that the element of struggle had disappeared, of course—in fact, it was only in the years around 1886 that the High Victorians really began to appreciate the extent of the poverty and squalor which lay at the roots of their society. There was a positive outpouring of books, reports and pamphlets exposing and analysing the miserable state in which the great mass of people spent their existence—Henry George's *Progress and Poverty*, the Rev. Mearns's *Bitter Cry of Outcast London*, the Salvation Army's *Darkest England —and the Way Out*, the first English edition of Marx's *Capital*, and above all the first cool, clinical and shocking volumes of Charles Booth's *Labour and Life of the People*. Later these were to provide a large part of the documentary backbone and statistical stuffing for the twentieth century's welfare legislation—pensions, labour regulations, health and unemployment insurance, family allowances and all the rest. But in the 1880s, when total government and local authority spending, on everything from torpedo boats to street lighting, stood at under 10 per cent of the national income—about £3 per head per year—their impact was merely descriptive. And with plenty of people around to whom the pound at that time represented anything up to four week's wages, the descriptions are frequently hair-raising.

Take, for instance, Booth's family, the R——s, who 'furnish an example of what I mean by "very poor" '. The father is old and blind, with a weekly pension of 5s. 6d.; his wife only earns money at 'hopping' or 'fruiting'. There are five daughters, but one is married and gone away. The eldest at home, a rough girl, who ruined her health at the Lead Works, does sack-making or bottle-washing, but (in March) had only earned 2s. since Christmas. The second and third girls work in a seed factory and each gives their mother between 5s. and 6s. a week. This makes the total house-income about 17s. 7d. a week. The fourth child is a girl at school.

'This family live', says Booth, 'to the greatest extent from hand to mouth. Not only do they buy almost everything on credit from one shop, but if the weeks tested are a fair sample of the year, they every week put in and take out of pawn the *same set of garments*, on which the broker every time advances 16s., charging the, no doubt, reasonable sum of 4d. for the accommodation. Fourpence a week, or 17s. 4d. a year, for the comfort of having a week's income in advance! On the other hand, even on credit they buy nothing till actually needed. They go to their shop as an ordinary housewife to her canisters: twice a day they buy tea, or three times if they make it so often; in 35 days they made 72 purchases of tea, amounting in all to 5s. 2¾d., and all most carefully noted down; the 'pinch of tea' costs ¾d. (no doubt this is ½ oz. at 2s. per lb.). Of sugar there are 77 purchases in the same time.'

The R——s appear to have disposed themselves somehow in two rooms, neither of them exceeding 10 feet square—bedroom (used sometimes as parlour) to the front, kitchen, where they ate and sat, at the back—for which they paid 17s. a month. Insurance cost 10d. a week (they were all in a burial club) and the girls at the seed factory took 2d. a day each, and bread and butter, to feed themselves at work. For the rest, Booth assessed the cost of meals at 3d. per head for Sunday dinner, 2d. a head for dinner on other days, and 1½d. a head for other meals.

Booth started his great investigation into the way Londoners live from a position of considerable scepticism. He himself had built up a substantial fortune in the shipping business, both in Liverpool and in London, reckoned that he knew the sober, hard-working and by and large cheerful people of the docklands pretty well, and was greatly incensed by the stream of revolutionary propaganda poured out by H. M. Hyndman's Marxist-orientated Social Democratic Federation, suggesting that over a million inhabitants of the capital lived in 'great poverty'. Early in 1886, he called on Hyndman—a strange, erratic, Victorian *grand seigneur*, as rich as Booth himself, and in many ways less sympathetic to the workers he claimed to represent— and complained that the SDF, in its London surveys, had 'grossly overstated the case'. He proposed, therefore, to launch his own inquiry, in which he confidently expected to expose the palpable exaggerations of the Socialists and refute their 'incendiary' statements once and for all. As his latest editors, Albert Fried and Richard Elman, dryly remarked, it took him 'seventeen years and seventeen volumes to complete the project, and in the process he was surprised to discover that, if anything, the Social Democratic Federation had erred in underestimating'.

Booth started in the East End, which he knew best, and among the 909,000 inhabitants of Shoreditch, Bethnal Green, Whitechapel, St George's-in-the-East, Stepney, Mile End, Poplar and Hackney, he identified eight main groups, ranging from the 11,000 loafers and semi-criminals of Class A whose 'life is the life of savages, with vicissitudes of extreme hardship and occasional excess' and a comfort-standard based on the possession or non-possession of 3d. a night for a bed, through Class E, with its 377,000 regularly employed artisans and their families earning between 22s. and 30s. a week, up to the lower and upper middle classes G and H, who even in this relatively impoverished part of London accounted already for some 100,000 people.

The R——s fell into Class B, the casually employed, who as Booth said, were 'at all times more or less "in want". They are ill-nourished and poorly clad. But of them only a percentage—and not, I think, a large percentage—would be said by themselves, or by anyone else, to be "in distress".' On the other hand, the 200,000 'poor' (classes C and D), though they would be much the better for more of every-thing, in any sense, he felt, were not 'in want'. 'They are neither ill-nourished nor ill-clad, according to any standard that can reasonably be used. Their lives are an unending struggle, and lack comfort, but I do not know that they lack happiness.'

What happiness there was, though, had to be sought pretty close to home—there was little margin for extravagance in the kind of cash-flow available to these sober, well-managed, working-class homes, and none at all if the family breadwinner decided that he needed a few drinks to get through the day. This is the bare-bones budget that Hyndman put up for a London working man, with a wife and two children, when he was arguing the case for a 30s. a week minimum wage before the Royal Commission on Labour. Admittedly, this was a few years later, in 1892, but prices had, if anything, fallen still further by then. No one challenged his figures at the time. And I have added a broad idea of what the various amounts would actually buy, at the levels obtaining in East End shops in the middle 1880s.

	s.	d.	
Rent	5	3	(three rooms, if lucky)
Firing	2	9½	
Light		8½	
Soap, soda, etc.		10	
Bread	1	8	(slightly under four quartern loaves, @ 5½d.)
Oatmeal		4	
Grocery	2	6	(tea @ 4s. a lb.; sugar @ 2d.)
Butter, cheese, etc.	2	0	(cheese @ 7¼d. a lb.; butter @ 1s. 3d. a lb.)

	s.	d.	
Flour		4	
Meat	3	0	(New Zealand lamb @ 7½d. a lb.)
Vegetables & fruit	2	6	(potatoes @ ½d. a lb.)
Club, union			
sickness & death			
benefit, etc.	3	3	
Total	25	2	

The balance, of 4s. 10d., had to cover everything else—clothes, furniture, repairs, recreation, books, newspapers, holidays; and in 1886 Robert Gigffen, the leading Victorian statistician, estimated that no less than 82·6 per cent of the working population were below Hyndman's 30s. minimum. Even the most sanctimonious of Victorian employers (like Joseph Parker, the chairman of the Congregational Union, who in 1884, had announced that 'I cannot but believe that the world would be poorer, but for its poverty. . . .') were beginning to accept that such budgets left little room for riotous living. But few of them went so far to follow the suggestion of an 1885 leader in the *Methodist Times*, that the modern formula for salvation might be amended to: 'Believe in the Lord Jesus Christ and adjust your wage sheets.' In 1890, the Anglican Christian Social Union tried to prepare a 'White List' of manufacturers who paid and treated their employees well and whose products could be bought by Christians with a clear conscience. Unfortunately the list was so sparse that the whole idea had to be dropped.

Such consideration, however, did little to quench the enthusiasm of the average, respectable Victorian shopper. For her there was no 30s. barrier—almost by definition her husband was enjoying an income above the income-tax limit of £200 a year. And although, by one of those unhappy accidents of politics, the great election campaign of 1874, when both Gladstone and Disraeli outbid each other with promises to abolish that hated tax, had not actually resulted in its disappearance, it was still only 7d. in the pound, and the following year it came down to 6d. again, as a gesture by the Tory Chancellor, Goschen, to 'the struggling middle class'.*

The nature of the struggle can be inferred from the tone of Mrs J. E. Panton, who in the late 1880s produced a handbook entitled

* Lord Randolph Churchill, who in 1885 had had the effrontery to raise it to 8d. and suggest the abolition of items like the tea duty to provide 'a free breakfast . . . for the masses at the cost of taxes put on the luxuries of the rich', had been unceremonially ejected from political life. If he had stayed in office, as Lord Rosebery acidly remarked, 'he was prepared to tax the very cartridges with which the Tories killed or maimed their game'.

E

From Cellar to Attic which is essentially a study in the delicate pros and cons of marrying on an income of between £300 and £500 a year.

'Dress and house-rent', she writes, 'are the two items that have risen considerably during the last few years, otherwise everything is much cheaper than it used to be before New Zealand lamb came to the front, and sugar, tea, cheese, all the thousand and one things that one needs in the house became lower than they had ever been before. . . . For example, when I was married, sugar was 6d. a lb. and now it is 2d.; and instead of paying 1s. 1d. for legs of mutton, I give 7½d. for New Zealand meat which is as good as the best English mutton that one can buy. Bread too is 5½d.—and ought to be considerably lower—as against the 8d. and 9d. of 17 years ago; and besides this there are a thousand and one small things to be bought that one never used to see, and fish and game are also infinitely less expensive.'

By her reckoning, £2 or at the most £2 10s. a week would keep a young couple 'and the model maid' in comfort, and yet allow of no scrimping. 'Meat for three people need not be more than 12s., 4s. for bread and flour, 2s. for eggs, 4s. for milk, half a pound of tea at 2s. 6d.—if they will drink tea—1 lb. of coffee made with equal proportions of East India, Mocha and Plantation comes to about 1s. 7d., sugar 6d., butter (2 lbs., enough for three people) 3s., and the rest can be kept in hand for fruit, fish, chickens, washing. . . .' Fish, she informs her readers, can be contracted for at the rate of 2s. a day, thus providing 'an ample for dinner, breakfast and sometimes enough for schoolroom tea, too' and chickens can be produced 'from delightful people in Liverpool' at prices ranging from 4s. 6d. to 5s. 6d. the couple.

Even clothes, which were allegedly much more expensive than heretofore, seem to have been a relatively tolerable burden. 'A man can dress himself well on £30 a year, and a woman do likewise on £50, but this requires in both cases the most careful management, while the average cost of a child is from £10 to £25. . . .' And although the rents of the new suburban houses and the more convenient London districts may have been going up, the cost of furnishing them seems to have been admirably economical. Mrs Panton quotes a precise sum of £145 18s. 3½d., for dining-room, kitchen, two drawing-rooms, best bedroom, spare room, servant's room, dressing-room and the passages and staircase. The black and brass bed in the best bedroom cost £3 5s., with £3 10d. for the hair mattress; while the model maid was accommodated with a 13s. 6d. bed, a 6s. 9d. palliasse, a 10s. mattress and a 9s. bolster. An arm chair, custom-made for the master of the house, cost £8–£10 and the three cups and saucers for the kitchen 8¼d.

The really big decision, however, still concerned the thorny matter of transportation. You could fit out two drawing-rooms, from carpet to chandeliers, for £35 12s. 6d., with the help of Mr William Whiteley, the Universal Provider, but a horse and carriage was a very different matter—£261 1s. 6d., even allowing for a £50 horse bought cheap in the country, and a discount on the coachman's £3 boots. And that was only the beginning—the annual cost of running the equipage, with coachman's wages at 23s.–25s. a week, and allowing 20 per cent depreciation on the £175 brougham or victoria, averaged out at £164 8s., or well over £1,100 a year at today's prices.

In many ways it was cheaper to use cabs, which cost 6d. a mile, day or night, for one or two persons, and could be hired for the day at only 18s. to £1. Even for special occasions, requiring a coach or large barouche, the daily charge was not usually more than 25s. ('with a gratuity—always expected—of 5s. to the driver'). And for those in less opulent circumstances, the by now quite extensive London underground would take you long distances for only 1d. a mile (against 3d. for the old horse omnibuses).

Major cross-country journeys were even more economical. 'The entire length of Great Britain may now be traversed for a few pence under three pounds sterling,' wrote T. H. Sweet Escott in 1885. 'The price of a single third class ticket from London to John o'Groats —from King's Cross to Wick or Thurso station—is two pounds nineteen shillings and fourpence. The distance is as nearly as possible six hundred and fifty miles. The time spent upon the journey will be something less than 25 hours, and the journey itself will be accomplished, whatever class the traveller may choose, with comparatively slight fatigue.'

Railway tickets were a cash transaction, of course, and most of the great London and provincial department stores, built in the last third of the nineteenth century, worked on the same basis— by demanding cash at the time of purchase, they were able to undercut all the traditional tradesmen who allowed long credit, and spent most of their time pursuing their customers' unpaid bills. But in 1886 that hard line of demarkation was beginning to waver— Harrods, the previous Christmas, had relaxed its rules and opened accounts for a list of approved customers which included (so much for the percipience of their credit manager) Lily Langtry, Ellen Terry and Oscar Wilde.

Hire purchase, too, which had been available in embryonic form for many years, was beginning to amount to quite a considerable business. Most of the pioneering had been done by firms set up to finance the buying of railway wagons. But 1877 saw the founding of the first HP company aimed specifically at the domestic consumer.

This was the Civil Service Mutual Furnishing Association, established by a group of senior Whitehall men who saw a profitable use for their spare cash in assisting junior colleagues to deck out their homes in becoming style. And by the 1880s the courts were full of cases like the unfortunate Mr Giles (*Cramer* v. *Giles*, 1883) who lost his piano, under the onerous 'punctual payment' regulations then in force, because he was late with the last two instalments.

Credit was one way to loosen the purse strings of the previously thrifty Victorian consumer. Another was the provision of decent facilities for lady shoppers, like the opening of the first Aerated Bread Company tea-shops in 1880 and the inauguration of the palatial and much-applauded establishment of The Ladies' Lavatory Company in Oxford Circus in 1884. And a third was the beginning of recognizably modern advertising. Jesse Boot, founder of today's massive Boots Cash Chemist chain, sent 200 of the Post Office's new-fangled telegrams to selected customers in Nottingham in 1886, telling them to hurry and buy his cheap sponges. And Lever Brothers, the soap people, who had only budgeted £50 for promotion that year, were so impressed by the success of the Millais *Bubbles* campaign for their great rival, Pears, that they raised their sights and spent £2 million over the next twenty years.

Almost as soon as it started, though, this trend towards freer spending and wider choice brought out the moralists and the economic jeremiahs. Escott struck the only-too-familiar note right at the beginning of the decade when he wrote expressing grave concern at the 'tremendous drafts' on British wealth 'represented by adverse trade balances of hundreds of millions sterling', and concluding that 'with our growing taste for luxuries as a people, and the enormous additions to our national expenditure in consequence, we have to occupy a position where we are no longer progressing but rather appear to be standing still, if we are not even falling back'.

Certainly this was the way things seemed to the farmers and landowners, who were particularly hard-hit by the combination of circumstances which were visibly easing the conditions of life for their by now much more numerous urban cousins.

Most of the massive investment in agriculture in the mid-Victorian years had gone into corn land, and English farming, it was widely accepted, was at that time the best in the world—it had to be, it was said, because with wheat at 50s. a quarter, super-high yields, then designated as over 28 bushels an acre, were needed to make it pay at all. In 1874, when prices reached 58s. 8d.—the highest level since the Napoleonic Wars—it looked as though it had all been worth while. But few delusions have ever been more complete or more short-lived. The much vaster, but slower-maturing investment in the grain-carrying railways of Canada, Russia, India and the American mid-West, and in the grain-carrying ships of the British merchant navy was about to flower. Suddenly, the broad, smiling acres of East Anglia were buried in a flood of cheap, free-trade, *laissez-faire* wheat, such as the world had never seen. By 1886 the price was down to 31s. a quarter, and worse was to come—the bumper harvest of 1894 sold at a panic-stricken 19s. As G. M. Young wrote in his classic *Victorian England*: 'Great wars have been less destructive of wealth than the calamity which stretched from 1879, the wettest, to 1894, the driest, year in memory.'

The destruction of wealth was real enough. Algernon West, chairman of the Board of Inland Revenue, told the Royal Commission on Trade Depression that 'comparing 1884 with 1879–80, the net assessments of landed property show a decline of 5,000,000 pounds and capitalizing that sum at thirty years' purchase, we have a total depreciation in the capital value of land of 150,000,000 pounds'. And by the mid-1890s it was estimated that the total capital value of farmland in the UK had been halved in the past twenty years, from £2,000 million to £1,000 million.

As the rents came tumbling down, so did the incomes of those members of the aristocracy and landed gentry who had not had the foresight to transmute their wealth into stocks and shares. The Earl of Verulam, for instance, whose domestic and financial troubles were mentioned in the last chapter, had by now seen the rent roll for his Essex estates collapse from £1,964 in 1878 to only £547 in the mid-eighties. His Consols and other stocks had recovered slightly, and thanks to a £100,000 legacy he managed to avoid actually selling any land. But a rigorous economy campaign had had to be inaugurated in 1881—stable staff cut; London season slashed from five months to two, and spent in a 36 guinea a week rented house instead of an all-the-year-round residence; sherry and brandy drinking down by over 50 per cent, from 845 bottles a year in 1870 to 373 (though claret was slightly up). And although falling prices helped to clip the London and St Albans tradesmen's bills from £2,300 to £1,700, it was still necessary in 1887 to reduce the allowance paid to his eldest son for running the shooting from £500 to £320 a year.

Not that £320 a year was insufficient to support a very tolerable mode of life in the 1880s, particularly for a young and single man. With Consols yielding around 4 per cent, the novelist E. M. Forster received just such an income from the £8,000 legacy left to him when his aunt, Marianne Thornton, died in 1887. And as he wrote much later: 'Thanks to it I was able to go to Cambridge—impossible otherwise, for I failed to win scholarships. After Cambridge I was able to travel for a couple of years, and travelling inclined me to

write. After my first visit to India and after the First World War the
value of the £8,000 began to diminish and later on it practically
vanished. But by then my writings had begun to sell and I have been
able to live on them instead. Whether, in so stormy an age as ours,
this is a reputable sequence I do not know. Still less do I know how
the sequence, and all sequences, will end, with the storms increasing.
But I am thankful so far, and thankful to Marianne Thornton, for
she and no one else made my career as a writer possible, and her
love, in a most tangible form, followed me beyond the grave.'

For those, however, who saw the value of their family estates
decimated at this time, such grateful reflections were few. The whole
basis of country life seemed to be going sour, as the corn rotted in the
wet, miserable fields. Barbed wire, a diabolical American invention
introduced by the fifth Earl Spencer in 1880 to protect his Leicester
estates, was ruining the hunting, and in the end 'did more to destroy
the ties of country life than death duties'. Even that supreme status
symbol of the aristocratic garden, the pineapple ('At Burton Hall the
pines were listed and numbered for Lord Monson long before maturity
so that they could be dispatched with all haste to relatives, friends
and others whom it was desired to impress.') was being ousted by
the cheap, refrigerated imports appearing on every suburban
table. And although the decay of corn brought its long-term com-
pensations—the desperate search for alternatives caused the
introduction of the tomato to the Vale of Evesham in 1887 and the
large-scale growing of strawberries for the British tea-table—this
seemed very scant consolation at the time.

But the plight of the landowners and their half-million tenant
farmers was only one wave in a sea of economic troubles. The
Britain which had effortlessly led the world in the early days of
coal and steam, and which had casually arrogated to itself, against
a background of essential self-sufficiency, the lion's share of that
world's international trade, was now coming up against the harsh
realities of competitive life. The population, now swollen to 35
million, was almost double that at the time of Waterloo, and two-
thirds of them were already irrevocably town-dwellers, pressed
together in the teeming back-to-back alleys and middle-class suburbs
of London and the nineteen great cities. Just to feed itself, let alone
to improve its national standard of living, the country was inextricably committed to the vagaries of the international market-place.
And the painful realization that there is no law which guarantees
British success there dealt a blow to national self-confidence from
which, in some ways, it often seems we have never fully recovered.

Lord Randolph Churchill graphically expressed the growing feeling of self-doubt in a speech of 1884. 'We are suffering from a

depression of trade extending as far back as 1874 . . . and the most hopeful among our capitalists or our artisans can discover no signs of a revival. Your iron industry is dead, dead as mutton; your coal industries, which depend greatly on the iron industries, are languishing. Your silk industry is dead, assassinated by the foreigner. Your wool industry is *in articulo mortis*, gasping, struggling. Your cotton industry is seriously sick. The shipbuilding industry, which held out longest of all, is come to a standstill. . . .'

And he continued, on this occasion, to consider one of the many anguished suggestions put forward as to the cause of Britain's malaise: the fact that, while she held firm to the true gospel of free trade, the rest of the world—Austria and Russia in 1877, Germany in 1879, France in 1881, Italy in 1882, the United States ever since the Civil War—had relapsed into ever-increasing tariff protectionism. 'With the state of British Industry', he inquired, 'what do you find going on? You find foreign iron, foreign wool, foreign silk and cotton pouring into the country, flooding you, drowning you, sinking you, swamping you: your labour market is congested; wages have sunk below the level of life; the misery in our large towns is too frightful to contemplate, and emigration and starvation is the remedy which the Radicals offer you with the most undisturbed complacency. But what produced this state of things? Free imports? I am not sure; I should like enquiry; but I suspect free imports of the murder of our industries much in the same way as if I found a man standing over a corpse and plunging his knife into it I should suspect that man of homicide, and I should recommend a coroner's inquest and a trial by jury.'

Lord Randolph's jury in the event brought in a verdict of not proven—Britain withstood the tides of protectionism for another thirty years, until the wall was quietly breached by the McKenna Duties in 1916. But there were plenty of other explanations for the coroner to consider. And there were plenty of other coroners, too— the steady, inexorable decline in prices was not a British, but a world-wide, phenomenon, and the reasons offered, at various times, and in various places, form a positive anthology of economic soothsaying. As W. T. Layton wrote in his *Introduction to the Study of Prices* (1912): 'In the investigations by the US Commissions, the causes suggested by witnesses are classified under 180 heads, while the opinions expressed before British Commissions are almost as divergent.' And he goes on to quote a formidable list of the most 'potent' suggestions, which range from war, strikes and the concentration of capital to 'the excessive drinking and general improvidence of the working classes'. 'A Danish Committee in 1886 found an important cause in the low price of German vinegar.' And a German investigation the same year lumped together 'the inflammable condition of international affairs', 'looming war', 'a great decline in the price of beetroot sugar' and 'the immigration of the Polish jews'.

Controversy still ranges over the whole period. Was the Depression real? Or was it just farmers and businessmen grumbling because life had suddenly become more difficult? But one factor of the situation does now seem to be fairly well established—a large part of the world-wide decline in prices between 1873 and 1886 can be attributed pretty directly to changes affecting the value of money itself; and in particular to the resurgent significance of one commodity—gold—in the international monetary system.

The era of the International Gold Standard, like the Feudal System, or the Renaissance, or the Dark Ages, is one of those histori-cal concepts which lie almost out of time, colouring people's im-pressions of past events to a degree out of all relation to its actual extent or detailed evolution. As we shall see in later chapters, the idea of a Return to the Gold Standard, implying a return to a lost, heroic age of economic milk and honey, has exercised a most power-ful influence, not only on modes of thought, but on major political decision-making (frequently with fairly disastrous effects all round). But the golden age, in so far as it existed at all, was in fact a relatively short-lived affair—a matter of forty years, from 1873 to 1913, at the outside. And for most of that time contemporaries, far from cele-brating their good fortune, were in one way or another questioning the whole capitalist, free-enterprise system, which by then was generating far more problems than any monetary conjuring tricks could be expected to solve.

Britain itself, of course, had adopted gold as the basis of the currency as far back as 1717, when Sir Isaac Newton had laid down that the guinea should contain 129·4 grains of 22-carat gold, with values of the penny, the shilling and the pound to be calculated by arithmetical proportion accordingly. With breaks for the Napoleonic Wars (1795–1821) and the Great War (1914–25) this remained the ac-cepted definition for over two hundred years, until 1939. But the Gold Standard, as an internationally accepted discipline, linking the currencies of the major trading countries into a single homogeneous, mutually adjusting web, started to develop seriously only during the 1870s. Germany, newly unified under Bismarck, introduced a gold-backed mark in 1871. France, Italy, Belgium and Switzerland, then forming a group called the Latin Union, followed suit in 1873. Denmark, Norway and Sweden (the Scandinavian Union) joined the party in 1875–6. But the most important link of all, the United States, only fell into place with the restoration of the gold dollar in 1879, after eighteen years of 'greenback' paper money. Japan,

India, the South American countries, Russia, all finally shuffled
into line. But some very important nations never made it at all—
Austria-Hungary was still preparing to change over from paper to
gold when the 1914 War finally blew it apart for ever.

The success of the Gold Standard lay in ensuring that the relative
values of the world's major currencies should remain virtually
fixed. For as long as it lasted, in its pre-1914 form, the pound
exchanged for 4·86⅔ dollars, 22·22 French francs, 20·433 German
marks, 9·86 yen and so forth, and the thought of the possibility of
devaluation or revaluation in the system never for one moment
crossed anyone's mind. Confidence, at least as far as the stability of
exchange rates was concerned, was complete; and world trade,
which is sharply affected by such confidence—people who sign
contracts to buy or sell, or borrow or lend, in foreign currencies
naturally like to know exactly what they are letting themselves in
for—flourished as never before.

But this confidence was bought at a fairly considerable price. The
theoretical essence of a full international Gold Standard system—
and indeed of the kind of internal, domestic Gold Standard evolved
by Britain during the eighteenth and nineteenth centuries—is that
the amount of currency and credit circulating in a country should
be more or less rigidly determined by the size of its bullion reserves.
When the country runs into balance-of-payments problems—that is,
its imports and its overseas investments and payments exceed its
exports and its overseas earnings—then gold flows out, the reserves
shrink, and the 'money supply' based on those reserves decreases.
Ultimately this will mean that the costs, both of materials and of
labour, must fall, as that diminished amount of money is stretched
to finance the same volume of trading transactions. However, this
is a pretty slow process, and in the short-term it needs to be reinforced. The routine method of doing this is to raise Bank Rate, and
to restrict credit. This, in the text-book examples, normally has three
effects—first, to bring the kind of 'hot money', which is normally
invested at the best short-term interest rates, pouring into London;
second, to reduce the number of new bills of exchange being discounted in London; and third, to make foreign borrowing in the City
more expensive and less attractive. All these would, in one way or
another, tend to boost the demand for currency and diminish its
supply, thus reinforcing the long-run downward pressure on prices
and wages. In the end these fall so far that exports become sufficiently
competitive again to restore the balance of trade, gold flows back,
reserves rise, the money supply expands, and wages and prices are
free to rise until the cycle is ready to start all over again.

It is quite a pretty mechanism, on paper. And because people like bankers and businessmen believed in it; and because it was favoured by circumstances, such as the long, uninterrupted years of late nineteenth-century peace, and the unchallenged pre-eminence of the London money market, it tended, on the whole, to work—even though there is plenty of economic argument to demonstrate that several bits of the model were put in back to front, and plenty of historical evidence that in practice the process was rarely allowed to work itself out to the bitter end.

The point is, however, that it only worked as far as its own particular task was concerned. Foreign exchange stability was effectively complete. But the other factors of economic life which concern people so much nowadays—prices, employment and overall growth —fluctuated violently. And for contemporaries, at any rate, the Gold Standard era looked anything but golden throughout most of its life. The nostalgia, as usual, came only when it was gone beyond recall.

Almost every aspect of that life came under scrutiny, as we have seen, during the years around 1886. And a central factor, compounding the impact of the social investigations and the growing political discontent, was a continual nagging worry over the part that money itself seemed to be playing in deepening and darkening the general malaise.

More specifically, there just did not seem to be enough gold to go round, in a system whose entire functioning now depended on it. And the anguished play of argument and counter-argument put up before the Royal Commission appointed to inquire into the Recent Changes in the Relative Values of the Precious Metals form a concentrated distillation of the monetary thinking of the time. In the end it was totally inconclusive, and the whole basis of the problem vanished with a whoop when the vast Rand goldfields were opened up in 1887 (see next chapter). But while it lasted it provided an almost inexhaustible series of examples of the way in which people can get hung up on the semantics and metaphysics of monetary theory.

The starting point of the argument was the observed fact that prices in those countries which were on a gold or mixed gold-and-silver standard rose from the time of the Australian and Californian discoveries of the 1850s until 1873, and then fell, continuously, after the widespread adoption of the Gold Standard, until 1886; while countries which had remained on a pure silver standard, notably India, had seen no such fall. 'The unchanged purchasing power of the rupee' impressed and infuriated the Victorian businessman, and the general feeling was that there was just insufficient gold for the job it had to do. The bare figures certainly tended to support this view— the sterling value of world gold production, the Commission were told, after reaching an annual peak average of £28·14 million in

1856–60, had steadily declined to a mere £20·80 million in 1881–5, while the value of world export and domestic trade had multiplied several times. And after subtracting the large amounts absorbed, for various reasons, by India and the US, the surplus available for all the other nations had dropped even more dramatically—from a total of £209 million in the decade 1866–75 to an almost nominal £85 million from 1876–85.

As in a medieval theological debate, the Commission begins by stating a deceptively simple proposition. 'Because the prices of commodities are expressed in terms of gold, it has been assumed that a transaction of sale or purchase is in substance what it purports to be in form, namely an exchange of commodities against gold; and this assumption, it is said, necessarily underlies all the arguments with regard to the supply of gold which are drawn from considerations affecting the prices of commodities.'

Against this, on the one hand, lie the following set of arguments: that the nominal value of all transactions going on at any given time or place is always enormously greater than the quantity of gold available, so that it would be impossible for most of them to be carried out in the terms in which they are formally expressed; that in fact only a minute proportion are ever actually settled in gold; that in most arrangements what passes is not gold but a promise to pay gold; that prices, therefore, are really regulated not by the quantity of gold, but by the quantity of such promises which is generally regarded as acceptable; that the quantity of such promises, or in other words the volume of credit, has only the most complex and obscure relationship with the quantity of gold, varying with different countries, different times and even different states of society; and that the relationship between gold supply and price levels is therefore so indirect that a rise or fall in the second proves absolutely nothing about the adequacy or otherwise of the first.

Taking a deep breath, the opposition then ripostes as follows: first, that a distinction must be drawn between the portion of the gold supply circulating as coin, and that portion held in reserve by banks as a basis for the credit which they create; second, that between gold in the latter form and the quantity of credit there is a direct arithmetical relationship, which may differ from society to society, but is locally tolerably uniform; third, that whatever the relationship of credit to gold base, the former must in the long run conform to the value of the latter; fourth, that the gold supply also acts directly on prices through its effect on interest rates; and that, fifth, in face of the fact that in the twenty years to 1886 there had been a 30 per cent alteration in the relative value of gold and silver, and a precisely similar alteration in the prices of commodities exchanged between the gold-using and the silver-using countries, it was impossible to deny 'that the standard of value is intimately connected with prices'.

Inflation, as we all know from recent experience, hits people with fixed incomes, as against those whose bargaining power enables them to offset the falling value of money with higher wages; it also favours the borrower, who pays his debt in depreciated pounds, as against the lender, who gets back less in purchasing power than he originally parted with; and in general it tends to strengthen the new men as against the established rich, and break up the citadels of entrenched financial power. Deflation, however, when the value of the pound in purchasing power terms is steadily appreciating year after year, should theoretically have just the reverse effects. The Forsytes (and the Forsters) flourish on the gilt-edged stocks and their 5 per cent funds, and enterprise is, at any rate relatively, stifled by the *status quo*. Much of the anguished argument before the Gold and Silver Commission naturally concerned itself with just how far this was working out in practice in the mid-1880s.

'The depression caused by falling prices', says the Report in one of its more eloquent passages on the subject, 'is partly due to material and partly to sentimental causes. . . . Falling prices will, if other things remain the same, involve a reduction in profits and a consequent indisposition to continue producing; but this reduction is to a certain extent only apparent. In so far as the profits, though smaller, have the same purchasing power as before, the person who receives them is, no doubt, in the same position as before; but he is more impressed with the decrease in their nominal amount than with the maintenance of their purchasing power. . . . Moreover it is found that wages, which must necessarily form a large proportion of the total cost of production, fall less rapidly than prices. For all these reasons the necessary adjustments in the cost of production which, to maintain real profits at their normal rate, should be going on *pari passu* with the fall of prices, is always deferred, and is frequently deferred to a point where production ceases to be remunerative.'

Needless to say, this did not pass unchallenged. One influential group of witnesses held that falling prices were a lesser evil than rising prices because they led to a more even distribution of wealth and higher real wages; that trade corresponds more closely to real need when prices are falling ('Great commercial crises rarely come in times of so-called depression.'); that falling prices encourage labour- and capital-saving inventions, and also raise the real rate of return on foreign investments; and that drooping profits are at least partially compensated by falling interest rates.

Nonsense, said an equally influential group on the other side. The extra real wages are only temporary and will be reversed and wiped out when prices rise; in any case they are effectively neutralized by the unemployment and uncertainty that go with the falling prices; and it is hard to believe that, in a situation where the owners of capital are getting most of the benefit, the workers are going to get much permanent advantage out of the reduced share left for producers and wage earners. In addition, the much-vaunted inventions only cause more friction and uncertainty, on top of the trouble generated by the constant effort to lower wages. And several of the more cynical doubted both the degree to which the benefits of falling prices actually filtered down to the workers ('much being intercepted by other classes first') and the moral basis for the rise in foreign investment returns—'a large portion of this gain is made at the expense of British colonies and dependencies, such as India, and does not accrue to the country at large but to a very limited clan'.

By the light of hindsight most of the doubts summarized in the last paragraph would seem to have been thoroughly justified. But they were little direct help in solving the problem before the Commission—whether the apparent shortage of gold in the system was primarily or even partially responsible for the 'depression' (if there was a depression) and whether or not there was a case for bringing in silver, as the other main precious metal, to eke out the Victorian money supply.

Bi-metallism never became a popular (not to say hysterical) rallying cry in British politics, as it did in America*—possibly because we had no silver mines tucked away in our more distant counties—and on the whole it was rejected on the practical grounds that, whenever gold and silver had been set up to provide a joint monetary standard, the normal fluctuations in market price ensure that one of them was always relatively profitable to melt down. That meant that the profitable one promptly disappeared into the hands of the metal dealers and the situation was left rather worse than before. Alfred Marshall put up an ingenious solution, Symetallism, to get round this problem, which involved setting up a standard based on

---

* This did not, however, save the perfidious British from getting a large part of the blame for what the Americans like to call 'The Crime of 1873' when a law discontinuing the coinage of the silver dollar was quietly slipped through Congress. By 1875, when the silver price had moved down, and the mine-owners realized it would have been profitable to send the stuff to the Mint under the old laws, it was too late. The popular theory was that the demonetization was planned by evil London bondholders, with the object of ensuring payment in gold and thus raising the value of their US holdings. In Populist and 'silverite' literature, Britain shared the obloquy and the conspiracy honours with Wall Street and the international Jewish bankers.

bars of metal where set amounts of gold and silver were indissolubly welded together. But the intellectual and practical effort involved was too great, and the Commission broke up inconclusively, hoping for the best, which duly arrived with the news that the Rand was an even bigger bonanza than California and Kalgoorlie thirty years before.

Even now, the mechanism of Britain's late-nineteenth-century slow-down remains deeply obscure—technological arthritis, the changing balance of long- and short-term investment, entrepreneurial decline,* the relationship of productivity to hours of work and increasing holidays: all these, as well as the money-supply position, have been put forward as partial explanations, and almost certainly all of them played some part. Railways were giving way to consumer durables (virtually all the modern household electrical gadgets, from heated blankets to cook-at-the-table saucepans, were on show at the Vienna Exhibition of 1883). Britain was missing out on important innovations, from basic steel to organic chemicals. Developments like the Nine Hour agitation, and the grant of paid holidays (South Metropolitan Gas Co. gave a week at double pay in 1886, and the Gas Light & Coke Co. had granted a week with 4s. 6d. gratuity, for men not absent more than seven days in the previous year) was beginning to cut down the average working day. But it does seem that the sheer shortage of money—not only in Britain but in the world at this time—was a prime cause, at least in the twelve years from the mid-1870s to 1887.

In those years the world's monetary stock, in the form of circulating currency and bank deposits, which in the 1850s had been growing at 8 per cent per year, slowed down to a mere 1 per cent. And in Britain, from 1877 to 1887, it did not, according to the latest measurements, grow at all.

This certainly seems the likeliest explanation for the length and steadiness of the 1873–86 price drop. The alternative causes suggested —economies of scale, technological change, belated pay-off on the great railway boom, improvement of the terms on which British exports could be exchanged for foreign raw materials—obviously all reinforced the effect. But they have all been duplicated, often to a substantially greater degree, in recent years without noticeably slowing down the rate of twentieth-century inflation. And, indeed,

---

* The most extreme form of this is the false-teeth theory of British decline, which holds that the older, staider and less adventurous industrialists were enabled by this invention to attend board-meetings without embarrassment, to a ripe old age, and hence to slow down the whole national speed of change. Unfortunately it has been observed that Germans, Americans and even Japanese have a similar advantage now, with no noticeable braking effect on their endeavours. Back to the drawing board!

in their latest pronouncements Dr Milton Friedman* and the Chicago School of monetary theorists are advocating precisely that we should go back to the situation of the 1880s and halt the growth of the money supply altogether, if we want to reverse (or even halt) the constant erosion in the buying-power of our currencies.

However, the situation is in many ways very different today. In 1886 no one deliberately made any decision about the state of the money supply: it was an automatic result of the working of the International Gold Standard in a situation where world trade, both export and domestic, was expanding fast and very little new gold was coming into the system to sustain it. And the side effects were in many ways a good deal less than wholly satisfactory.

National income, admittedly, was continuing to expand at a very fair rate—per head of the population, and at constant prices, it grew by over 30 per cent between 1870 and 1886. But although, as we have seen, some of the fruits of this were beginning to seep down to the lower reaches of society, the discrepancies remained enormous, and in some directions were even widening at this time.

Miriam Beard, in her *History of the Business Man* (New York, 1938), estimates that in the 1880s Britain had 200 dollar-millionaires —twice the number in either Germany or the United States at the time. But such statistics can have been of poor comfort to the people of Bermondsey, parts of which, according to Lord Shaftesbury's evidence to the Royal Commission on Housing in 1884, were 'a large swamp where a number of people live, as they do in Holland, in houses built upon piles. . . . So bad was the supply of water there that I have positively seen the women drop their buckets into the water over which they were living, and in which was deposited all the filth of the place, that being the only water they had for every purpose of washing and drinking.'

There were certainly housing acts and health acts and artisans' dwelling acts already on the statute books. But they tended only to help the established working man, earning between 25s. and 30s. a week. Below that—and almost 60 per cent of the manual labouring population was below that—the laws of the *laissez-faire* jungle had free rein.

Even the Church offered little in the way of comfort, apart from the ubiquitous charitable soup, and even that was reserved exclusively for the 'deserving' poor, who could be relied on not to grumble too loudly about their lot. The Salvation Army, in the true commercial spirit of the times, advertised 'The Hallelujah Railway Ticket', with a timetable for 'The Up Line to Heaven and the Down Line to Hell' and a prospectus offering 'Shares in the Salvation

* Milton Friedman: *The Optimum Quantity of Money* (Princeton, 1969).

Mine . . . 100 per cent guarantee in this life, and in the world to come everlasting'. But the respectable Christian owners of actual railway stock and 5 per cent bonds, being not particularly anxious to share the act of worship with the Army's 'submerged tenth of humanity', found that pew-rents and accepted standards of dress provided a perfectly adequate way of keeping them out.

Pew-rents were particularly vicious—Anglicans, Methodists and Congregationalists all had them, and once a family had paid its dues for the year, it was as much as anyone's life was worth to attempt to sit in one of their seats, even if the whole pew was vacant. The Church of England's Free and Open Church Association, set up by those few members who disliked the system, was always fighting cases—in 1885 they were defending three pensioners served with writs of trespass by a pew-holder; helping in a case where a church-warden tried to allocate seats after a notice had declared them 'free to the parishioners forever'; and appealing on behalf of a lad convicted under the Brawling Act after attempting to pray where the church-wardens did not want him to. And the snobbery of clothes provided an even more pervasive defence. In the mid-eighties the Catholic paper *The Month* held an inquiry into the reasons why poor people failed to go to Mass, and the typical response, which could easily be duplicated for all the churches, was: 'Oh, we don't go out on Sundays at all; we just stop quiet in bed in the morning, and in the evening the little ones crawl about in the court and we stay inside: we don't want to be laughed at among well-dressed people.' Methodism had long entered into its mahogany age ('We got our mahogany pulpits and the preachers found their way to the mahogany tables of wealthy laymen.') and an 1888 *Guide to Manchester* spoke of 'Dissenting ministers in the place who enjoy incomes which sound almost fabulous to those who believe in the tradition of a Dissenting clergy-man's dependence upon the hardly-extracted contributions of the tradesman and the artisan. When it is mentioned that . . . the income of one popular Dissenting preacher is stated to be £1,500 a year, it will readily be understood that the dissidence of Dissent in Manchester does not imply sitting and waiting upon Providence.' Cardinal Manning was not alone in his bitter comment on the comfortable Catholic laity: 'What are our people doing? Oh, I forgot; they have no time. They are examining their consciences or praying for success in finding a really satisfying maid.' But that provided little spiritual consolation to the maids, who had probably only entered service, at £10 to £12 a year, as an alternative to one of Booth's sweated East End trades, such as making the insides of match-boxes at 1d. a gross, or boiled sweets at between 3s. and 6s. a week (except for the Christmas season when it rose to a munificent 16s.).

The extraordinary thing to a later, more affluent generation, tuned to protest at the slightest excuse, is just how little real unrest or active discontent there was in these conditions. Sidney Webb was clearly right when he told the Royal Commission on Labour in 1892:

'It appears to me that if you allow the tramway conductor a vote he will not be for ever satisfied with exercising that vote over such matters as the appointment of the Ambassador to Paris, or even the position of the franchise. He will realize that the forces which keep him at work for 16 hours a day for 3s. a day are not forces of hostile kings, or nobles, or priests; but whatever forces they are he will, it seems to me, seek as far as possible to control them by his vote. That is to say, he will more and more seek to . . . obtain some sort of control over the conditions under which he lives.'

But that was still some time off. In 1886, when a Royal Commission witness was heard to describe Socialism as 'the state of things where there is not the respect for the classes above . . . that I think there ought to be', the ice was hardly even beginning to crack. And gaslight still flickered over all.

The Pound in

was worth £7 6s. in 1970 money

It may make little difference to the fullness of
life of a family whether its yearly income is
£1,000 or £5,000, but it makes a very great
difference whether the income is £30 or £150;
for with £150 the family has, with £30 it has not,
the material conditions of a complete life.

Alfred Marshall: *Principles of Economics*
(1895 edn.)

The only people that my book will disappoint
are those anti-Christian economists who . . .
believe that once a man is down the supreme
duty of a self-regarding Society is to jump upon
him.

William Booth: *In Darkest England* (1890)

In 1896 retail prices for many items reached the lowest levels touched in the last two centuries. The Great Depression, such as it was, began to lift. The Empress of Russia ordered a wedding dress in gold and pearl for £40,000. Lady conjurers could earn 10–15 guineas a week, entertaining at school treats and church bazaars. A Dogs' Toilet Club opened at 120 New Bond Street, offering shampoos at 5s. and chiropody at 2s. 6d. Programmes at the more fashionable balls included a transparency showing, when held up to the light, a view of the gardens, and cost 3s. 6d. a dozen. Female police searchers received 4d. a time (6d. after 10 p.m.) for the technical feat of dismantling suspected shoplifters' buns. And a sturdy, thrusting member of the exploited majority advertised on 11 January: 'Socialist, small capital, is desirous of entering into business; any line if prospects good.'

All sorts of pregnant events were taking place that year—the launching of the first mass-circulation popular newspaper, in the shape of the ½d. *Daily Mail*; the repeal of the Red Flag Act, which finally allowed the private motorist to drive on the public highway; the arrival of Marconi in London to sell his first wireless patents to the General Post Office; the first showing of a cinematographic moving picture in England. But as far as the basic structure of society was concerned, little appeared to have changed. Tories and Liberals disputed the political terrain as they had done since the days of James I. The birth of the Labour Party was still five years away. The Conservative Prime Minister, Lord Salisbury, enjoyed a personal landed fortune estimated in the region of £6 million. The ageing Liberal leader, Mr Gladstone, had retired to his estate at Hawarden, with its 7,000 acres, its 2,500 tenants and its £10,000–£12,000 a year rent roll. And a future Labour Foreign Secretary, Ernest Bevin, switched jobs in Bristol from being a 6s. a week bakehouse boy (twelve hours a day, six days a week) to the 10s. a week splendours of Brooke & Prudencio's mineral-water wagons. The rich, apart from the irritating introduction of Lord Harcourt's 1894 death-duties (running up to 8 per cent on estates of over £1 million) retained their normal arithmetic relationship with the poor, while an ever-growing middle class flourished in between. On average, everyone in the country was probably slightly better off than they had been ten years before. Even the farmers had more or less come to terms with their diminished lot, as fruit and jam (with sugar at a 'ridiculous' 2d. a lb.), vegetables and the new 'railway milk' increasingly took the place of the old rolling cornfields.

Naturally, with no great advance yet in welfare spending, the improvement was pretty minute at the lower end of the income scale. It cannot have meant much, for instance, to the old man whose

troubles were reported in the *Northern Echo* in August 1896. He was
in process of being committed to prison by the Middlesbrough
magistrates for non-payment of an outstanding debt (the lawyers
having by now found half a dozen ingenious ways round the debtors'
charter of 1869). The amount involved was the staggering sum of 11d.,
which had been raised by court costs to a total of 5s. 8d. When the
local good samaritan who finally paid it called on the victim, he told
the newspaper, he 'found him sitting up but unable to walk about,
his legs being much swollen with dropsy. In reply to my questions,
without any excitement or bitterness, he said: "I am 70 years old
on the 20th of next January. For the last four years I have not been
able to work regularly. I have no children of my own but my stepson
pays the rent and brings my coal. I pawned nearly all my clothes
before I would apply for parish relief; but I have had 3s. a week for
the last three weeks."' From the court records it emerged that the
original debt had been 2s. 11d. of which 2s. had already been paid.
When he could not meet the difference the magistrates awarded him
seven days' hard labour. And his rescuer discovered 'to my horror'
that such sentences were a frequent occurrence that year in the North
Yorkshire area.

That was the penalty for the sin of poverty. It was far better to
go in for something socially respectable like fraudulent company
promotion. The issuer of a prospectus for a new bank, of which the
judge said: 'For all any investor can tell, this bank might be set up in a
line of balloons strung between here and the moon', got off without a
stain on his character or a dent in his purse. And even the sober, and
utterly respectable, *Congregational Year Book* found it necessary to
advocate the abolition 'of the unwritten law that the first qualification
to be a deacon is that the man should possess a cheque-book'.

To those who did possess cheque-books, however, the world in
1896 was a wide and handsome place. The women's magazines were
full of bargains that year. Harrods offered a full-scale trousseau,
starting at £7 7s. 8d. Messrs Smee & Coburg, in Moorfields, undertook
to furnish a complete house, to the highest standards, on a price
scale ranging from £100 to £500. Silk brocade, stiff enough to stand
on its own, was selling at 4s. 11d. a yard, 'this being stuff that could
not be bought five years ago under three times the sum'. Children's
dresses, from the Shakespeare Manufacturing Co., Mill Street,
Manchester, were obtainable for 1s. 9d., and D. H. Evans, in Oxford
Street, had elaborately ruffled pinafores 'suitable for either maid
or mistress' for 1s. 11¼d. and caps 'with streamers of abundant
length' for no more than 1s. 4¾d. each. But it was sometimes as well
not to inquire too closely into the conditions under which such
bargains reached the market.

Up in Manchester, for example, there was a case before the City Police Court, where a young woman was charged with stealing shirts from her employer's warehouse. 'It was stated', tartly reported Robert Blatchford's weekly *Clarion*, which cast an acidulous eye on such matters, 'that the philanthropic employer who allowed the woman to work for him gave her in return 1½d. per shirt!' Hardly surprisingly, the Federation of Women Workers for the Prevention of Sweating thought it worth while to take space in the same issue to recommend the products of The Shirt Manufacturing Co., with retail branches all over the North, which, they said, 'for the past 10 years have paid the Highest Prices in the Trade to their Shirt-makers'.

But there is little sign that this announcement, or similar efforts, often elaborately tendentious, appealed to more than a tiny fraction of the hard-headed *fin-de-siècle* Victorian public.

Normally, when papers wrote about wage levels at all, it was more in the flat, neutral, oh-isn't-that-surprising tone adopted by the trade magazine *Athletic Sports, Games & Toys* when it informed its readers that 'for hand-painting, birthday and Christmas cards, young artists are paid at the rate of 12s. a gross or 1d. each. Yet the manufacturers say that a skilled hand can make quite £1 a week with constant work even at this price.'

Even an unusually perceptive publication, like Harmsworth's *Women's Life*, with its Economic Menus for Working Wives and its, at the time, very advanced series on Careers for Women, shows only a limited comprehension of the great gulf between its relatively comfortable readers and the rest. Its piece on laundry work, for instance, describes in excellent and useful detail the training scheme run by Miss Louisa Jones, at the 'Mirror' Steam Laundry, Putney, where the daughters of gentlemen could learn to become manageresses and superintendents, with the prospect of earning 30s. a week to start with, two guineas after three months, three guineas in a year's time and up to seven guineas thereafter. One firm in Wimbledon, it was said, paid its lady superintendent as much as £500 a year, though that was 'exceptional'. And indeed it must have been, in the same trade which that October produced the case where a young laundress, Norah Higgs, sued her employer, Thomas King, for back wages in one of the London county courts. Asked by Judge Emden how much she earned and how long she worked, she said fourteen hours a day, from 8 a.m. to 9 or 10 p.m., during which time she was never allowed to leave the works. For this she received 10s. a week plus commission, making 14s. in all. The employer, on inquiry from the judge as to whether he considered such conditions 'Christian-like', said: 'We have numbers of girls who do it' and added that:

'They are quite a happy family.' Judgment was given for the plaintiff, with costs, and Judge Emden said: 'I hope such happy families won't last long in this country.'

There were plenty of them about, though, as you can see from the 'Jobs Wanted' columns—like the entry from the *Clarion* on 25 January: 'Brother, 20, who has been employed by a certain sewing machine company from 8 a.m. to 10.30 p.m. for 8s. weekly [!] seeks employment as carter, porter, labourer or anything. Member SDF. A. J. Cass, 3 Poplars, Coplow St., Birmingham.' And to put such figures into perspective, one need only quote the careful footnote which Alfred Marshall wrote to his famous *Principles of Economics*, which came out in the 1890s and established itself as the outstanding text-book of its subject for the next three generations: 'Perhaps at present prices the strict necessaries for an average agricultural family are covered by 15s. or 18s. a week, and the conventional necessaries by about 5s. more. For the unskilled labourer in the town a few shillings must be added to the strict necessaries. For the family of the skilled workman living in a town we may take 25s. or 30s. for strict necessaries and 10s. for conventional necessaries. For a man whose brain has to undergo great continuous strain the strict necessaries are perhaps two hundred or two hundred and fifty pounds a year if he is a bachelor; but more than twice that if he has an expensive family to educate. His conventional necessaries depend on the nature of his calling.'

Marshall's 'strict necessaries' covered the minimum amount of food, fuel, clothing and shelter required to maintain 'merely physical efficiency'. And when Seebohm Rowntree came to conduct his elaborate survey of living conditions in the city of York—a pretty typical sort of place, neither particularly rich or particularly poor— in 1899, he found that some 15 per cent of the population were living at this sort of standard, and another 28 per cent actually below. Of course, most of them did not spend their whole lives in this condition —for periods shortly after marriage, and then again after their children had grown up and before old age set in, most of these households could reasonably expect to get their nose briefly above the poverty line—but in between these periods conditions were obviously pretty grim, even with cigarettes at six for 1d. and beer at 2d. a pint.

Just how grim, Rowntree summarizes in a classic passage on what life on 'the minimum' really implied: 'A family living upon such a scale . . . must never spend a penny on railway fare or omnibus. They must never go into the country unless they walk. They must never purchase a halfpenny newspaper or spend a penny to buy a ticket for a popular concert. They must write no letters to absent children, for they cannot afford to pay the postage. They must never contribute anything to church or chapel, or give any help to a neighbour which costs them money. They cannot save, nor can they join sick club or Trade Union, because they cannot pay the necessary subscriptions. The children must have no pocket money for dolls, marbles or sweets. The father must smoke no tobacco and must drink no beer. The mother must never buy any pretty clothes for herself or for her children. . . . Should a child fall ill, it must be attended by the parish doctor; should it die, it must be buried by the parish. Finally, the wage earner must never be absent from his work for a single day.'

However, while society at large was prepared, from time to time, to take note of such observations, it was not yet ready, in 1896, to do much about them. In fact, quite often the reverse. There was the case, which caused a certain amount of comment that spring, of the sixteen-year-old boy admitted, at the public charge, to Hoxton Workhouse Infirmary. His leg had been crushed by a quarter-ton bag which he was unloading, unaided, as part of his 8s. a week job for a firm whose ultra-cheap tenders had won it a contract working for the Hoxton Guardians, who were supposed to be administering the poor relief in that area. One of the more conscience-stricken Guardians, the Rev. Cartmel Robinson, pointed out that 'by encouraging such conditions of work as obtained in this case, and then repairing the damage at the public cost, we are simply literally helping to break up useful citizens and grind them into paupers'. He suggested that in future the Board should insist on the payment of trade-union wages by all traders which it employed. But he was ruled firmly out of order by his colleagues.

They must have been rather the same sort of people as the magistrates who heard the case of Henry and Mary Ann Harris at Southampton that June. The Harrises were had up for cruelty to their seven children, which turned out, in evidence, to mean failing to provide sufficient food out of their 15s. a week income. So the court, in its wisdom, agreed to fine them £9 to be paid by instalments over nine months, thus neatly reducing their already inadequate income to 10s. a week. Mrs Harris was described by the inspector as 'not a good manager' and the *Clarion*, predicting her inevitable reappearance on a similar charge, commented: 'As the magistrates will, by their action, be aiding and abetting Henry and his wife in their cruelty, won't it be possible to punish them as accessories? Or will the fact that they are not of sound mind, and therefore not responsible for their actions, be a sufficient defence?'

In the gay and merry nineties, though, there was little money to spare for the assistance of such as Mr & Mrs Harris. Lord Harcourt's death-duties were earmarked for defence expenditure (Dr Jameson

and his friends were currently on trial for their ridiculous raid into
the Transvaal, and the South African war was brewing up), and the
£6 million budget surplus of 1896 was largely dispensed as a consolation prize to the irate landowners who had helped to vote Lord
Salisbury's Tories back into power. Total social service payments by
the State and local government totalled under £1 per head that year.
And there were plenty of places like St George's-in-the-East, the
poorest parish in London, where 'it cost a great deal more than 20s.
to distribute 10s. to maintain the poor in workhouse, infirmary and
schools'. St George's Guardians only distributed £165 that year, in
fact, while spending no less than £1,663 3s. 4d. on the administration
required to keep the relief figure down to that amount. 'That is to
say,' as one contemporary commented, 'for every £1 given in relief,
£10 is spent in trying not to give it.'

Still, even £1 was well worth having in 1896—it would buy you
eighty two-pound jars of fruit jam, six bottles of whisky, 1,440
herrings (at six for 1d.), thirty gallons of fresh milk, the rent of a shop
and house for nearly a month, three and a half 28lb. pails of dripping,
fifteen pairs of serviceable ladies' shoes, or two-sevenths of an
emigration passage to America—a trip which some 100,000 people on
average were still taking every year. And many of those who stayed
at home had little cause for grumbling.

The Archbishop of Canterbury, for instance, was at that time
collecting a stipend of £15,000 a year. The Speaker of the House of
Commons (though the members were still unpaid—their £400 a year
only started in 1912) received £4,500 a year and a £4,000 a year
pension on retirement. Mme Adelina Patti, the leading opera singer
at that time, who had settled in Wales, was reputed never to set foot
on the stage for less than £1,000 a night (though Melba, at £200, was
a good deal more reasonable). Lord Overton, the owner of the Show-
field Chemical Works, in Glasgow, was able to give £10,000 a year to
charity, while paying his workers 3d. an hour for a twelve-hour day,
seven days a week, and fining them a day's wages if they took Sunday
off. And the census of 1891 had shown that in the country at large
there were 250,000 males of between twenty and sixty-five without
trade or profession. These, to a large degree, constituted 'the idle rich'.

But even the idlest rich were increasingly coming to terms with
the new world of company flotations, stock exchange financing and the
broad acres, not of land, but of the board room table. This was
the way that the third Lord Verulam, who by now had succeeded the
hard-pressed second Earl whom we met in earlier chapters, set about
restoring the family fortunes. He kept his total spending rigidly
down to £15,000 a year, rationed his own personal expenses to £3,600,
let the main family house, Gorhambury, with its shooting for around

£1,500, and systematically set about collecting directorships. In 1896 he added the lustre of his name to the Colchester Brewery (fee £50 a year), the Imperial Life Insurance Co., Harrietsville Housing, and Accles Ltd (which paid a handsome £500). The next year he added two more—Palmarejo Mexican Mines and the South African Gold Trust, in which he already held 605 shares, paying a useful 100 per cent in 1895–6—and by 1913 he had thirteen of them, representing, in fees and dividends, a full third of his income.

He was not alone. This was the era of Ernest Terah Hooley, the Nottingham lace manufacturer who, between 1895 and his spectacular bankruptcy in 1898, made an incandescent career out of company promotion, largely on the basis of offering 'large gifts to obtain the services of titled and other persons as directors'. In three years he floated twenty-six corporations with a net capital of £18 million and a personal, if short-lived, profit of £5 million (his great coup was Dunlop, which he bought from its founder shareholders for £3 million in the summer of 1896 and re-sold to the public six weeks later for £5 million). And Hooley was only one of a flamboyant group—Lawson, H. O. O'Hagan and later Horatio Bottomley—who between them channelled more than £1,000 million of capital into domestic British industry and commerce via such operations in the two decades up to 1914.

This was a pretty new development in the 1890s. Although there had been a fairly steady trickle of big, household-name companies to the Stock Market from 1862 onwards—Cammell Laird and the Aerated Bread Co. in the sixties, Cunard and BSA in the seventies, and a gaggle of brewers, Bass, Guinness, Whitbread and Ind Coope in the eighties—the really heavy money was all routed overseas. In the early 1880s, out of the £5,800 million worth of securities quoted and dealt in on the London Stock Exchange, only a minute £64 million represented investment in British industry.

The near-smash of Baring Brothers in 1890, after an excessively enthusiastic venture into Argentinian Railways, sharply reversed the moneyed public's preference for foreign enterprises. Net lending abroad dropped from almost £100 million in 1890 to £22·9 million in 1898. At the same time, an unprecedentedly long period of cheap money—bank rate stayed at 2 per cent from February 1894 to September 1896—stimulated interest in anything which would produce a yield better than the somewhat unexciting 2·47 per cent average return available on Consols. O'Hagan, who floated off many of the big brewery concerns, regarded them as 'high-paying and speculative' because of the political danger from the highly organized teetotaller movement. But that did not prevent the public from eagerly shelling out some £80 million in the period 1893–7 for a stake in Watneys, Barclay, Perkins and the like. And a whole host of other blue-chip concerns—J. Lyons, the caterers, International Tea, the grocers, Stewarts and Lloyds, the steel tube makers, English Sewing Cotton, and J. & P. Coats, the thread manufacturers, all took the opportunity to go public in the mid-nineties; often to the great fury of the Fabians and the Social Democratic Federation, who were already detecting strong signs of a tendency to monopoly in these moves.

However, such dangers, though potentially real enough, had yet to reveal themselves in the price tickets in the shops. Things were cheap everywhere (if you had the money). And in the growing retail chains and the booming department stores they were even cheaper. Even as far back as 1886 Lewis's of Liverpool had demonstrated the power of the big buyers, when they purchased a quarter of a million felt hats direct from the makers, and sold them for 3s. 11d. instead of the usual 6s. 6d. At first the Hat and Cap Traders' Association threatened to boycott Lewis's and have all their supplies cut off, but the new facts of life soon began to sink in. 'Lewis's', said the trade press, 'sell more hats in a week than most middlemen can buy in a month, and the manufacturers know too well who are their best Customers to allow themselves to be dictated to in this manner.' And thus all the riches of the earth were made available, at a very reasonable figure, to any late-Victorian shopper whose income kept comfortably clear of the 21s. 8d. a week Rowntree–Marshall poverty line.

From Sloan & Smith in Oxford Street, for example, you could acquire a 101-piece dinner service, decorated with your own crest or monogram, for the sum of £4 18s. 6d., and an additional £3 10s. would bring you eighty-seven matched and assorted wine glasses, engraved with your personal coat of arms. The Irish Linen Co. in Bond Street would supply you with highest quality blouses at 49s. 6d. the dozen, and silk stockings, still very much a luxury item, were obtainable, in five sizes and 300 different shades, at 5s. a pair (where cotton—though admittedly only the best cotton—would have set you back 4s. 11½d. forty years before). Messrs Wilson & Gill, in Regent Street (as they still are today), were offering solid-silver cigar lighters, shaped like a hunting horn, starting at 25s. According to a trade estimate, 'In London on an average one person in every three carries a watch, and of these two-thirds pay from 25s. to £3 for them.' And a pocket Kodak camera, complete with twelve exposures of film, could be bought from Messrs Eastman at 115–117 Oxford Street for £1 1s.

You did not need to restrict your shopping activities to London, either. What was described as 'The Cheapest Continental Holiday' would take you to the Ardennes and back for 35s., or to Brussels (for the Field of Waterloo) for 20s. The straight return fare from London to Paris at this time, by the London, Brighton & South Coast Railway, was 58s. 3d. first class, 42s. 3d. second and 33s. 3d. third. And for those fastidious families who preferred to see Britain first, and did not wish to sully their fingers with the crude commercial act of buying a railway ticket, it was common enough to charter a special private train, at an average price of around £25.

Only horses, and everything that went with them, remained really obstinately dear. Even in 1896, the first year that private cars were allowed on the road without a red-flagged chaperone, it was reckoned that the running costs of a one- or two-cylinder model, which could be bought for between £100 and £200, worked out at only 4d. a mile, where the most modest pony and trap averaged 6d. And for anything really ostentatious the sums involved became, by the standards of the time, quite astronomical.

As *Women's Life* said, in an article on 'The Cost of Riding in Rotten Row': 'Riding under the cheapest conditions is an expensive luxury; but in Rotten Row it becomes even more so, as you see there only the finest cattle.' The 'cattle' ran out at anything between £100 (considered 'cheap for a saddle-horse') and 250 guineas, for a thoroughbred with a pedigree. As such animals were only ridden during the Season, and never for more than two or three years, the minimum cost of the horseflesh alone was £50 a year, which was raised to £150 a year, after adding in shoeing, harnessing, forage and the services of the 'vet', and probably to £200, after investing in at least three smart riding habits at £5 each, and the groom ('a necessity') whose annual licence fee was 15s. and whose wages came to at least 25s. a week. And that only covered one person's recreational riding—a well-appointed one-horse brougham cost at least £150 a year to keep on the road, with coachman's wages at anything between 25s. and 50s. a week, and a crack carriage and pair (with 'indispensable' footman at another guinea) something in the region of £315. Naturally, this did not include anything for initial investment in the motive power or in the vehicle itself. 'The carriage horse is a costly animal—one of 17 hands would be valued at quite 150 guineas, and as at least three are wanted, one being kept in reserve, a large cheque is required in this direction.' No wonder there was a substantial trade in hiring out such equipment. A carriage and pair, complete with coachman, could be rented from stables in most towns at a figure in the region of £250 a year. But even that can hardly have appeared cheap at a time when at least five million manual workers in the country (including most of the soldiers, sailors, policemen, farm labourers and domestic servants) were subsisting with their families on something under one-fifth of this sum.

However, such considerations only intermittently troubled those happier few who could afford to find work for the 75,000 private coachmen and grooms recorded in the 1901 census, or even make frequent use of the 113,000 whose services were available for hire. Their money, their clothes, their servants, their well-bred voices insulated them from the hand-to-mouth miseries of other people's lives in a way that a later generation finds it difficult to comprehend. As K. S. Inglis wrote in his *Churches and the Working Classes in Victorian England*: 'For most of the nineteenth century Englishmen looked at poverty and found it morally tolerable because their eyes were trained by evangelical religion and political economy. A preacher could spend his life surrounded by the squalor of a manufacturing town without feeling any twinge of socially radical sentiment, when he believed that many poor people were suffering for their own sins, and that the plight of the rest was the result of spiritual ordinances which it would be impious to question and of economic laws which it was foolish to resist.'

Such an argument probably justifies a good deal of the moral myopia of the time; but it is hard to stretch it to cover some of the more direct confrontations of rich and poor, like the East Denbighshire case in 1896, when a magistrate's court was considering whether Emily Jones, a girl 'with the mind and body of a child' should stand trial for killing her seven-month-old illegitimate baby. Her sister had been keeping Emily, herself, an earlier infant and the new addition on a total income of 9s. a week, out of which rent took 3s. 6d., and it emerged in the course of the hearing that the father of both children was a married man of the middle class, who had contributed 2s. 6d. a week to the support of the first, but withdrawn altogether on the arrival of the second. 'His name', solemnly reported the contemporary newspapers, 'was respectably kept out of the affair.' And the penalties were very little harsher for the Birmingham pen-nib manufacturer who, in the same month, was found guilty of welding a couple of two-ounce lead weights to the underside of the scale pan which he used in the works. As his work-people were paid on the weight of steel which they converted into nibs each day, this meant that he was screwing an extra $12\frac{1}{2}$ per cent of production—109 nibs per lb.—out of his wage bill every time the scales were used. The fine for this charming practice was fixed by the understanding members of the Birmingham Palace bench at £5 and costs.

That was the summer that Lord Rosebery, one of the twelve men in England (seven dukes, three marquesses, a baron and a baronet) who could call upon a landed income of £100,000 a year, decided to ignore the standard 6s. a head dinner at the newly opened Hotel Cecil in the Strand—'the Largest and Finest in Europe'—and order something a little more recherché. He insisted on the provision of 25 lb.

of out-of-season strawberries for his guests, and although after extensive search it turned out there were only 20 lb. in the country at the
time, even that was sufficient to set him back the modest item of £66.
It was no doubt after a somewhat similar meal at Sir Julius Wernher's
Bath House, in Piccadilly, with a company of assorted financiers and
hangers-on that Beatrice Webb wrote: 'There might just as well have
been a Goddess of Gold erected for overt worship—the impression of
worship, in thought, feeling and action could hardly have been
stronger.'

This was the new gold, pouring out of the Transvaal in an ever-
growing flood. In the 1890s world production doubled, to around
£400 million, against £200 million in the 1880s. And in the first decade
of this century, following the invention of the cheap cyanide process,
which revolutionized mining costs from 1896 on, it doubled again.
The main beneficiaries, like Wernher (who continued to scandalize
Mrs Webb by employing fifty-four gardeners, ten electricians and
twenty to thirty house servants for his 'occasional week-end'
house at Luton Hoo) and Barney Barnato (who captured the
headlines by entertaining his friends to dinner at the unheard-of
expenditure of £4 a head, including the flowers), contributed largely
to the legend of the Gay Nineties. But the gold itself tended rather
to confound the money theorists. Its shortage, from 1873 on, certainly
seemed to have helped drive prices lower. So why, in its abundance,
did they so obstinately refuse to rise?

In the United States this conundrum occupied a central place in
the political scene. Throughout the early nineties the battle raged
between the 'populists' and the 'silverites'. On the one side stood a
formidable amalgam of the National Bi-Metallic Union, the American
Bi-Metallic League and the National Silver Committee, backing
William Jennings Bryan in his complaint that mankind was being
'crucified upon a Cross of Gold'; on the other the 'sound money'
party glowered four-square behind the ultimately victorious Repub-
lican McKinley on a platform rather reluctantly favouring the gold
standard (which was not fully and irrevocably accepted in the USA
until 1900).

The campaign, fought out against a background of agrarian unrest,
the Pullman railroad strike, martial law, the imprisonment of
Eugene Debs, and a secret Treasury bond issue, largely handled in
London, which brought renewed and furious accusations of 'international bankers' conspiracy', was conducted, as Milton Friedman
and Anna Schwartz say, with 'notorious bitterness' and with 'fear
and smear techniques . . . freely used on all sides'. And although
Britain offered no direct parallel at the electoral level—the main
issues at the polls in 1895 were more concerned with the relationship

of religion and education than with overt economics—most of the underlying discontents were as naggingly present in East Anglia and the colliery towns of the North East as they were in the farming Mid-West and industrial New England.

In many ways, in fact, they were worse. For although at this period the peculiar monetary worries of the 1880s had dissolved, they had given way to a much more generalized uneasiness about Britain's competitive position in the world. The pound sterling stood at its zenith, both in purchasing power and in domination over the international financial system—the newly emergent Japanese, in an extreme example of respect, preferred to ship their gold and their export bills physically to London (switching in 1904 to the interminable distances of the trans-Siberian railway) rather than to rely on any form of local intermediary for their trade and governmental transactions. But everywhere else national self-confidence was under attack, both within and without.

Just why, and how far, Britain's industrial leadership slipped in the last thirty years of the nineteenth century is still the subject of fierce and unresolved debate. Technological lethargy, slack management, poor salesmanship, other people's protectionism, institutional rigidity, misguided investment policies, all these were put forward, at the time and later, as possible explanations (just as roughly the same list has been produced to explain Britain's post-1945 performance) and almost all of them must have played some kind of part. But just how they combined to produce the effect that emerged, and whether the ultimate picture will appear as one of inexorable decline, uneasy stability, or the beginning of an extended pause preliminary to renewed growth, remain essentially open questions. According to taste, it can be presented as greatness in decay, random muddle, or realistic adjustment to a flow of social, political and economic forces which transcend national frontiers. And even the choice of units in which 'it' should be measured—average *per capita* real income, rate of growth of national product, spread from richest to poorest, acreage of Empire, annual murder rate, degree of environmental pollution, defence and strike capability, number of Easter Sunday communicants, relative export costs and prices, propensity to enjoy leisure and exotic foreign foods—presents a spectrum of almost infinite controversy.

For the British public in 1896, however, the problem crystallized itself in the rising strength of Bismarck's Prussia. The year's non-fiction best-seller was a book by E. E. Williams called *Made in Germany*, which deliberately set out to chill the flesh of the patriotic consumer. 'In your own surroundings', it said, 'you will find that the material of some of your own clothes was probably woven in Germany.

Still more probable is it that some of your wife's garments are German importations; while it is practically beyond a doubt that the magnificent mantles and jackets wherein her maids array themselves on their Sundays out are German-made and German-sold, for only thus could they be done at the figure. . . .' And the list goes on, in a manner only too reminiscent of more recent anti-import tracts, to point out the sinister Teutonic origins of the toys and the fairy books in the nursery, the piano, the Black Forest mug cunningly inscribed 'A Present from Margate', the drain pipes, the poker in the fireplace, the opera and its singers, the text on the wall and, final insult, 'the German band that rouses people from sleep in the morning'.

Such diatribes helped to stoke up the demand for increased naval and military spending which burdened mid-nineties budgets (and had recently led to Gladstone's final resignation from the leadership of the Liberal party). And they were certainly taken seriously enough to produce a heart-cry from the 1897 *Library Year Book*: 'The refining, stimulating and refreshing influences of the novel are being positively swallowed in the feverish anxiety of young people to equip themselves in technical and other subjects to enable them to fight competing Germans, and it looks as if imaginative literature, whether in poetry or prose, would lose its hold in the face of urgent commercial needs.' But it required more than the sales of a few more textbooks on chemical engineering and the new-fangled internal combustion engine to halt the rot that was beginning to show up in Britain's export figures, and by 1898 it was possible for the young American Henry Adams to be writing from London to his brother, Brooks: 'The secret of it all lies in the returns of the Board of Trade, which show that this year at last settles the fact that British industry is quite ruined and that its decline has at last become a débâcle.'

The exultation was unbecoming (after all, even the *New York Times*, on the occasion of Queen Victoria's Diamond Jubilee the year before, had been proud to subscribe itself 'a part, and a great part, of the Greater Britain which seems so plainly destined to dominate this planet') and also a trifle premature. But the underlying facts were clear enough. Britain's overseas sales, which had risen by 4·8 per cent a year from 1854 to 1872, had dropped back to an average rate of only 2·1 per cent from 1876 on. Although the growth of world trade itself had slightly slackened, it was still progressing at 2·55 per cent a year, and by 1896–8 the progressive shrinkage of the UK share in the total was already an established phenomenon. In 1899 a furious row over the Midland Railway's first purchase of a US-made locomotive underlined the extent to which Britain felt its traditional specialities were being eroded.

Even banking, the greatest of the late-Victorian growth industries, was felt to be obscurely at risk. As J. W. Cross wrote warningly in *The 19th Century*: 'In the City of London today there is not a single English firm among what might be called the *haute finance*. If a large financial operation has to be concluded we first go to Messrs. Rothschild, then to Messrs. Raphael, both German Jews; then to Messrs. S. P. Morgan & Co., an American House; after that, probably, to Messrs. Speyer or Messrs. Seligmann or Messrs. Stern, also German Jews; then perhaps to Messrs. Hambro, a Danish firm; then to houses like Messrs. Frühling & Goschen, and so on, all foreign houses and mostly Jews; but there is no strictly English name among them since the unlimited Barings ceased to exist in 1890; and that period during which the Barings' business was best managed was while it was under the direction of Mr. Joshua Bates, an American.'

Such xenophobic heart-cries punctuated the preparations for the Jubilee, whose endless processions of exotic and far-flung dignitaries first opened the eyes of the great British public to the fact that they had rather absent-mindedly acquired hegemony over an Empire some fifty times larger than their own foggy and overcrowded island. And although it was cheering to be able to claim overlordship of Sarawak, Zanzibar and the Turks & Caicos Islands, it failed to deflect attention for long, either from 'the fact that, in the richest country in the world, the great mass . . . live without the knowledge, the character, and the fullness of life which are the best gift of this age';* or the even more cogent fact that the commercial supremacy which had produced these riches was under strenuous world-wide attack.

For the moment, though, English society, despite its many strains and inequities, was able to maintain some sort of uneasy balance. The 'new unions', which emerged in 1889–90 to represent the great unskilled, unorganized, industrial groups like the gas-workers, and to win the 'docker's tanner'† from the intransigent employers of the

---

* Canon Samuel Barnett, founder of London's Toynbee Hall settlement, where young men from Oxford tried to tackle the plight of Booth's East End poor.

† Ten thousand men, including many of the unemployed from other trades, competed each day for 3,000 casual jobs in the docks, where even the 2,188 regulars only averaged 12s. to 15s. a week. The brilliantly organized five-week strike finally won a 6d. an hour minimum, 8d. for overtime, no signing on for less than four hours and the abandonment of contract and piecework. John Burns, one of the leaders, reminded his men in a triumphant speech on Tower Hill of the Relief of Lucknow in the Indian mutiny, when the garrison strained its eyes for the gleam of the rescuing bayonets, and exulted: 'This, lads, is the Lucknow of Labour, and I myself, looking to the horizon, can see a silver gleam— not of bayonets to be imbrued in a brother's blood, but the gleam of the full, round orb of the docker's tanner!'

G

Port of London, had now temporarily subsided. The skilled men, averaging 38s. a week in jobs like compositor or engineering fitter, were collecting the highest dividend ever—2s. 8½d. in the pound—on their accounts with the Co-operative Societies, and enjoying 'unstinted food, clothes of the same pattern as the middle-class, when house rents permit, a tidy parlour, with stiff, cheap furniture which, if not itself luxurious or beautiful, is a symptom of the luxury of self-respect, and an earnest of better things to come, a newspaper, a club, an occasional holiday, perhaps a musical instrument' (E. J. Hobsbawm: *Labouring Men*). Profits, as measured by the gross amounts liable for Schedule D income tax, had grown by a third, from £267 million to £352 million over the two decades of the 'Great Depression'; wage earners, thanks to falling prices, more than maintained their share; and the 'Depression' itself was finally evaporating in a roaring boom set off, at first, by the cycling craze which kept Birmingham and Coventry working overtime during 1895–6, and then sustained by a major house-building surge, whose somewhat dingy and dilapidated progeny now represent the 'inner twilight zone problem' for most of Britain's larger industrial cities. Building costs in the mid-nineties reached their lowest level since the Great Exhibition (despite an 80 per cent increase in wages) and output, after a long, stagnant period closely linked to the rate of emigration to the United States ('It was the prosperity of the Dakotas, so to speak, that brought building to a standstill in Dalmarnock.') jumped from an average of 80,000 dwellings a year to over 140,000 in the decade from 1896 to 1905.

The activity was by no means overdue. The 1891 census had shown that 11 per cent of the population in England and Wales were living two or more to a room, and in the worst parts of London the figure jumped to 40 per cent. In Scotland over half the people lived *more* than two to a room, and there were few towns or cities that did not have one family in five living in hovels without either separate privy, water-supply or through ventilation. It was such conditions, in the richest country in the world, that, in 1883, had caused even the very conservative John Morley to say that: 'I believe we shall have to bring to bear the collective forces of the whole community, shortly called the State, in order to remedy things against which our social conscience is at last beginning to revolt.'

The revolt was an unconscionably long time in the incubator, and in 1896 it had hardly begun to stir. Fashionable life provided far more interesting topics than the state of the Hoxton slums, even for the people paying 5s. per week per room to live there. There was the cost of fashionable weddings for example—a colonel of the Blues, married from the Langham Hotel, laid out £100 to hire thirty-seven carriages for the day, and his wife's wedding dress was made from lace at 300 guineas a yard. There was the burning question of what the Queen paid for her tea, on which the royal tea merchant, Mr Gibbs of Pall Mall, was able to throw considerable light—'Although reports have been frequently circulated about the extravagant prices paid by her, such sums as 15s., 20s. and even 30s. a lb. being freely stated, she seldom pays more than 6s.; 5s. 6d. is her usual price and the tea is a special scented blend; for a change her favourite is a very fine souchong at 4s. 8d.' There was the chance to learn to skate for 5s. a session at the Niagara Rooms in York Street, Westminster, with a hope of seeing Lily Langtry, Lady Randolph Churchill and the Honourable Bridget Bulkeley 'looking lovely, pretty and festive in deep cardinal with gold-embroidered yoke'. There was the question as to whether one's daughter should become a private secretary (average salary £150 a year) after mastering Pitman's Phonographic Teacher (price 6d.). And for those of a more political turn there was always the perennial topic of the pampered, overpaid, working classes.

As the *Sheffield Daily Telegraph* resoundingly trumpeted that winter, after hearing that the Japanese cotton workers in Osaka were content with only 3s. 6d. a day: 'The foreign manufacturer is in a position to undersell his British rival. It does not seem possible to suggest a remedy until the petted British artisan has been starved into realization of the fact that he must work at the same rate of labour and remuneration as his continental brethren.' The fact that these continental brethren included Germany, where Bismarck had introduced old age pensions in 1889, and the beginnings of a fully comprehensive system of social insurance, was not regarded as relevant to this kind of argument.

It was to be another thirteen years, as we shall see in the next chapter, before a British government agreed to back the revulsion of Morley's social conscience with a serious disbursement of public pounds. And by then the whole world would be on the edge of change.

The Pound in 1909

was worth £6 10s. in 1970 money

I remember listening for many hours, on the
journey over the St Gotthard to Milan, to a
fluent English traveller explaining to some aston-
ished Italians that England was steadily growing
poorer year by year, less money accumulated,
less money spent.

C. F. G. Masterman: *The Condition of England*
(1909)

We all thought Papa would die. He looked too
ashen to recover.

A daughter of the Duke of Rutland, after
hearing that the Liberals had raised
the income tax to 11d.

The first payment of Lloyd George's Old Age Pension—virtually the first disbursement of Britain's public funds which did not depend on proof of total destitution—was on 1 January 1909. A huge bonfire was lit on the White Horse Hills. In Bromsgrove the streets were hung with bunting, and bands paraded the streets. In Walworth one old woman offered the postmaster two rashers of bacon in gratitude for his help in filling up the necessary forms. In Spalding people said they would keep the money as a memento for their grandchildren, and in Bishop's Stortford a seventy-five-year-old farmhand died as he signed the receipt. The National Society of Amalgamated Brassworkers sent a congratulatory New Year's telegram to the Prime Minister and the Chancellor of the Exchequer in gratitude for 'Glorious Pensions Day'. And the Lord Provost of Glasgow, echoing the sentiments of the House of Lords, the Charity Organisation Society, and most leading figures in the City, told a savings-bank meeting that such pensions could only tend to encourage the thriftless, and to dissipate the proud spirit of Scottish independence.

As the sum involved was precisely 5s. a week—at Burton Latimer the first pensions were paid in crowns, which the lucky beneficiaries promptly sold at a premium to local souvenir hunters—and you had to be over seventy, with an income of under £31 a year, to qualify at all, it was hard even for contemporaries to take such attacks very seriously. But the *Woman Worker*, one of the crusading weeklies set up to support such advanced causes as Votes for Women, the Women's Trade Union League and the Anti-Sweating League (that same week it was advertising 'Rushing the House'—a Grand, Exciting, Suffragette Game—Price 6d.), took the trouble to report a sample 5s. budget, as laid out by one of those profligate and abandoned Glasgow widows whose moral and spiritual welfare the Lord Provost was so concerned about.

The money was expended as follows: rent, 2s. 3d.; pint of paraffin, 1½d.; 14 lb. of coal, 2½d.; 2 oz. of tea, 1d.; ½ lb. of sugar, 1½d.; 2 lb. of potatoes, 1d.; 2 lb. loin of mutton, 1s.; half-bag of flour, 1d.; pint of porter (for Sunday's dinner), 1¾d.; pepper, salt and vinegar, 1¼d.; one loaf, 2½d.; Total, 4s. 5¼d. The old lady, in typically thriftless manner, said that she intended to have a first-class dinner on Sunday, with perhaps 1d. worth of cheese. Later in the week, she would purchase 'a ha'porth of beans' together with 'a pennorth of onions', and after that, she calculated, she would have enough over to afford '1d. for a herring on Friday, and then it will be time to draw my pension again'.

Flora Thompson's *Lark Rise* graphically describes what the money, even in such tiny amounts, meant to the hundreds of thousands of old people who previously had had to spend their declining years in a grim struggle to keep out of the workhouse. 'When the Old Age Pensions began, life was transformed for such aged cottagers. They were relieved of anxiety. They were suddenly rich. Independent for life! At first when they went to the Post Office to draw it, tears of gratitude would run down the cheeks of some, and they would say as they picked up their money, "God bless that Lord George! (for they could not believe one so powerful and munificent could be a plain 'Mr.') and God bless *you*, miss!", and there were flowers from their gardens, and apples from their trees for the girl who merely handed them the money.'

Such was the golden dawning of the Welfare Age, the beginning of the process of social and economic change summed up by Lord George Hamilton, chairman of the Edwardian Poor Law Commission, when he wrote, in his *Reminiscences*: 'The object and incitement of the nineteenth century was to accumulate wealth, while the duty of the twentieth century is the far more difficult task of securing its better distribution.' And although the start, as usual, was somewhat grudging, and hung about with bureaucratic meannesses—like the rule which forced many people to pay 3s. 6d. out of their first 5s. for a birth certificate, in order to prove that they really were seventy, and the exclusion of anyone who had drawn poor relief in the last year, or been in prison in the last ten years—they could have been a lot worse. The original proposal had been to exclude anyone who had been in trouble or on relief since 1889, to deprive all pensioners of the vote, and to give married couples only 7s. 6d., on the carefully documented grounds that two could live cheaper than one; but all these were dropped, either in drafting, or in House of Commons amendments. Even the belated and scandalized revelation by the Tory newspapers that it was possible for a man with £3,000 deposited in the bank at 1 per cent to qualify for a 1s. a week pension (the precise basis of dispensation being that you got the full 5s. if your income was below £21 a year, and less, by units of 1s., as you ascended towards the £31 pinnacle) failed to jolt the Government from the paths of relative generosity. Some 650,000 people collected their money in the first full year—nearly 150,000 above the original official estimates, which helped to demonstrate just how much concealed poverty lay beneath the swelling Edwardian tide-line—and the cost came to £8 million, swiftly rising to £12 million by 1913. With the beginnings in 1911 of national health and unemployment insurance, on a partially contributive basis, the total new social expenditures by government had by then reached over £20 million—almost as much as the State had spent altogether in the years before the Napoleonic Wars.

In many ways, these were the last and least pleasant days of *laissez-faire*. In the years from 1870 to 1896, as we have seen, the trend of prices, wages, profits and technologies was such as to put slightly more money, a lot more purchasing power, and a great deal more choice into the hands of ordinary people, while concealing, behind a somewhat depressing monetary curtain, the amount of real economic progress which business and the landowning interests had enjoyed. But from 1896 to the outbreak of the first World War the process had gone smartly into reverse. Prices and profits had started to rise again. Business, despite its hectic tendency to be either booming or busting, was on the up and up. Even the farmers, after their long late-Victorian gloom, had successfully made the transition from corn to beef and milk and the more profitable forms of horticulture, and could face the future with at least a faint smile. The ever growing numbers of the middle classes, of which by now there were an estimated 1·4 million belonging to families with an income of over £700 a year, and another 4·1 million above the 'gentility' line, represented by the £160 a year level at which income tax started, saw an average increase of around a quarter in their salaries, rents and dividends during the decade 1900–10. But for the great 39 million mass of the working populace, progress had slowed to a halt, and even, in some cases, started to run backwards. Real wages, after adjusting for unemployment, had risen by an average 1·85 per cent a year from 1874 to 1900, according to Bowley and Wood. But from 1901 to 1914 they actually dropped, by an average 0·71 per cent a year. And even allowing as much as possible for the fact that men lucky enough to be in steady work tended to move during the period from lower-paid to better-paid occupations, it remains clear that for the great mass of working families the first decade of the twentieth century was a time when pay failed pretty consistently to keep up with the cost of living.

The pound in the worker's pocket, in fact, was now already worth a good deal less than the Victorian 20s. According to the Labour Department of the Board of Trade, its purchasing power in terms of twenty-three selected articles of food fell from 20s. to 18s. 5d. between 1896 and 1900, and by 1912 it was down to 16s. 3d. Life was offering more possibilities of enjoyment—the ½d. newspapers, the football matches, the early, flickering cinema screens—but for a growing number each year, the price, except very occasionally, was prohibitive. Unemployment, which in 1900 had been low, rose to 6·4 per cent in 1904, dipped slightly, and then, after the big American crisis in 1907, rose to 8·7 per cent, its highest level since 1886. It held there for nearly three years, till some sort of recovery set in in 1910. The workhouses, even after the first pension payments, were fuller than they had been for fifty years, and signs of real poverty were visible to anyone who cared to look. Eric Hobsbawm in *Industry and Empire* quotes a trade union man saying of those years: 'It will give you some idea of the conditions in Liverpool, it was quite common for a farthing's worth of milk to be sold; not merely bought and sold, but carried to the house too. At the end of the week you would collect a penny three farthings for seven farthings' worth of milk. This was in the poorest part of Liverpool. . . . I remember once I was working for Smithdown Rd. depot on the tram to Pier Head and I had seventy-five passengers and they all paid 2d., and when I came to cash up I only had one threepenny bit, all the rest was coppers. That was a sign of poverty.'

Yet these were the same years of which George Cornwallis-West, the husband of Lady Randolph Churchill, and then of the actress, Mrs Pat Campbell, wrote in his memoir, *Edwardian Hey-Days*: 'I doubt whether in any period of history of the modern world, except perhaps that immediately preceding the French Revolution, has there been such a display of wealth and luxury as during King Edward's reign. Not even the death duties brought in by Sir William Harcourt a few years previously, or Mr. Lloyd George's rabid anti-wealth speeches in Limehouse and elsewhere, acted as a deterrent to extravagance. If Socialism was in the air, no one, in the class I refer to, bothered to think about it. The possibility of a Socialist government was the last thing that entered into any one's mind.'

The irony was that by this time Britain had clearly begun to slow down. The annual growth in national income, which had been over 2·5 per cent in the nineties, was now down to only 1·75 per cent. But the combination of rising prices and stationary labour costs meant wider profit margins, with the result that virtually the whole of the national growth went into the pockets of those classes of society— traders, speculators, entrepreneurs, the holders of ordinary shares and their professional advisers—who were in a position to benefit from inflation. And to turn the screw a little further, the cost of food, which could still be expected to absorb something between 60 and 70 per cent of a low income in Edwardian days, was going up appreciably while the price of personal service, which accounted for a very substantial fraction of middle- and upper-class spending, remained effectively stationary.

This was no marginal matter, either. At the peak of Edwardian affluence, there were something like 1·5 million domestic servants in Britain—more than the number employed in the whole of the engineering industry. Even then the demand far exceeded the supply of girls and boys who were prepared to accept the long hours, attic bedrooms, coal buckets, black-leading and rules about 'no followers' which went with Edwardian housekeeping. So that the fragmented, unorganized horde of parlour maids and under-footmen probably maintained their standard of living, such as it was, rather better than the increasingly bitter, strike-prone and heavily unionized labour forces in the mines and the factories. The rigid, hierarchical career structure of kitchen and pantry ran from hall-boys and between-maids, at £8 to £10 a year, through head housemaids and under-footmen at £25 to £30, up to cooks at £80 and butlers at £100, and the big department stores had whole sections devoted to the outfitting of servants and their quarters—all the way from 'Bed (2'6") with Plain Woollen Flock Mattress for Servants—35s.' to Stockinette Directoire Knickers, 3s. 11d. new, or 1s. 6¾d. slightly soiled in autumn sales, and Special Servants Non-Creaking Boots, 2s. 11d. But even in 1902 Mrs C. S. Peel's comprehensive guide *How to Keep House* was complaining that girls would do anything—board-school teacher, post office clerk, shop girl or worker in a factory—rather than enter domestic service. And by 1909 even the *Woman Worker*, while editorially advocating the notion of a servants' trade union, was suggesting in its careers column that the best thing a girl could do was to scrape together £50 and set up in the registry office business.

Servants were now recognized as providing an index of a family's, or a district's, prosperity more accurate even than acreage, size of house or means of transportation. The census authorities coined the phrase 'standard of comfort'—the number of servants per hundred separate occupiers (excluding hotels)—and Hampstead came out at 80 against Rochdale's 7. Westminster could boast as many as 12 menservants per hundred, leaving out the innumerable females alto-gether. And in the 'servant-keeping' areas of London, every other house had more than one living-in help, and one in ten had three or more.

In such circumstances, it was a moot point whether Lady Wim-borne and her son were more to be envied in 1909 for their fleet of two Daimlers, two Mercedes, three Darracqs and two Napiers, or for the fact that they employed a platoon of chauffeurs, in the charge of a 'chief of the engineering department'. There was plenty of significant truth, both social and industrial, in the story of the American who tried at this period to sell the idea of a self-starter to Britain's fledg-ling motor industry. His big line was that by providing press-button ignition they could save their customers the inconvenience of getting out to crank the handle in the prevailing British rain. But he was told loftily: 'Our customers have drivers to do that sort of thing.'

Customers, in fact, found the drivers a great deal cheaper than the vehicles. Even the most skilled and reliable man could scarcely com-mand more than £40 a year, while the most modest cars on the market, like the 'wee but wonderful' 8 horse-power Humber, cost between £150 and £200. The new 45 horse-power Mercedes, proudly announced the week after Lloyd George's 1909 Budget introduced the first road-fund licences (six guineas) and the first petrol tax (3d. a gallon, on top of a basic price ranging between 1s. a gallon in the Isle of Man, 1s. 2d. in Central London and 1s. 6d. in North Scotland), came out at a basic price of £900—though the Car Mart advertisement in the *Autocar* had the cautious grace to add 'or near offer considered'. Even in the second-hand market it was hard to come across anything much below £100, and the motoring magazines found it worth while to offer a vetting service of travelling experts who charged three guineas to look at vehicles costing under £150, four guineas for those between £150 and £400, and five guineas over £400 (plus 5s. third-class railway fare, where applicable). It was almost as expensive as experimenting with one of the new-fangled flying machines, which were now on offer to the more intrepid members of society at between £400 for a Farman biplane and £1,000 for a Wright, complete with guarantee that the machine would get off the ground. Blériot flew the Channel solo that summer, to win the *Daily Mail's* long-standing challenge prize, and *The Economist* predicted that 'when a sufficiently hardy and reliable type of machine, suitable for carrying one or two persons, has been evolved for ordinary use, the price will probably be in the neighbourhood of £150'.

But even £150 looked a good deal of money when compared with the average household income of 45s. a week—equivalent to around £15 at 1970 prices. That was reckoned to be the earnings of 1½ wage earners (husband and one elder child), which had to support three or four others (wife, younger children or elderly relations). It bought 32 lb. of bread and flour, 3 lb. of rice, tapioca or oatmeal, 17 lb. of potatoes, 9 lb. of meat, ¾ lb. cheese, 12 eggs, 2 lb. butter, 10 pints of fresh milk, 5 lb. of sugar, ½ lb. tea, and small quantities of jam, marmalade, treacle, fish, dried fruit, vegetables, pickles and condiments. That took up 20s., and, after paying out 7s. 6d. for rent, fuel and light, there was 17s. 6d. left for clothes, furniture, soap, matches, drink, tobacco, newspapers and medical care, not to mention the journey to work, stamps, holidays and any form of entertainment. And the diet, though no doubt an advance on the bread-and-scrape of earlier decades, still looked like pretty-unrelieved stodge—fresh fruit and green vegetables were so infrequent that they did not appear in the first official cost-of-living index, started in 1914, based on 1904 budgets. And, indeed, one of the more surprising items of sociological discovery is the fact that the now omnipresent greengrocer's shop only really started to spread in the years following the Great War. Before that, it was street markets or nothing, and for many town children apples were almost as rare and exotic as the dessert mangoes which the Army & Navy Stores were offering at 2s. 2d. a bottle, or their guavas at 1s. 10d. a tin.

The Army & Navy catalogues (one of which was recently reproduced in loving facsimile as *Yesterday's Shopping* at the not insignificant 1970 price of £8 8s.) give a superbly opulent conspectus of this extravagant age. But even in the Special Notices at the beginning of the 1909 edition it is made quite clear just who is expected to enjoy the goodies listed in the succeeding 1,282 pages. 'Complaints have been made of persons entering the Stores to make purchases who are not members and who are not of cleanly appearance and respectably clad: Members will oblige by making their own personal purchases and by not sending servants or messengers for them.' However, once within the magic circle of cleanly, and monied, respectability, the pleasurable world had few bounds. There was golf, with four clubs and a bag for 29s. 3d., balls at 24s. a dozen,* and a patent device for 42s. enabling you to practise your swing in your drawing-room. There was yachting, with a fourteen-foot spruce dinghy for £23 15s., and the magic lantern, at 92s., in Russian iron and brass, with eight slides on Life in the British Navy for 2s. 6d. There was the gramophone— 'Monarch' Senior, with 'Morning Glory' Horn, £11, and records at 7s. 6d. (though Melba, Patti and Caruso cost 21s.) and Charles Parsons's patent 'Auxetophone', worked by electricity, could set you back £100. There was big game hunting (hammerless 'Jungle' guns from £30) and there was billiards, with a best oak, twelve-foot table, plus balls and twelve cues, for £109 10s., there were bicycles at between £6 and £15 15s. with three-speed gear £2 extra and there were Bechstein concert grand pianos at 300 guineas (though you could have a lady pianist for four hours for 9s. 6d. and the cab fare, if you lived within ten miles of the store).

Electricity was at last beginning to take hold, as the price, which had been between 4d. and 6d. per unit in 1902, came down to 2d. in 1906. Back in the nineties Lord Salisbury had been among the pioneers, when he installed a lighting system at Hatfield (his family threw cushions at the wires to make it spark). But now it was becoming fully accepted. The King's yacht had 'a complete electrical outfit, including soup and coffee boilers, hot plates, ovens, grills and hot closets'. The Army & Navy could not offer all that until 1911 or so. But they had the Pulvo Portable Air Suction Dustifier, at £26 4s., which had recently replaced the Empress Electric Aspirator Air Suction Cleansing Machine for £23 2s. (even if the Low-Vacuum Pneumatic Dust Extractor, which took a maid and a footman to

* Down from £1 each, when the Haskell rubber-cored 'Bounding Billy' first replaced the old 'gutty' in 1898.

work it, but only cost £5, was the more popular). And there was a three-pint electric kettle for 43s. 6d., an electric iron for 23s. and an electric shaving pot in polished copper for 21s. 6d.* Ediswan lamp bulbs, up to 25 candle-power (watts only came in later) cost 11s. a dozen (down from 13s. 9d. in 1907) and there was an illuminated electric table-cloth for 68s. 3d. ('Care should be taken to use the 2-pin plugs across metallic lines in cloth and not lengthways.') But the electric washing machine and the modern refrigerator were still some way off. The best you could do in 1909 was a Bradford Vowel A Washing Machine at 63s. 9d. and a fiendish 'Raplin' ice maker at 190s. ('Sulphuric acid . . . is the only chemical required.'), both of which required someone to turn a heavy cast-iron handle for twenty minutes or more to produce any effect.

Still, there were plenty of worse ways to make a living in 1909 than turning an ice-machine handle. A good deal had been done, on paper, in the way of alleviating some of the more brutish excesses of the industrial revolution—the first Employers' Liability Act, giving compensation in accidents; the 1901 Factory Act outlawing the truck system, where workmen were often paid in kind, or in vouchers on a company shop, or in a pub where they drank the proceeds away; various laws curtailing the employment of children; and the Eight Hours Act, setting an often rather theoretical limit to coal-mining shifts. But it was only in 1909 itself that the Trade Boards Act finally laid down some legal standards for the badly sweated trades, starting with tailoring, and the makers of lace, chains and paper boxes. And bad as the individual mistress might be, it is hard to believe that many were as harsh and tyrannical as some of the employers who got into the courts, and the newspapers, during that year.

One favourite ploy was to charge workers for the materials which they used; a fairly undesirable practice at any time, but doubly so when applied in the manner of one large Leeds tailor, reported by the Women's Trade Union League, who charged his men and girls 3s. 6d. a day for reels of cotton which could have been bought retail at the shop round the corner for 2s. 9d. Then there was another Yorkshire factory which charged its girls 2d. a day for 'cooking', or in other words boiling the water for the tea they brought themselves. The union reckoned this out as a profit of £150 a year. And even that paled into relative acceptability against some of the compulsory 'hospital contributions' and fines for lateness and allegedly poor work. The unions fought—and lost—the case of a girl, on 5s. a week,

---

* Two cut-throat razors, in crocodile leather case, with strop and manicure kit could be had for 29s. 6d.; but Gillette's new safety razor, still recognizable as near-cousin to today's model, cost 21s. with twelve blades.

who was fined 5d. for being five minutes late—a fine which, as their lawyer said, rated her absence at something like sixty times the price of her presence. And a Leicester hosiery worker who submitted imperfect goods because of a defective needle found herself at the end of the week with an empty pay envelope and a debit slip for 3s. 9d. All this passed virtually without comment in an age when trades-men even made a practice of swindling their customers over the farthing change from those 'Best silk gloves 1s. 11¾d.' bargains. The favourite gambit was to offer the purchaser a packet of pins instead of the coin. But as you got 52 pins in the packet, while ordinary pins cost 1d. for 250, the draper reckoned to make 6d. out of every 144 transactions in this way.

Even in those trades where the employers were not actively engaged in defrauding their employees, the normal reaction to a temporary decline in business was a proposal to cut wages, backed up if necessary with a train- or boat-load of blacklegs, supported by police and troops. The supplying of blackleg workers, by organiza-tions like William Collison's National Free Labour Association, which had figured in the Taff Vale* affair eight years before, was in itself a substantial business. And it is hardly surprising that this period, particularly from 1910 to the outbreak of the war, should have been riven with a series of bitter strikes, riots, lockouts and the occasional shooting—particularly in the pits, on the railways, and among the still very lowly paid, unskilled men on the docks—which seemed to many contemporaries to threaten the blackest form of revolution.

Looking back, indeed, the most extraordinary aspect of the situa-tion is not the aggression, but the relative docility of labour at this time. Engineering and shipbuilding, iron and steel, printing, textiles, and boot- and shoe-making were all highly organized industries where wages and conditions were little if any better than among the

---

* The Taff Vale case, which in one way and another has embittered and distorted British industrial relations for seventy years, arose out of a strike on the Taff Vale railway in South Wales, where members of the Society of Railway Servants induced a gang of blacklegs sent down from London to break the contract they had signed before setting out. The local manager insisted against all legal advice in asking the courts for an injunction to stop the men picketing. The High Court granted it, to everyone's surprise, the Court of Appeal threw it out, on the grounds that a union could not be sued, but the House of Lords restored it on grounds of public policy. From then on any official's or member's action was in danger of making the union funds liable for damages, and all strike action stopped until the newly-elected Liberal government reversed the Lords' decision in 1906. And from then on, right up to 1969, any suggestion of bringing the unions under the law has created a pathological opposition in Britain.

Darlington railwaymen or the South Wales colliers. But apart from the very occasional outbreak, like the Dudley girls in 1913 who walked out one day with the flat announcement that they could no longer keep alive on their wages (and thus precipitated a more or less successful demand for a 23s. a week minimum in the Midlands) there was little real trouble outside the main storm centres. Certainly nothing like enough to explain the reaction of the better-off sectors of society, who were starting to grow positively hysterical at this time in defence of their social and economic privileges.

The true extent of this hysteria was first exposed in the reception accorded to Lloyd George's 1909 Budget—the 'People's Budget', designed to produce the £16 million of extra revenue needed to pay both for the Dreadnought battle-cruisers demanded as part of the defence build-up against Germany and for the programme of reform inaugurated by the Old Age Pensions Act, which by 1914 was destined to encompass labour exchanges, subsidized school meals, juvenile employment bureaux and the beginnings of the full-scale national health and unemployment insurance schemes. As the Welsh Chancellor said, this was a war budget, a means of raising money 'to wage implacable warfare against poverty and squalidness'. But it was immediately interpreted as warfare against the rich and comfortable, in a way which is now almost impossible to comprehend.

The proposals themselves covered three main areas. Income tax, which had been 1s., was reduced to 9d. on lower incomes, and raised to 1s. 2d. on higher ones; child allowances, initially £10, were introduced for the first time; and, most dramatic feature, a 'supertax' of 6d. was imposed on incomes of over £5,000, to the extent that they exceeded £3,000 (so that the man with £5,001 paid £50 0s. 6d. more than the man with £4,999). Additional indirect taxes were placed on beer, spirits, tobacco, cars and petrol, but to a degree which looks minuscule by today's standards. And, worst of all, there were to be 'land value duties', levied on the unearned increment every time land was sold or leased, and including even a proportional contribution from undeveloped ground. This was the first attempt to grapple with a problem which is still only very partially resolved: the proper way to tax the windfall benefits of property ownership. Coupled with a proposal for a new 'Domesday Book' survey and valuation of all the land in Britain, which seemed to open up vistas of ever increasing imposts of this kind, the plan sent the Tory, and even some of the Liberal, landlords close to the borders of open rebellion.

In the end the Budget was thrown out by the House of Lords, in defiance of long-standing tradition, and the resulting political crisis, fuelled by growing trouble over Ulster and the Suffragettes, could only be resolved after a General Election and the passing of the 1911

Parliament Act, which trimmed the Lords' powers of disruption
down to acceptable levels. But ultimately most of the Budget provisions, apart from the land tax sections which turned out to be
largely unworkable, went through without any noticeable savage
effect on the standard of well-to-do living, and even to many people
at the time it was difficult to see what all the fuss was about.

A large part of the trouble, though, was undoubtedly the very
mixed motivation of Lloyd George himself. By the light of free
trade finance, rejection of tariff protection and on general grounds of
equity, his proposals were modestly and sensibly designed. But he
went a long way round to ensure that at the same time they were as
provocative as possible towards the chief financial supporters of the
Tory opposition, in the hope—wholly justified as it turned out—that
they would thus be trapped into some major tactical error, like the
Lords' veto. And he rammed the point home in a series of flaunting
speeches calculated to fan every available flicker of criticism into
flame.

Even his own Cabinet, on being shown the Budget proposals,
deliberated over them, according to John Burns, the ex-Labour
Chairman of the Local Government Board, 'like nineteen rag-pickers
round an 'eap of muck'. And emollient Liberal assessments like that
of *The Economist*—'The long-expected supertax is reasonably simple,
and is less than the Socialists hoped, or the contributors apprehended'
—were blown briskly aside when the Chancellor went down to Limehouse to tell Booth's still-struggling East Londoners that 'a fully
equipped Duke costs as much to keep up as two Dreadnoughts. . . .
He is just as great a terror and lasts longer.'

By temperament, Lloyd George was quite sincerely on the side of
the underdog. As he once said, after a long colliery wage conference:
'There were the employers on the one hand, plump, full-fed men,
well-dressed men who had never known what it was to go short in
their lives. On the other side were the men, great gaunt fellows, pale
with working underground, their faces all drawn with anxiety and
hard work. I know which side I'm on when I see that kind of thing.'
But now this boiled over into a sustained and deliberate campaign to
stoke up class hatred. And one of the abiding mysteries of British
politics is why at least one of his oratorical efforts that summer did
not end with a mob marching to burn the Bank of England, or at
very least the Junior Carlton Club.

However, for the Liberals' purpose it was sufficient that plenty
of Tory peers, encouraged by *The Times* and the *Morning Post*, should
think that they might. The noisy charade continued, with the *Daily
Mail* yelling about 'the plundering of the middle class' (though in
fact the new duties hardly touched them at all—even the tobacco

tax hit the workman's Black Cat cigarettes, at ten for 3d., propor-
tionately much harder than the businessman's 10s. cigar), and others
joining in with a by now only too familiar chorus—British capital
was the most heavily taxed in the world; the man who prospers and
accumulates money was treated as an enemy of the country; the
government was bleeding the upper classes to provide largesse for
the proletariat, and so forth. It sounded even more hollow than
nowadays in the summer of 1909, when in the four months following
the Budget, seventeen people left estates of over £250,000 (including
one of £2 million and one of £6 million) while the going rate for a
seamstress to make a pair of trousers was 4½d.

A quarter of a million pounds was a great deal of money at a time
when death-duties were still little more than nominal, and when you
could sail first class by the NYK Line to Japan, with a round-the-
world return, for £107. But 4½d. was not, especially with prices showing an inexorable tendency to rise over the past twelve years, and
economists like W. T. Layton and J. A. Hobson were already starting
to wrestle with the problem of twentieth-century inflation and the
apparent failure of a gold-based currency to maintain its value in a
gold-rich world. But their efforts sparked little in the way of official
interest or support, and the un-burned Bank of England basked in a
splendid Imperial haze, at the heart of a system where the Gold
Standard represented the unquestioned ark of the economic covenant.

To outward view, few institutions could have appeared more
secure, or more righteously resistant to unnecessary change. The
United States had only finally settled its gold and silver problems as
recently as 1900; the founding of the Federal Reserve System, which
would ultimately take over the leadership of the monetary world,
was still four years away; and as recently as October 1907 the entire
New York banking establishment had seized up as the $62 million
Knickerbocker Trust closed its doors and the panic-stricken American public rushed to convert its bank deposits into cash, in a way
which Britain had not seen since 1866. Not a bank had closed in the
UK since the City of Glasgow crash in 1878, while anything between
70 and 150 of the 20,000 US banks could be relied on to suspend
payments every year during the early years of this century. The
gentlemanly smothering of the Baring débâcle in 1890 tended to be
contrasted very complacently with the hectic and disruptive way in
which Wall Street handled such affairs. Altogether it was widely felt,
both at the time, and in later accounts of the period, that London was
in effect managing a sterling-exchange system for the rest of the
world, and benevolently monopolizing the short-term loans business,
which provided the essential lubrication, for the benefit of the Gold
Standard at large.

H

Few of the major central or near-central banks of the world at that time published—or in some cases even kept—the kind of statistics calculated to tell the public or the politicians how they really operated, and in the Bank of England the doctrines of secrecy and 'the hidden hand' were more deeply entrenched than anywhere. But patient work by financial researchers, cross-checking and co-ordinating those sparse and incomplete figures later made available, has fairly conclusively demonstrated that the Gold Standard was in fact already diverging a good deal from the pure, automatically operating text-book model. It was indeed, in many ways, getting very close to the Gold Exchange, or 'key currency' system of the inter-war years, which so painfully emerged from the efforts to 'get back to gold'. And it is one of the many tragedies of the twenties and thirties, underlying much that we shall be discussing in the next two chapters, that the men of 1925 understood so little of what the men of 1909 (even when they were the same people, just sixteen years and a great war later) had actually been practising.

In 1965, when Britain's then Chancellor of the Exchequer, James Callaghan, was in Washington, an earnest reporter asked him, 'Why do you have balance-of-payments problems now, when you didn't have them fifty years ago?' To which Mr Callaghan replied with some feeling, 'There were no balance-of-payments problems fifty years ago because there were no balance-of-payments statistics.' But Peter H. Lindert, who picked up this exchange as a main theme in his recent study, *Key Currencies and Gold 1900–1913*, shows fairly conclusively that the Chancellor was in error—the problem was there all right, and in considerable magnitude, but in the golden Edwardian sunset no one recognized it, or bothered their heads about it.

The beauty of the Gold Standard mechanism was always supposed to be the smooth, automatic manner in which it corrected any temporary international economic aberrations. And indeed, in 1907, during the American panic, there had been a classic demonstration. In sixty days, as US banks and private holders fought to lay hands on every scrap of liquid capital available, some £17 million worth of gold, equal to almost half the Bank of England's entire reserve, had flowed across the Atlantic. But a swift touch or two on the traditional switches, pushing the London Bank Rate up to 6 per cent on 6 November and to 7 per cent (the highest since the foreign loan collapses of 1873) on 7 November, had brought the whole lot, plus a couple of extra million, rolling back, and within six months the rate was back to an equable $2\frac{1}{2}$ per cent once more. That was in fact the last serious strain to which the system was subjected up to the outbreak of war (though there were smaller irruptions, equally smoothly dealt with, in 1906, 1910 and 1911) and its successful outcome acquired an almost mythological force in the minds of the post-war monetary authorities.

Unfortunately, as we can now see, it was only a success on a very narrow front—the protection of the Bank of England's reserves, which even contemporaries often thought dangerously slender for the country which was now universally recognized as 'the clearing house of the world'. It did virtually nothing to impose the kind of financial discipline that nowadays causes so much international concern. And in particular it allowed Britain to build up a deficit position, and an 'overhang' of short-term overseas liabilities, of a magnitude almost as huge, in proportional terms, as those which precipitated the sterling collapse of 1931 (see pages 136–58) and the US balance-of-payments upheavals in the 1960s.

According to the investigations of Peter Lindert and Arthur I. Bloomfield (*Short-Term Capital Movements under the Pre-1914 Gold Standard*) gold had by now long ceased to be the only form in which reputable trading nations held their reserves. Already something like 20 per cent of the total—roughly the same proportion as we shall find in the totally transformed situation of 1925—were in foreign currencies, notably sterling, French francs and German marks, in that order. Largely as a result, the substantial current account surpluses which all three achieved during the thirteen pre-war years were converted, after taking account of the relevant capital movements, into sizeable deficits. Britain, whose huge £270 million a year earnings on shipping, banking, insurance and other 'invisibles' comfortably took care of the long-established excess of imports over exports, had the whole of her average £125 million surplus wiped out by such capital flows, leaving an overall shortfall of at least £5 million a year (and probably twice as much if the figures were complete) on both the 'liquidity' and 'official settlements' method of calculating such things.

More important, though, was the relation of foreigners' sterling holdings by this time to the country's so tenderly cared-for reserves. Here there had been a really formidable build-up. Even on those items which have been positively identified, the total—nearly £100 million—was more than two and a half times the amount of gold in the Bank of England, and in fact rather more than all the gold in the country. To put the figures into perspective, it is only necessary to recall that the ratio of US overseas short-term liabilities to reserves in 1967, after eight years of mounting concern over the dollar and its balance-of-payment backing, was still appreciably below the two and a half mark. And at the peak of the panic which tumbled the pound in 1931, the equivalent figure, with no errors and omissions, was only just over four.

Why then was the Edwardian pound so strong, and the Kennedy-Johnson dollar and the Ramsay MacDonald pound so weak? And was it, in the long run, a good thing or a bad thing that in the 1900s Britain (and to a lesser extent, France and Germany) should have been allowed by the no-longer-quite-a-Gold Standard system to run persistent payments deficits of the kind which the post-1945 world has found intolerable?

The answer to the first question almost certainly comes down to a pure case of confidence. As it never remotely crossed anyone's mind to imagine that the pound could be in danger, or, after 1907, that the Bank of England could fail to conjure gold from the moon, if need be, by the wave of a discount-rate wand, so no one bothered to inquire at the time just what was happening to the structure of international sterling liabilities. So to that extent the nostalgic obfuscators are right—no statistics is good statistics, so long as no prod-nosed economist comes along to rock the boat.

But 'good', in such a context, is a very question-begging adjective. The even, equable tenor of Edwardian international finance was certainly good for the livers of the directors of the Bank of England and for the current earnings of the City, and in the short term it was good for exports, for prices, and for industrial investment. But whether it was good for Britain's long-run economic health is another matter.

What seems clear is that in this financially halcyon period life became very pleasant and easy for the monetary authorities, and the really rigorous part of the Gold Standard mechanism, if it had ever existed, fell into disuse. As we saw in the 1886 chapter, its main component, the raising of Bank Rate in times of trouble, was supposed to work in four main ways—pulling in short-term capital, chiefly gold; discouraging long-term foreign issues in London; cutting London credits to importers, and forcing them to sell stocks and lower prices; and, finally, by reducing total demand in Britain, to lower domestic prices and incomes and thus improve the trade balance. But given the apparently unlimited willingness of the rest of the world to hold pounds it was only really necessary to bring the first of these cards into play. Even in a major upheaval situation like 1907, a short, sharp dose of high bank rate was enough to bring the foreign exchange market back on an even keel, and the rest hardly mattered. In fact, as Lindert shows, foreign issues were rarely curtailed—why should they be when the whole massive £1,600 million build-up of Britain's overseas investments between 1900 and 1913 was more than covered by the dividends and interest produced by its Victorian forerunners. Import prices, if anything, rose rather than fell during all but one of the major Edwardian bank rate upheavals.

And the long-run effect on labour and material costs, though ultimately more or less in the direction predicted by the theory, were never pushed home, as they were to be during the 1920s, by employers trying to impose an actual wage cut on their men.

In effect, Britain was basking on a Gold Standard air cushion. Credit was easy; there was plenty of expansion, despite the occasional burst of unemployment; the massive import bill and the huge outflow of overseas lending both helped to boost foreign purchasing power and to sustain the country's traditional export industries. The continuing rise of competition, particularly from the US and Germany, which had caused so much despondency in the 1890s, could now be complacently ignored, as all the old staples—coal, cotton textile machinery and capital funds—enjoyed an Indian Summer boom. From 1905 to 1907 Lancashire opened 95 new mills, with $8\frac{1}{2}$ million spindles, and boosted its spinning capacity by over a fifth. Coal, employing 1,118,000 men and £135 million of capital, was experiencing the fastest growth and the highest returns in its history (though only three mine managers in the UK were earning over £1,000 a year, and more than half were getting under £300). New industries, like Courtaulds' artificial silk, were achieving a fantastic success, and obscuring the fact that in many other soon-to-be-important areas, like cars, chemicals and electricity, Britain was now lagging far behind. Full knowledge and appreciation of the worsening balance-of-payments position would no doubt have led to much sharper deflationary policies, and a much harder look at the island's aging industrial structure, but their absence, meanwhile, produced much higher incomes both for Britain and for the rest of the world. Even with all the benefits of hindsight, it is hard to be too harsh on the Edwardians—by the light of the information available to them, cotton and coal were the right and profitable things to invest in, and the benevolent dominance of the Bank of England merely represented the reward of generations of sound financing, on which it would have been the height of ingratitude to turn one's back. But the net result, after the supervention of an apocalyptically monstrous war, was an economic framework—and a set of economic attitudes—so fractured and distorted that Britain has been suffering from the effects ever since.

However, in 1909, that was all in the future. What interested the pound-using public was not any fine nuance of monetary theory, but the obvious fact that the gold sovereign, after its long period of Victorian appreciation, was now steadily losing a penny or two of its value every year. The most likely reason seemed to be that there was now a great deal more of the yellow stuff around—the gold stock in the world is estimated to have approximately doubled between 1890 and 1914, growing at a rate of over $3\frac{1}{2}$ per cent a year. And Britain was not alone in suffering from this: US prices during the period went up by a clear 40 per cent, while the Board of Trade in London made the English experience only 26 per cent.

The result, unmodified by anything very serious in the way of Government tax policy, followed the classic inflationary pattern. Farmers, mine-owners, manufacturers with fixed rent and interest charges and large wage bills all benefited, as did their shareholders and anyone paid a commission on profits or involved with a profit-sharing scheme (of which some 56 survived in 1909 out of the 224 started in British firms in the previous eighty years). People like stockbrokers and auctioneers, paid commission on turnover, were unaffected, except in so far as they benefited from higher sales. And landlords with long leases outstanding, holders of gilt-edged and other fixed-interest securities, lawyers and civil servants, and all ordinary wage earners—particularly the unorganized ones—tended to be distinctly worse off.

Most leading opinion agreed that this was, on the whole, a bad thing. But apart from Lloyd George's attempts to ease the worst effects on the near-destitute, no one had any very serious ideas what to do about it. Alfred Marshall suggested that in an ideal currency system, things should be so arranged that the receivers of fixed incomes, as well as those more fortunately placed, should 'secure a fair proportion of man's increasing control over his material environment', but he failed to provide any practical blueprint. Professor Jevons proposed a 'tabular standard of value', which involved a periodic revaluation of the sovereign to take account of any changes in the prices of goods and services—a notion of mind-boggling complexity—and W. T. Layton, in his pioneering *Introduction to the Study of Prices*, leaned more towards linking wages to some kind of cost-of-living index. On a completely different tack, Professor Irving Fisher wanted to divorce the nominal value of gold coins entirely from their fluctuating value in the open bullion market, and work on a restricted and 'managed' currency of the kind which India at that time had recently introduced with the gold rupee. This collapsed fairly comprehensively, however, as soon as the major governments started calculating the cost of buying in their depreciating currencies at face value, against a steadily falling gold price (a declining gold price, of course, being the automatic obverse of a rise in the price of commodities).

As Layton rather gloomily summed up: 'Seeing that almost all such attempts to control artificially the value of currencies have had unforeseen consequences it would not be surprising if the public preferred rather to bear those ills they have rather than to fly to those they know not of.' And a public moving inexorably towards Sarajevo, and a whole new, different, blighted world, preferred for the moment to do just that. The gold sovereign enjoyed its last years untrammelled by any official attempt to control its purchasing power. And in August 1914, after the pound in July had soared to $7 on the New York Exchange—the highest figure recorded since the darkest days of the Civil War—the worried Bank Holiday public queued up in the courtyard of the Bank of England to help perform what turned out to be the final obsequies for the country's 657-year-old gold coinage.

At that time the only notes circulating in England were of £5 or over, and most members of the general public never saw one from one year's end to another. Even when they did have occasion to cash one there was an elaborate business of signing on the back, which trades-men reckoned gave some protection against accepting forgeries, and for practical purposes gold and silver were the essential components of everyday finance.

As people prepared to go on holiday on the Friday and Saturday, 31 July and 1 August 1914, and the farm-workers assembled to collect their harvest money, some of the banks, in panicky expecta-tion of an ominous and uncertain future, refused to pay out more than half their customers' needs in gold. The rest came in notes, which were virtually useless for the ordinary purposes of shopping or bus fares or settling up small debts, so the crowd moved *en masse* to Threadneedle Street, there to exercise the Englishman's inalienable right to convert his paper currency on demand into gold.

The Times described the scene. 'The courtyard and the Issue Department of the Bank of England presented a remarkable spectacle. From noon onwards it was occupied by a changing queue of people, desiring to change notes, which stretched in a double line from the counter of the Issue Department to the pavement of Threadneedle Street. On the opposite side of the road, on the steps of the Royal Exchange and the triangular space before it, a much larger crowd stood and with some amusement watched the proceedings.'

On the following day things were worse. The ordinary banks were now only disgorging a minute trickle of gold, and at the Bank of England 'the courtyard contained two distinct queues between half-past eleven and one, and a number of policemen were employed, not from any fear of disorder, but to protect the visitors themselves against possible robbery'. Within half an hour of the normal closing time, everyone within the gates had been dealt with, and the last pre-war sovereign had passed into circulation. On Sunday Germany declared war on Russia; Monday was Bank Holiday, and on that evening a Royal Proclamation declared a moratorium on bills of exchange, and prolonged the holiday till Thursday the 6th; on the 4th, Britain declared war.

By the time the banks opened again, the government had rushed through a Currency & Bank Notes Act, which authorized the issue for the first time of Treasury (rather than Bank) notes, in the everyday denominations of £1 and 10s. (People called them 'Bradbury's' after the secretary of the Treasury who signed them, and collected them as souvenirs.) In the Act it was laid down that the notes were still convertible into gold on demand, but there was nothing on the notes themselves to say this, and few people ever realized that they had this right. Sovereigns continued to circulate fairly freely till 1915, but from then on they were progressively withdrawn. And by 1918 it was only too clear that a new monetary era—as well as a new political, social and economic era—had decisively dawned.

The Pound in 1925

was worth £3 10s. in 1970 money

Whatever its imperfections, gold has for centuries commanded the confidence of the civilized world and has continued to command it. If the gold standard fails to give complete stability its adoption is nevertheless the most simple and direct method of obtaining a high degree of stability. It is not proved that any other standard would give even as good results. All countries which have successfully restored stability and confidence in their currencies after the disturbances of the last ten years have done so on a gold basis.

Treasury White Paper accompanying the
Gold Standard Bill (1925)

There's no escape; you have to go back; but it will be hell.

Reginald McKenna to Winston Churchill
(spring 1925)

On 28 April 1925, in the Budget that cut income tax from 4s. 6d. to 4s., introduced widows' and orphans' benefits, and set the new, contributory old age pension levels as 10s. for everyone at sixty-five, the Chancellor of the Exchequer, Winston Churchill, made the expected, and in the event almost off-hand, announcement that Britain intended to return to the Gold Standard, at the full pre-war exchange rate of $4·86¾ to the pound. It was a supreme effort to turn back the clock, to 'return to 1913', and to call back yesterday. It signalled the opening of one of the most miserable, and to many minds, criminally mismanaged decades in British history.*

To what extent the decision actually caused or intensified that misery is a matter which has consumed a great deal of ink over the last forty-five years, and we shall return to it ourselves shortly. But for the moment, let us first consider what kind of a changed world it was around which Churchill and his advisers wished to rebuild their golden cage.

In many ways, of course, it already looked very much like our own world. By the end of 1924 there were 1·3 million cars and lorries on the road and the horse was rapidly becoming a picturesque relic. There were full-page advertisements for Omo ('Gives out oxygen which puts the final touch of absolute whiteness to household linen. . . .') and Lux, in the big, new 10d. packet. You could buy an Atco sixteen-inch motor mower, at the distinctly high price of £50, or a Qualcast hand machine from 38s. You could sport a Parker Duofold pen at 37s. 6d., or a Consulate shirt at between 6s. 6d. and 1 guinea; nibble a Lyons Swiss Roll at 1s. or a plate of Shredded Wheat at 8d. a packet or a bar of Cadbury's Fruit & Nut at 1s. 1d. a ½ lb; and if you were a woman you could have a Harrods Permanent Wave (4

---

* Formally, Britain only abandoned the Gold Standard in 1920, when the Gold & Silver (Export Control) Act specifically forbade the shipping of bullion from the UK. During the war, although it was theoretically possible to move gold out of the country, in fact the German submarine threat effectively prevented anyone doing so, and the only currency that mattered was the paper pound, whose foreign exchange value was pegged by the Government at the rate of $4·76$\frac{7}{16}$. Supporting even this rate, 2 per cent lower than the traditional $4·86¾, cost the Treasury some £420 million, and it was reckoned that in practice sterling had depreciated by between 10 and 15 per cent against the dollar by the time support ended on 20 March 1919. Gold sales were then temporarily banned under the ubiquitous Defence of the Realm Act until September 1919, when a licensing system, later consolidated under the 1920 Act, was introduced to restore at least some faint semblance of the old London gold market. This Act was due to expire on or before 31 December 1925. While it existed, the Gold Standard, which depended essentially on free movement of bullion in response to market forces, was effectively moribund.

gns. for shingled head; 5 gns. for long hair) or invest in André Hugo's
much more expensive Permanent Steam Waving at 15 gns. A third
of the population of London, it was estimated, went to the cinema
every week (cheapest seats, 6d.) and nearly two million people had
bought sets which enabled them to listen to the still pre-BBC wireless
('G & S one-valve loudspeaker model—why Worry With Crystals?—
£10 10s.' or, alternatively, 'Greatest Wireless Bargain Ever Offered—
three-valve set for £7 15s. 0d.—Will Work!'). You could even acquire
a Rolls-Royce Silver Ghost if you were prepared to put down £1,850
for the chassis alone.

All this sounds a long way from the mellow, lavender-scented,
long-skirted certainties of 1913 to which Churchill and his Treasury
advisers were directing such nostalgic backward glances. But if anything the changes in Britain's fundamental economic and financial
position were even more striking than the contrast of the streets and
shopwindows would suggest.

These changes stemmed only very partially from the war itself.
Certainly Britain had lost men—745,000 killed, or about 9 per cent
of all the men between twenty and forty-five, and 1·7 million
wounded—and a fair amount of money: net liquidation of privately
held overseas investments probably ran to some £550 million, plus
some substantial confiscations in Russia and East Europe. But we
actually ended the war owed more—by a matter of £485 million—by
our allies than we had incurred in new debts, largely to the United
States. It was only during the intensely complex and fractious debt-
repayment negotiations after the war that this positive balance was
whittled away.

When all the dust had settled, though, one positive and highly
significant factor emerged: the long-term capital position of the
United States, which had shown a net debit of well over £400 million
in 1914, was by 1922 in overall credit to the tune of £1,200 million,
and New York had decisively taken over London's position as the
world's largest source of international capital. And although, on
paper, the new Federal Reserve authorities claimed that they were
on the Gold Standard, in fact they had no intention of submitting the
US currency to any such automatic discipline—for practical purposes
they were operating a Dollar Standard, closely managed in the
interests of the US, and gold was already playing a very circumscribed and subservient part in their calculations.

The relative eclipse of London as a finance centre was only one
facet of Britain's burgeoning post-war difficulties. While the war
monopolized the country's effort, major trading markets in Canada,
South America and the Far East were lost, sometimes irrevocably, to
the highly active and expansive Americans and Japanese. And at the

same time the weakening position of the old staple exporting industries, coal, cotton and engineering trades, which had already started
to show itself well before the war, was now a great deal worse. After a
wild, hysterical boom in 1919–20, and a burst of activity in 1923,
while the Ruhr was effectively shut down by French occupying
troops, the mines and mills and yards of the North relapsed into a
general condition of slump, which kept the national unemployment
figures almost continuously above the one million mark—often well
above—until the dark days of 1940. War had something to do with
this, of course—the shattered European countries, which would
willingly have bought more British goods, were often totally unable
to pay for them, in the economic and political chaos which followed
the Armistice and the Treaty of Versailles—but the decline in
demand for coal and cotton would have happened anyway, and so
would the rise of new competitors. Failure to recognize this, and the
accompanying hope that all would be well if only the (often mythical,
and almost universally rose-coloured) conditions of 1913 could be
restored, condemned most of the policies and initiatives launched in
the early 1920s to sterility or worse.

For the bulk of the population in 1925, however, it was perfectly
possible to ignore the situation, and live life as it came. Unemployment, by and large, was something that happened in Scotland and
Wales and along the Mersey and the Tyne—areas which had
flourished during the Industrial Revolution and which still believed
that it was only a matter of a few small adjustments before they
flourished again; while in London, where the biggest concentration
of misery, evil conditions, and ill reward had existed for generations,
people were just beginning to enjoy the swing in Britain's prosperity
axis which has now constantly favoured the South-East for almost
fifty years.

Even the current crop of swindlers had a crisp, up-to-the-minute
touch about them. In the spring there was Mr Bud Pollard, an enterprising gentleman who advertised in the *Daily Mail* (now 1d.) that he
was casting a new and splendid motion picture, offering jobs at £10
to £15 a week, and conducted nearly two hundred screen tests, at a
'nominal' fee of £2 5s. a time, before it was discovered that he, with
his cameras and his Soho 'studio', had silently vanished away. And
in the summer there was the sad affair of the well-known baronet,
who persuaded a syndicate of London investors to put up £60,000
('guaranteed annual dividend of 120 per cent') to finance the illicit
export of whisky to Prohibition-racked America. Unfortunately he
fell out with his bootlegger contacts over a little matter of a £2,000
bribe, and lost the lot.

It was possible to shrug off such misadventures, though, so long as one was safely in a job. For although the 1925 cost of living, according to the February *Ministry of Labour Journal*, was a clear 79 per cent above the figure for 1913–14, most people's money wages had more or less kept up with this, and some had done a good deal better. Dockers, printers, bakers, boot and shoe makers and the less skilled railwaymen were well ahead, with increases of over 100 per cent; and the municipal employees, gas workers, electricity wiremen, seamen, tramway drivers and painters were close behind. Even more important, the traditionally low-paid workers, like labourers in the engineering industry, shipyards and the building trade, had sharply improved their position as compared with the skilled grades. At the base of the railway pyramid, there were widespread rises of 150 per cent or more above the pre-war level. It was only in the heavily exposed and unemployment-prone export industries, like shipbuilding, cotton spinning, coal mining and parts of engineering, that pay and earnings had clearly failed to keep up with prices. And the victims there, apart from the occasional hunger march, mostly remained at this time safely out of sight, and out of mind.

Certainly the woes of the coal industry received a certain amount of attention, as they could hardly fail to do when there were over 600 Welsh pits shut down by the end of 1925 and when in towns like Blaenavon virtually the whole male population—in this case 3,500 miners—had been thrown on the dole by local pit closures. The Blaenavon men, in their first week out, drew an average of 23s. a head from the Ministry of Labour. But the *Daily Mail*, while recording the fact, was much more interested in its long-running and slightly hysterical campaign against 'Dole Dodgers' of which the following letter, from a reader in Nottinghamshire, is one of the more sober examples:

'At the court of petty sessions held at Wellingborough on Friday last a painter was fined for being drunk and disorderly. He stated that he was out of work; he admitted that he received a dole of 33s. a week and a pension of 19s. In this district painters are in good demand and likely to be as long as they can get 52s. a week without working. It is not a princely income as things go now but sufficient, it seems, to find ample beer money.'

With beer now costing between 10d. a pint for porter and 1s. 2d. a pint for bitter or bottled light ale (against a range of 1½d. to 6d. in Booth's 1890 London), the wretched painter can hardly have made a daily occurrence of such behaviour, and his pension, which presumably related to war wounds of some kind, does not seem very relevant. But the whole idea of 'the dole' caused continual controversy during the twenties and thirties. Under its official name of 'uncovenanted benefit'—as opposed to the 'standard benefit' of 18s.

a week, covered by contributions of 8d. a week from the employer and 7d. from the employee—it was introduced as a 'temporary extension' of help by the Shaw Act of 1924, under Ramsay Mac-Donald's first Labour Government. This was one of no fewer than twelve unemployment measures passed by a now thoroughly panicky Parliament between 1920 and 1927, and its purpose was an attempt to prevent too many of the chronically out-of-work, whose contributions were quickly exhausted, from falling into the hated (and already financially overburdened) hands of the Poor Law authorities. Given as it was, as a grudging hand-out rather than a natural right, it probably generated more bitterness than any other social measure between the wars.

The basis for the whole post-war unemployment insurance mechanism had been laid down in 1918–19, mainly to tide over the difficult resettlement period for men returning from France. For largely administrative reasons it looked sensible to extend the scheme (which on its inauguration in 1912 had covered only a very narrow band of around 2·4 million workers) to include virtually everyone except farm labourers, domestic servants and the civil service. At the same time provision was made for the rise in the cost of living (the original payments had been only 7s. a week for men and 5s. for women), for dependant allowances and for an 'out-of-work donation' for anyone temporarily unemployed and uncovered by contributions. All this fairly generous figuring was based on the assumption of a 'normal' unemployment rate not exceeding 4 per cent. When the great 1920 slump introduced a twenty-year period during which the rate was not once to drop below 10 per cent, it naturally threw a great strain on the Exchequer—especially as it was not until 1934 that the government finally gave in and accepted that extended unemployment was not a matter of temporary, hand-to-mouth expedients which must somehow be repaid within the system, but something that would have to be met as a direct charge on the taxpayers.

Still, notwithstanding the muddle and bitterness, there is little doubt that, even allowing for the extent of long-term unemployment, the general condition of what were still unhesitatingly called the working classes was a good deal better in 1925 than it had been in the Edwardian 'golden age', let alone the Victorian 'golden age' which had gone before. And there is little doubt that it was the existence of 'the dole', ramshackle and unhappy as it was, that prevented an all-round slashing of wages, of the kind that the coal-owners and many other employing groups really wanted. There was one big downward readjustment between 1920 and 1922, when the Ministry of Labour's index of earnings, taking 1913 as 100, collapsed from 244 to 147, but this was largely as a result of agreed sliding-scale arrangements linked

with the cost of living, whose own index over the same period
dropped from 276 to 180. All further serious moves in this direction
were effectively blocked, despite the apparent failure of such direct
confrontations as the 1926 General Strike.

Meanwhile, when the country's most eminent statistician, Sir
Arthur Bowley, came to inquire in 1924 *Has Poverty Diminished?*,
his answer, based on a careful study of Reading, Northampton,
Bolton, Warrington and Stanley, was a clear 'Yes'. 'The proportion
of families in which a man is normally working found to be in poverty
was in 1924 only one fifth of the proportion in 1913 if full employment is assumed; whilst if the maximum effect of unemployment is
reckoned, it is a little over half.' Admittedly some part of this is
probably due to a general decline in the size of families. But even
there some improvement was noticeable: the 'usual' wage of 21s.–
23s., which the Bowley investigators had found in Reading in 1913,
was only sufficient to support, at most, a man, his wife and two
children; now the 'usual' wage there was up to 42s.–46s., and allowed
for one additional child of school age. The only serious exception to
this improving trend was the Durham mining village of Stanley,
which had been the most prosperous of all the five sample communi-
ties before the war, but now showed a $7\frac{1}{2}$ per cent poverty rate,
against the previous 6 per cent. And indeed it was the miners—the
pre-war 'aristocrats of labour'—who were taking the brunt of intransigent employers,* of worsening coal-seam conditions, of falling
world demand, and soon of Churchill's new Gold Standard move.

But elsewhere, the most striking thing that Bowley found was the
steady upward mobility in his working-class terraces and tenements.
This made his inquiries particularly difficult at the top end of the
income scale. 'When the working class approximates the middle class
it frequently acquires the secretiveness of the latter on questions of
income', he complained, after a particularly frustrating time in
Northampton. 'A bay window is always a barrier.'

The bay windows were becoming more numerous as the 'tax-line'
disappeared and nearly six million people came to enjoy the bour-
geois privilege of contact with the Inland Revenue Department. The
early twenties indulged in a modest housing boom (though nothing
to compare with the brick-and-mortar-mad thirties) and it is possible
at this distance of time to penetrate a good deal further than
Bowley's university inquirers, behind the aspidistras and the thick
net curtains of that genteel suburban life which was now springing

---

* In the acidulous words of Lord Birkenhead: 'It would be possible to
say without exaggeration that the miners' leaders were the stupidest
men in England, if we had not had frequent occasion in the course of
these negotiations to meet the owners.'

up. In places like Hendon (reached by the Hampstead underground-railway-line extension from Golders Green in the summer of 1923), it was putting up land from two or three hundred pounds an acre to well over one thousand pounds, and the same sort of thing was happening in similar retreats round all the great cities.

The general impression at the time was that 'unlike those of the working classes, middle-class and especially professional standards seem still to be below pre-war level, but this has undoubtedly improved as compared with the close of the war and the post-war boom'. Certainly the standard rate of income tax, which had reached a peak of 6s. in the pound in 1918, plus a supertax of up to 6s. for really high incomes, had now come down sharply. Churchill's new budget brought standard rate down to 4s., the lowest rate for the past half-century (it lasted until 1930). And everybody with less than £15,000 a year received a cut of between 6d. and 1s. in his relevant supertax rates.

Not everyone, though, had managed to engineer a successful adjustment to the nearly doubled cost of living. The Chancellor of the Exchequer, for instance, was still getting the same £5,000 that he had received in 1913, as were the High Court judges. Before the war these had been really princely salaries—equivalent to something like £30,000 tax-free at 1970 prices—and their effective purchasing power had now been slashed by something like two-thirds. Of course, their possessors were still very comfortable and no one but their families worried much about their plight. But slightly lower down the pyramid, people like higher civil servants, particularly principals and assistant secretaries, had done very badly. The shopping value of their £1,073 and £1,382 salaries in 1924-5 was also only two-thirds of the £855 and £1,150 they had been paid in 1913; and no one in the civil service above the rank of executive officer appears to have actually beaten the cost-of-living index over the period.

Partly this seems to have been deliberate Treasury policy, based on a particular interpretation of the way prices were moving. The theory was that it was food prices which had advanced most spectacularly, while the other elements of respectable suburban existence had held relatively steady. For this reason, a complicated cost-of-living bonus was introduced by Whitehall in 1920 (at which time the index was 130 per cent above its pre-war level). Essentially people got 130 per cent extra on the first £91 5s. of their 1913 pay; 60 per cent on anything between £91 5s. and £200; 45 per cent between £200 and £500, and nothing thereafter. Additionally, as the index rose and fell, so did the first slice of bonus—by five one-hundred-and-thirtieths for every five point move. So by 1925 the bonus effectively amounted to something like 80 per cent for the really low paid—the

The first gold souveraigne, issued by Henry VII in 1485. Its purchasing power was equivalent to about £50 at 1970 prices. Wolsey, when Archbishop of York in the next reign, was considered the richest man in England with an income of £10,000 a year

The Newark nine penny piece, coined in 1645 from silver plate when Charles I ran out of money during the Siege of Newark. Equivalent to around 7s. 6d. in 1970 money

The first gold guinea. It started life as a £1 piece, but the African gold (indicated by a little elephant below Charles II's head) was so fine that the British public thought it was worth more. Gamblers pushed the price to 30s. before it settled down at its traditional value of £1 1s. The name guinea comes from Guinea in West Africa, the source of the African gold

The Hangman's Pound. George Cruikshank drew this Bank Restriction Note, signed by Jack Ketch, the public executioner, at the time of Waterloo, when 307 Britons had been hanged for counterfeiting

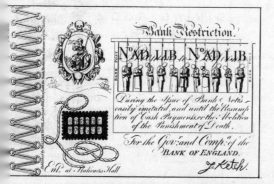

1 Photo: Peter Clayton
2 Photo: Peter Clayton
3 British Museum
4 British Museum

1870

The Marshalsea Debtors' Prison in London's Southwark, part of the world that 1870 was leaving behind

Peter Jackson Collection

The inescapable water-filter was a required fitment everywhere, above and below stairs: 14s. 6d. for the servants, 70s. in the dining-room . . .

SILICATED CARBON WATER-FILTERS.

THE MOST EFFECTIVE MEANS KNOWN OF PURIFYING WATER FOR DOMESTIC, MANUFACTURING AND GENERAL PURPOSES.

These are the only Filters capable of thoroughly removing the organic and saline impurities, animalculæ, &c., from water. The are adopted, in preference to all others, by the Government, the authorities of the General Post Office, the London and Provincial Hospitals, and many other large public and private establishments in all parts of the world.

PRIZE MEDAL, PARIS EXHIBITION, 1867.

THE DOMESTIC FILTER.

No. 27.

Made in cream-coloured Stoneware, and fitted with slabs of Patent SILICATED CARBON Filtering Media.

Complete with Cover and Plated Tap.

PRICES.

No. A, capacity 1 gallon ... ... 14s. 6d.
No. B, ,, 2 ,, ... 21s. 0d.
No. C, ,, 4 ,, ... 32s. 0d.
No. D, ,, 6 ,, ... 42s. 0d.
No. E, ,, 8 ,, ... 52s. 0d.
No. F, ,, 12 ,, ... 70s. 0d.

No. 27.

THE ONLY SILVER MEDAL, HAVRE EXHIBITION, 186

THE DINING ROOM FILTER.

No. 22.

Made in marbled china, chaste and elegant in appearance, and well suited for the Dining room.

Size A will purify six gallons per day; B, about twenty gallons; the water possessing that freshness which is always wanting in the ordinary Carbon Filters.

Prices, with Electro-Plated Tap.
A, 30s.; B, 70s.

No. 22.

The English Mechanic (courtesy: Miss Dorothy Hartley)

. . and a new adjunct to gracious
~ving was available in the 1870s for
£10 3s. 3d.

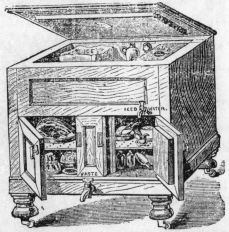
is was the 'Archimedean' Lawn
ower, made and sold, wholesale
d retail, by Walter Carson and
ns, of La Belle Sauvage Yard,
ndon E.C. For slightly broader
res, Messrs. Shanks of Arbroath
uld supply a 30-inch pony-and-
nkey-pulled machine for £15 15s.,
th boots for the pony (to protect
e grass) for 22s. extra

The Field, 1 January 1870

The Southern Veteran-Cycle Club

The 'Ariel' Penny-Farthing—£8 for the basic
model, £12 with gears

Photo: *100 Years of Soccer in Pictures* (Heinemann)

Aston Villa—Birmingham F.A. Challenge Cup Winners, 1880

870s		1970
2d.	Haircut	5/-
/10d.	Jersey	30/-
/-	Shorts	15/-
/11d.	Boots	120/-
6d.	Ball	210/-

othing inflates like leather—
or transfer fees

Chelsea—F.A. Cup Winners,
1970

Photo: Press Association

1886

The Victorian working man protesting—
at a 3s. cut in his basic wage of 30s. a week

' "At ten bob," said the Carpenter,
"I deeply sympathize!" '

THE·PENNY
ILLUSTRATED·PAPER
AND · ILLUSTRATED · TIMES

A SCREW LOOSE AT BIRMINGHAM: STRIKE OF MESSRS. NETTLEFOLD'S HANDS.

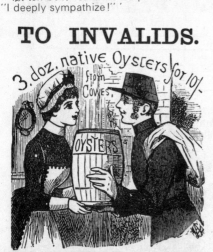
No late Victorian male needed to
suffer in this inelegant fashion.
Platt's Patent Trouser Rack was
available, in polished mahogany,
walnut or oak, for 9s. to hold six
pairs, 12s. for eight pairs, and 18s.
for a dozen

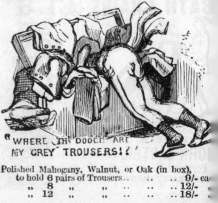

Photo: Cunard Line

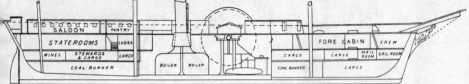

Photo: Arthur J. Maginnis, *The Atlantic Ferry* (Whittaker)

For those who sought refuge in America—a month to cross the Atlantic in the *Britannia,* at 10–15 guineas saloon class, 7 guineas intermediate, and steerage at 'lowest rates'!

For when the Gold Standard mechanism broke down

The last great age of oil and gas—by the 1890s even a Tory Prime Minister had seen the electric light

Peter Robinson's stylish silk costume with plush, jet or striped velvet cost 5 guineas in 1886, against Cardin's mini cocktail dress for £28 in 1969, at Miss Selfridge. The maxi, in the usual manner of the dress trade's topsy-turvy economics, was £24 10s. Victorian males were even better served, with a full morning coat at under 30s., where today it would be a bargain at £30

Part only of advertisement, The Daily Telegraph, 1 December 1969

MANUFACTURERS,
97, 99, & 101,
NEWINGTON-CAUSEWAY, LONDON, S.E.

Over 1000 Garments have already been made up this season from country customers' own measurements, and not one garment has been returned as a misfit. This fact shows the simplicity of our Easy Rules for Self-Measurement. All should try a single garment as a Specimen of the Style and Workmanship we give.

RINK SUIT, to Measure, at 29/6, 34/6, 39/6, 45/-, 50/-, 55/-, and 60/-.
TROUSERS, 8/11, 10/6, 12/6, 14/11, 16/9. Before ordering elsewhere, see our immense range of New Goods, at 12/6. No risk of Garments not fitting. See Easy-Measurement Form. Patterns post-free.

HOLIDAY SUITINGS.

Superior RINK SUIT, Made to Measure, from choice TWEEDS and INDIGO BLUE SERGES, at 29/6.

If Morning Coat Suit, 2/6 extra.

Single Jacket, 15/6; Vest, 5/11; Trousers, 8/11.

29/6

Superior MORNING COAT and VEST, Made to Measure, from good Black DIAGONAL and FANCY COATINGS, at 29/6.

Single Coat, 24/6; Vest, 6/11; Trousers, 12/6.

In consequence of the extra pressure of business previous to holidays, we regret that disappointment has occurred, and to avoid this Customers are requested to ORDER EARLY.

The Penny Illustrated Paper, 22 May 1886

1896

D. H. Evans's all-purpose 'pinnie'—equally suitable for mistress and maid, at 1s. 11¾d. The 'Doris' cap, remarkable, according to *Woman's Life,* for its quiet style and eminent suitability, cost 1s. 4¾d., together with 'streamers of abundant length'. Other caps could be had for the 'truly marvellous' sum of 4¾d.

IN CAP AND APRON.
Woman's Life, 18 January 18

ELLIMANS UNIVERSAL
EMBROCATION 1/1½

"IT
I WILL
HAVE
OR
I WILL
HAVE
NONE"

The wooden club, in 1896, was 5s. 3d.; the golf balls 10s. a dozen; the aches and bruises free

Prepared only by Elliman Sons & Co Slough.

FOR
STIFFNESS
SPRAINS
ACHES
BRUISES
The Queen, 6 October 1894

Photo: Abbot's Hall Museum of Rural Life of East Anglia

A doctor's gig like this cost £50 in the mid-1890s, with another £80 for the horse. The blacksmith, however, was prepared to do running repairs for 1s. a shoe

Photo: University of Reading, Museum of English Rural Life

Tied cottage 1896. Rent £3 8s. per annum. No damp course, no running water, no sanitation, privy within a stone's throw

1909

Happy Easter 1909. You could go to the seaside by rail (by 1870 the first-class return from London to Brighton had risen to 30s. and the second-class to £1) or by car. . . .

BRIGHTON & SOUTH COAST RAILWAY.

Easter on the Sunny South Coast.

FAST TRAINS FROM LONDON BRIDGE, VICTORIA and KENSINGTON (Addison Road).

CHEAP RETURN TICKETS.

By all Trains on every Friday, Saturday, and Sunday, available to return on the Sunday or following Monday or Tuesday.	Return Fares from London Termini to						1st Class.	2nd Class.	3rd Class.
	BRIGHTON	...	...	...	...	...	12/9	7/6	6/4
	WORTHING	...	...	...	...	...	14/-	8/3	7/-
	LITTLEHAMPTON	...	...	...	...		14/6	9/6	7/6
	BOGNOR	...	...	...	...	...	15/9	10/3	8/-
	HAYLING ISLAND	...	...	...	...		17/6	11/6	9/6
	SOUTHSEA	...	...	...	...	...	19/-	12/-	9/6
	PORTSMOUTH	...	...	...	...		19/-	12/-	9/6
	ISLE OF WIGHT	...	...	...	...		21/6	13/6	11/-
	SEAFORD	...	...	...	...	...	14/-	9/-	7/-
	EASTBOURNE	...	...	...	...		14/-	9/-	7/6
	BEXHILL	...	...	...	...	...	14/-	9/-	7/6
	HASTINGS	...	...	...	...	...	14/-	10/6	8/-

These Tickets will also be issued on April 8th, 9th, 10th, 11th, available to return by any train, according to class, on any day except day of issue, up to and including Tuesday, April 13th.

Day Excursions will be run on Good Friday, Easter Sunday and Monday.

Brighton in 60 minutes—Daily (except Easter Monday), The "Southern Belle," Pullman Express, comfortably warmed, leaves Victoria at 11.0 a.m. Single Ticket, 9s. 6d., Day Return Ticket, 12s., returning at 5.45 p.m. on Week-days and 5.0 p.m. on Sundays.

Eastbourne in 1½ hours by Pullman Limited every Sunday and Good Friday from Victoria 10.45 a.m. Returning at 5.20 p.m. Single Ticket, 11s. 6d., Day Return Ticket, 12s. 6d.

Details of Supt. of Line, L.B. & S.C.R., London Bridge.

The Tatler, 24 April 1909

The little 8 h.p. Rover two-seater, which cost £200 new in 1905, was advertised second-hand four years later in excellent condition, one owner, 23,000 miles, for £115

The Rover Company Ltd

Household Triturating Strainer.

For Soups, Sauces, Purees, Gravies, Jams, &c.

The object of the Patent Triturating Strainer is to enable cooks to reduce to pulp or liquid, and strain by the same operation, every description of animal and vegetable substances for making Soups, Sauces, Purées, Gravies, Jams, &c.

Each...... 16/9

Army & Navy Catalogue, 1909

Household triturating strainer— invaluable for the production of nourishing soup for the poor

Personal Weighing Machine

Designed for those overweight with Empire?

Army & Navy Catalogue, 190

Resonating Gongs on Oak Stand.

Army & Navy Catalogue, 1909

Household duties were still regulated by the bell and the gong. But the new consumer durables were beginning to creep in

The Low-Vacuum Pneumatic Dust Extractor.

With best fittings thereon, and supplied with one dust-bin, two dust-bag one 12 ft. length ⅞ in. bore flexible metallic tubing, a carpet sweepi nozzle, and two small nozzles (for cleaning upholstery &c.)

Price £5 0 0

Sent direct from Makers, Carriage paid.

Army & Navy Catalogue, 1909

Hats—

Army & Navy Catalogue, 1909

s worn by the well-dressed . . .   well-fed Edwardian man . . .

THE ONLY GENUINE IMPORTED

TURKISH CIGARETTES.

Guaranteed Hand-made in Turkey.

Sold by all Leading Tobacconists.

PRICES PER 100.

Yenidje	...	12/-	and	13/-
Special	...	9/-	10/-	11/-
En A'ala	...	7/-	8/6	9/-
Yaka	...	5/6	6/-	6/6
Nazir	...	4/-	and	5/-
Selam	...	3/6	4/6	5/6

Assorted Samples of 12 Cigarettes
post free on receipt of P.O. for 1/-

WEST END DEPOT: RÉGIE, 83, PICCADILLY, W.

TURKISH RÉGIE CIGARETTES

The Tatler, 13 January 1909

. . . before old age, malaria,
and far too many creature
comforts . . .

reduced him to . . .

PATENT LEITER

Army & Navy Catalogue, 1909

1925

But only 1½ million wage-earners got a~~n~~
paid holiday in 1925—the Holidays With Pa~~y~~
Act only went on the Statute Book in 193~~_~~

THE BROADS

200 MILES OF SAFE INLAND WATERWAYS   HOLIDAYS AFLOAT £4 PER WEE~~K~~

BOOKLET FREE FROM PASSENGER MANAGER LIVERPOOL STREET STATION LONDON E.C.2 OR ANY L·N·E·R INQUIRY OFFI~~CE~~
PARTICULARS OF YACHTS FOR HIRE FROM NORFOLK BROADS BUREAU 22 NEWGATE STREET LONDON E.C~~.~~

Photo: Kershaw Stud~~io~~

Reduction in Price of B.T.H. Headphones

"A cute aid to Acute hearing"

Ⓑ-Ⓣ-Ⓗ

Old Price   •   £1 : 5 : 0
NEW PRICE - £1·0·0
(per pair, 4000 ohms)

To go with your £3 10s. crystal
set—'no hair-catching projections,
no "scissors" movement of
headbands, permanent magnets
that are really permanent, and now
cheaper, too!'

POPULAR HOLIDAY
CRUISES TO
NORWAY

BY

R·M·S·P
"ARAGUAYA"
10,000 TONS

FROM LONDON
12 Days from 15 Guineas

FROM LEITH
10 Days from 13 Guineas
MAY TO AUGUST

Write for Brochure No. P. 12.

THE ROYAL MAIL
STEAM PACKET CO.

ATLANTIC HOUSE, MOORGATE, E.C.2 AND
AMERICA HOUSE, COCKSPUR STREET, S.W.1
LIVERPOOL · MANCHESTER · GLASGOW
BIRMINGHAM   SOUTHAMPTON

Bystander, 25 February 1925

Note the ominous sentence about
foreign Competition—two months
after the advertisement appeared the
Chancellor of the Exchequer, Mr
Winston Churchill, made it 10% worse

The wooden club was now 15s. 6d. and
golf balls between 13s. 6d. and 30s. a
dozen. Aches and bruises were still free

Car prices were beginning to come down, as Austin and Morris picked up the mass-market lessons taught by Ford in Detroit. But the Model T itself was already on its way to the museums

Easter in sight.──Order Now!

MORRIS

Still the best value

buy British-and be Proud of it.

PUBLIC CONFIDENCE in the value of Morris products and the stability of the Morris policy is evidenced by our sales record for January, which totalled 4,380 cars delivered. The equipment of all Morris cars includes Dunlop Cord Balloon tyres, Lucas twelve-volt lighting and starting, Gabriel Rebound Dampers and Every Necessary Accessory.

W HEN comparing Morris prices remember that they include a Full Comprehensive Insurance policy operative for one year. This gives the purchaser approximately £11 direct saving on Morris-Cowley models, and £13 10s. on Morris-Oxford cars.

Remember also that the 11.9 h.p. Morris-Cowley is a *full-sized* touring car with ample power. The engine develops over 25 b.h.p.

The 11.9 Two-seater MORRIS-COWLEY - - - £175
Fully insured for one year. Fully equipped.
Choice of Blue or Grey.
14/28 h.p. MORRIS-OXFORD models, with four-wheel brakes, from £260.

MORRIS MOTORS, LTD., COWLEY, OXFORD.

F.H.S.R.1.

The Bystander, 11 March 1925

Technological economy. Despite inflation and the war, the Remington Standard, £21 17s. in 1909, was still only £26 10s. And the cut-price competition was chopping these prices to ribbons

Harrods
INTRODUCE THE NEW
A.M.C.
TYPEWRITER

The Last Word in Durability, Convenience and Economy

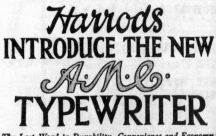

T HIS new Typewriter is identical in every feature with many higher-priced machine Standard size, with the standard keyboard, th 'A.M.C.' is soundly constructed throughout and thoroughly practical in every way.

A Marvel of Value!

It's safe to say that for Value this new machine stan absolutely alone. Nowhere else will you find its equ For use in the home, for social correspondence and cl affairs, for private business, for the student, for the pr fessional writer and for general office use, the A.M.C. is t ideal Writing Machine. Como to Harrods to-day and s for a Demonstration, or, if that is inconvenient, you m send your order by post assured of perfect satisfacti

Metal cover and baseboard supplied with each machine.

£6·10

Sent carriage p to nearest station England and We

Convenient Terms arranged if desired.

HARRODS LTD   LONDON S

Kendals Sale

NOW PROCEEDING

FOR TWO WEEKS ONLY . . .

Wonderful Opportunities from
THE LINEN HALL

Remarkable BEDSPREAD offers

Special Offer of PRINTED BEDSPREADS
...Jaspe, grounds in a ...od design. In pink, ...se, orange and green, ... single beds 70 x 90 ins.
...ual Price 6/11 SALE PRICE **4/11**
...r double beds
...LE PRICE **6/11**

Irish Embroidered BEDSPREADS on Jaspe Grounds
Effectively striped in blue, green, rose and gold.
For single beds 70 x 90 ins.
Usual Price 8/11 SALE PRICE **6/9**
For double beds
SALE PRICE **8/9**

PURE WOOL BLANKETS
...superior ...lity in ...ite, that ...give ...xcellent ...ervice. AT **15/-** per pair. Usual Price 18/9
...small single beds, ...approximate 60 x 80 ..., weight 6 lbs.
20/-

ALL-WOOL CLOTH BLANKETS
In all-white, with whipped ends. For single beds. Size about 63 x 83 ins, weight about 7 lbs. Per pr.
Usual price 24/6 SALE PRICE **20/-**
For double beds
SALE PRICE **29/-**

HEMSTITCHED LINEN SHEETS
A superior quality offered at a big price reduction. For single beds, size 2 x 3 yards.
Usually 25/9 SALE PRICE, per pair **20/-**
Also for double beds, size 2½ x 3 yards.
Usually 33/- SALE PRICE, per pair **27/6**

TABLE LINEN BARGAINS

O BLEACH CLOTHS O SERVIETTES
...h Linen Double Da... ... Tablecloths in a ...utiful Willow Pattern ...gn. Size 72 x 72 ins.
...al PRICE — **17/6**
...72 x 108 ins.
...al Price 37/-
...E PRICE — **25/-**
...IETTES to match.
...24 x 24 ins.
...al Price 37/6 per doz.
...E PRICE — **25/-**

TABLECLOTHS and SERVIETTES TO MATCH
In Irish Linen Double Damask. Rose and Scroll, as illustrated.
Size 72 x 72 ins.
Usual Price 14/6 SALE PRICE — **12/9**
Size 72 x 90 ins.
Usual Price 18/- SALE PRICE — **15/6**
SERVIETTES to match.
Size 24 x 24 ins.
Usual Price 21/- per doz.
SALE PRICE per dozen **19/6**

PURE LINEN DAMASK CLOTHS and SERVIETTES TO MATCH.
A good-wearing quality, with white ground and dainty border in attractive shades of blue, green or gold.
Size 36 x 36 ins.
Usually 5/11 SALE PRICE — **3/9**
Size 45 x 45ins.
SALE PRICE — **5/6**
SERVIETTES, 14 x 14 ins.
Usually 11d. each
SALE PRICE **7d.**

SPECIAL VALUE IN ALL-LINEN HOUSE CLOTHS
...n excellent quality, ...th red border, typed ...ea" or "Glass.
...al Price 12/9 per doz.
...ALE PRICE
...6 for **5/-**
...tter qualities at 15/-
...d 19/9 per dozen.

MARVELLOUS OFFER! REVERSIBLE WOOL MOTOR RUGS AT 9/11
These rugs are beautifully warm and cosy, and are available in assorted check designs, in brown, fawn, blue and grey, with coloured checks to tone. Full size. We have never previously been able to offer a rug of this quality under 15s.

Kendal Milne & Co
ANSGATE   MANCHESTER

1931

These were some of the bargains the housewives of Britain were missing in 1931

On the 15s. 3d. a week dole, of course, you just got wet

AN UMBRELLA WITH TWO MISSIONS IN LIFE

One, to protect you; the other, to complete your ensemble—does both with a quite remarkable degree of success, and more, is quite remarkably inexpensive!

A very chic, yet withal serviceable affair, of fashionable walking-length, it has a splendidly weather-withstanding silk-mixture cover on a slender, fine-rolling frame. You can choose from a varied collection of crook handles and an up-to-the-minute selection of covers, including striped and plaid effects—or, if your taste does not incline to patterns, there are plain covers in pure silk—brown, navy and black, all priced at **21/-**

A MAN'S UMBRELLA

that will appeal to the most discerning of men has an all-silk "Gloria" cover, on a fine-rolling Fox's "Paragon" frame, with a crook handle in Partridge, Whangee, Bamboo, or Crocus wood. **21/-**

The April 1970 price for a single room and a bathroom at Grosvenor House started at £10 a day—an example of the way that services have outstripped the general rise in the cost of living

The Manchester Guardian, 2 February 1931

'Not, of course, my friends in Jarrow, who are trying to feed their aged parents for a week on the price of the cheapest pair'

Slump medicine, delivered in bulk

This advertisement for the latest Paris fashions appeared on the same page in *The Times* as the report of Snowden's 21 September broadcast, in which he said: 'Let me appeal to those people who may be contemplating foreign travel for purposes of pleasure to return to this country if they possibly can; and British nationals who are abroad will render a service to their country by returning home and spending their money here.'

In the same issue a firm of practical patriots took the opportunity to suggest 'To Garden Lovers—a Double Road to Economy. Buy Bath's British-grown Bulbs and Keep Your Money in the Country'

The Times, 22 September 1931

1949

The Utility Years when coupons were currency

For men, the Lewis's £5 15s. sports jacket in real Harris tweed; for women the New Look—£30 for a Dior copy— and a squeeze by courtesy of Illingworth and the *Daily Mail*

LEWIS'S
FOR
SPORTS JACKETS

Hand-woven Harris Tweed, renowned for its warmth and hard-wearing quality and tailored to perfection in this smart Sports Jacket. In short and long fittings, and a range of plain colours, checks and herringbone designs, misty blues and greens and rich reddish-browns, Coupon free.

£5.15.0

The Manchester Guardian, 24 February 19

STILL THE SQUEEZE LOOK

The Daily Mail, 10 February 1949

—a very good reason for buying
UTILITY FURNITURE
from Goodalls

THERE is Utility Furniture *and* Utility ! Only the very best finds its way into Goodalls showrooms. Having a two-century's reputation for fine quality furniture, Goodalls are distinctly choosey where they buy . . . from the leading manufacturers in the land *only*. And it costs you not a penny-piece more for this assurance. Well then . . .

BELOW are details of typical Utility Suites from Goodalls selection, but it is well worth a visit to see the improvements in the new Utility designing.

The Bedroom Suite illustrated, in Australian Walnut, comprises 4ft. fitted Wardrobe, 2ft. 9ins. gents fitted Wardrobe, 3ft. 8ins. Dressing Table, 4ft. 6ins. solid panel Bedstead and Bedside Cupboard—the set **£96 0s. 0d.**

Quilted Mahogany and Sycamore Bedroom Suite—4ft. Wardrobe, 2ft. 9ins. gents Wardrobe, both fully fitted, 3ft. 8ins. Duchess Dressing Table, 3ft. Twin Beds with Vono side rails, **£90 13s. 4d.**

Figured Walnut Dining Suite, 4ft. 6ins. Sideboard, trestle-type Table, 3ft. 6ins. x 2ft. 6ins. extending to 5ft. 6ins. x 2ft. 6ins., 6 Chairs with upholstered backs and seats green leather-cloth. Complete **£48 11s. 4d.**

Reproduction Walnut Dining Room Suite—4ft. 6ins. Sideboard, concave front, Table 3ft. (extending to 5ft.) x 2ft. 9ins., 6 Chairs with upholstered seats and backs brown leather-cloth. Complete **£54 10s. 0d.**

GOODALLS
KING STREET
Telephone: BLA 2132
The fine art of furnishing

Manchester Guardian, 22 April 1949

PORTABLE BATTERY RECEIVER
ALL-DRY TYPE 'K'

SPECIFICATION

CABINET :	Blue weather-proof finish. Cream plastic escutcheon : fitted with a retractable carrying handle. Dimensions : 11 × 11½ × 6¾ in.
WEIGHT :	15½ lb. including battery.
AERIAL :	Self-contained, with sockets for external aerial and earth.
CIRCUIT :	4-valve superhet, covering medium and long waves.
WAVEBANDS :	194-550 metres and 920-2,000 metres.
SPEAKER :	Highly sensitive 6 in. moving coil speaker.
VALVES :	EVER READY DK91 Frequency Changer. DF91 H.F. Pentode. DAF91 Diode Pentode. DL92 Output Pentode.
BATTERY :	EVER READY "Batrymax" type B103, combined 90 v. H.T. and 1½ v. L.T., giving 300 hours normal service.

PRICE :		
Receiver, including battery ...	£10	10 11
Purchase Tax	£2	9 1
TOTAL ...	**£13**	**0 0**

Ever Ready brochure

---

3 major features of the new

"H.M.V." RADIOGRAM

TWIN LOUDSPEAKERS

EXTENDED RANGE SWITCH

DUAL TONE CONTROLS

th this latest "His Master's Voice" io-radiogram, you can enjoy the rld's finest entertainment. Switch to lio or records—whenever you wish.

MODEL 1608
£112.17.6 Including Tax

"HIS MASTER'S VOICE"

The Hallmark of Quality

THE GRAMOPHONE COMPANY LIMITED, HAYES, MIDDLESEX

Manchester Guardian, 24 January 1949

In 1949 the Ever Ready Model K Receiver cost £13 (including Tax) and would run for 300 hours on one battery. But the H.M.V. radiogram, Model 1608, cost £112 17s. 6d. (including Tax)—which in 1970 money was as much as any colour TV set

Air fares speed upwards more slowly than the general cost of life—Aer Lingus quote £18 2s. for the same trip in 1970, which is barely half as much as prices have risen overall

NOW! FLY TO DUBLIN

£11

RETURN FROM
LONDON

Special 30-day midweek excursion

every Tuesday, Wednesday, Thursday

Also £6.6.0 return from Liverpool, £6.12.0 from Manchester, £7 from Glasgow, £9 from Birmingham (starting May 2nd)—to Dublin's fair and friendly city by Aer Lingus airliner. No crowds, queues, fuss or delay. You need no visa, just a passport or travel identity card, and there are no currency restrictions. Phone Aer Lingus, BEA or your local travel agent for information and immediate bookings. Send your goods by air, too.

TRAVEL TO IRELAND THE **EASY** WAY

AER LINGUS
IRISH AIR LINES

'Only 3d. a packet' was thought to be a good slogan in 1949. But 'Only 5d. a packet' should ring with even more clarion force in 1970, when the value of money has dropped by 55%

SPANGLES
LUSCIOUS ASSORTED
CRYSTAL FRUITS

I'd love a BABYCHAM

The genuine
Champagne Perry

*

1/3 a bottle

1957

Thirteen years later the recommended price was 1s. 10d. (including Purchase Tax), plus 3d., returnable, on the bottle

GPO

NEW CHARGES

effective from 1st October, 1957

Some of the new postal charges are detailed below. Leaflets giving details of other new charges (including those for letters and parcels sent to H.M. Forces) can be obtained from any Post Office.

INLAND POSTAL SERVICES

Letters: Not over 1 oz.—3d.; not over 2 oz.—4½d.; each additional 2 oz.—1½d.

Postcards: 2½d.

Printed Papers: Not over 2 oz.—2d.; not over 4 oz.—4d.; each additional 2 oz.—1d.

Newspapers (regd. at G.P.O.): Not over 6 oz.—per copy 2½d.; each additional 6 oz.—per copy 1½d.

Parcels:

Not over 2 lb. . . 1s. 6d.	Not over 7 lb. . . 2s. 9d.
„ „ 3 lb. . . 1s. 9d.	„ „ 8 lb. . . 3s. 0d.
„ „ 4 lb. . . 2s. 0d.	„ „ 11 lb. . . 3s. 3d.
„ „ 5 lb. . . 2s. 3d.	„ „ 15 lb. . . 3s. 6d.
„ „ 6 lb. . . 2s. 6d.	(max.)

The above charges will also apply to postal packets and parcels for the Irish Republic.

OVERSEAS POSTAL SERVICES

Letters: BRITISH COMMONWEALTH: Not over 1 oz.—3d.; each additional oz.—1½d.

FOREIGN: Not over 1 oz.—6d.; each additional oz.—4d.

(*Commonwealth rate no longer applies to U.S.A. and a number of other countries.*)

Printed Papers:

ORDINARY RATE: Not over 2 oz.—2d.; each additional 2 oz.—1d.

REDUCED RATE: Not over 2 oz.—1½d.; each additional 2 oz.—1d.

BULK POST: Per lb.—8½d.

Registration Fee: 1s. 0d.

Insurance Fee: Carrying compensation up to £12—1s. 2d.; each additional £12—2d.

OTHER POST OFFICE SERVICES

Remittance Services: Poundage has been increased for certain values of Postal and Money Orders.

Inland Telephone Services: New charges are being notified to subscribers individually. Leaflets showing charges for exchange connexions and calls are also available at Post Offices.

Overseas Telegraph Services: Full particulars of new rates are available at Post and Cable and Wireless Offices.

These were the charges which over-compensated for inflation in 1957. In 1970 it cost 5d. to send a letter or a card by the quicker, first-class service, and 4d. by the slower, second-class, and by January 1971 it was to become 7d. and 5d.

d Parcels prices in 1970 were as follows:

Not over 1½ lb . . .	2s. 6d.
„ „ 2 lb . . .	3s. 0d.
„ „ 6 lb . . .	4s. 0d.
„ „ 10 lb . . .	6s. 0d.
„ „ 14 lb . . .	7s. 6d.
„ „ 18 lb . . .	9s. 0d.
„ „ 22 lb . . .	10s. 6d.

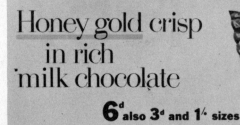

Honey gold crisp in rich milk chocolate

6ᵈ also **3ᵈ** and **1/** sizes

The Radio Times, 19 July 1957

1957 Fry's Milk Chocolate with Golden Honeycomb Crisp—2 oz. 6d.
1970 Milk Chocolate without Golden Honeycomb Crisp—2 oz. 1s.

NEW! KING OF THE MINSTRELS

YOUR PERSONAL
PORTABLE RADIO
at **12½ gns.** Tax paid
(Batteries Extra)

VIDOR CN 4
Weighs only 4¼lb.
only 10¾" x 3" x 2
2 Wavebands, 4" l
speaker. Ferrite
aerial built into
retractable har
(patents pendi
3-colour plastic cab

VIDOR

VAGABOND

BATTERY PORTABLE RADI

EXCLUSIVE (Patents Pending) **AERIAL FEATURE**
Ferrite rod aerial built into retractable handle which is spring-loaded to rise at a touch 3" above the receiver. This aerial displacement gives the Vagabond exceptional sensitivity and range.

NEW slender styling . . .
NEW colours, gay but cool . . .
NEW sensitivity because of exclu sive new aerial arrangement . . .
NEW hairbreadth tuning contr with Slow Motion Drive . . .
NEW robustness with gracious lir and lovely colours . . .

a personal portable that goes with you all the way.

See the Vidor Vagabond now in all the busiest radio shops

FOR PORTABLE PLEASU

The Vidor Vagabond cost 12½ guineas In 1957 before the transistor age really got going. Now, thanks to Japan and Hong Kong, 'personal, portable radios' start as low as £5

The Radio Times, 30 August 1

One place where prices have really come down. The average worker would have needed $7\frac{1}{2}$ weeks' pay to buy this 21″ model in 1957. In 1970 it would take him under three weeks to collect enough for its equivalent

Unfortunately the Swiss have inflation, too— and they don't devalue. Minimum all-in price for 12 days of Alpine sunshine in 1970 was £53

1967

Some of the new currency of the 1960s

Courtesy: Green Shield Stamps Ltd.

By 1970, GPO vans were all carrying big posters advertising the career of the £1,000 a year postman. Time marches on

Graduating 1967?

WHAT DO YOU EXPECT FROM YOUR CAREER...

A good starting salary?

How about £1,030 per annum? That's the present starting salary for graduate teachers with a good honours degree and a year's professional training. (Otherwise starting salaries range from £830–£950). Basic salaries then increase annually to £1,670 for good honours graduates and £1,550 for others (£1,620 or £1,500 if untrained). But few graduates stay on the basic scale for long.

Part only of advertisement, The Guardian, 20 January 1967

Council flats. National average rents in 1967, £3 8s. per week.
All mod. cons. including sometimes garage and piped TV

Photos. Combine: Farmers Weekly. Labourer: Hereford City Libra

Harvest 1870: Scythe 1s. 9d. Labourer's earnings 12s. a week.
Harvest 1967: Combine harvester £1,200–£4,000. Driver's earnings £15 4s. a week

Soon the 3d. bit, the old cupro-nickel penny—and maybe the 6d.?—will have gone the same way

House prices are a yardstick many people use to measure the value of the pounds in their pocket. But there are almost as many yardsticks as there are pockets

Photo: John Arlott and Sir Neville Cardus: *The Noblest Game* (H

The Rising Price of Eton

IN 1870, it was usual, on leaving, to place £10 inconspicuously somewhere in the headmaster's study, 'as with one's medical adviser';

IN 1896, the school fee was £8 8s. a term, and the house payment £110 a year;

IN 1909, school fees had risen to £10 10s. a term and house payments to £115 10s. a year;

IN 1925, the all-in annual charge was £230, where it remained into the 1930s;

BY 1949, the fees were £308 a year, plus a £10 games subscription;

BY 1957, the figures had risen to £400 for fees, £13 for games;

BY 1967, the overall cost of keeping a boy at Eton was officially £595 a year;

AND IN 1970, further increases were announced, raising the total to £765, which, by a happy coincidence, is almost exactly in line with the 1896–1970 decline in the value of money

executive officer was supposed to keep himself above graft and reproach on £195 a year in 1913—down to 33 per cent for the £500 men, and so on.

Some members of the professions failed to retain their place in the sun over this period—dentists, engineers and particularly the clergy all suffered a relative pay slide. But others did considerably better. Qualified teachers, particularly women, who had been lucky to make £2 a week in 1913, scored a considerable advance, despite the valiant efforts of Sir Eric Geddes and his 'axe' committee to economize on the rising cost of education. Barristers, solicitors, doctors, nurses and even army officers continued to stay at least slightly ahead of the game; and business managers, whose pay was sampled with some care by the Inland Revenue in 1924–5, all succeeded to a greater or less extend in holding their own. Admittedly it was the lower ranks—the men like Courtaulds' chief research chemist who had been recruited with a starting salary of only £200 a year in 1907 —who did relatively best. But even the top men—the four-thousand-odd executives in the country who at that time (1925) were averaging £8,290 a year—had managed to cover themselves against the full rigours of inflation, without any civil-service nonsense about reduced impact on higher income groups. United Dyestuffs that spring were looking for a managing director at a salary of £10,000 a year, and at that level a married couple, with no children, could expect to walk away with £6,408 8s. 9d. after tax—an amount of purchasing power which it would take a gross income of roughly £190,000 a year to generate at 1970 rates and prices. After Churchill's budget, that figure was increased by a handsome £577 15s. 9d.—enough to buy two Morris Cowley saloon cars, and almost sufficient for the cheapest house (£670) then on offer in the newly built Welwyn Garden City.

The full Welwyn price range ran from £670 to £3,250, and for £975, a reasonably average sort of figure, you could get three bed-rooms, a 13 ft. 6 in. by 11 ft. 7½ in. dining-room, a 13 ft. 6 in. living-room, kitchen, hall, larder, bathroom, covered yard and single garage. The minimum for which you could reasonably think of building your own, architect-designed home, according to Bateman's *How to Own & Equip a House*, published in 1925, was £1,000, but slightly above that figure there was plenty of scope. For £2,000, in Clarence Road, Dulwich, in 1924, the proud owners were able to provide themselves with three sitting-rooms, five bedrooms, a panelled hall, a dining-room and a drawing-room, both around 17 ft. 6 in. by 13 ft., with oak-block floors, a bathroom and two lavatories, all with marble terrazzo floor and tiled walls, an all-gas kitchen, electric light throughout and a large garage. Mr Bateman had to point out regretfully, however, that the basic price had not

I

included the laying of the tennis court, or the planting of the orchard.

Slightly more modestly, a new, custom-built, four-bedroom house in Guildford could be built at that time for £1,399, with maid's room, and garage (but unfortunately only with cesspit sanitation—the sewers had not reached that far). And at Oxhey, near Watford ('a convenient retreat from the City') a weekend cottage, four bedrooms, two with running hot-and-cold water, garage, central-heating radiators, and electric fires in all rooms, could be run up for £1,400.

David Caradog Jones carried out a survey, *The Cost-of-Living of a Sample of Middle-Class Families*, in 1925, based on a group of several hundred men in the same profession (not identified, but apparently accountants) and found that the median annual expenditure came out at £445 a year in London, £420 in towns of over 50,000 inhabitants and £422 10s. in smaller places. The London figure was made up as follows:

	£	
Rent & rates	82	
Fuel & light	18	
Housekeeping, food, service	186	
Clothing	41·5	
Education	—	(only families with over £500 spent anything appreciable on schooling, he found)
Doctors, dentist, chemist	7	
Insurance	23	
Holiday, clubs, car, leisure	39·5	
Subscriptions & charities	4·5	
Alcohol & tobacco	7·5	
Paper & stamps	4	
Travel expenses	17	
Repairs, renewals, sundries	15	

Such, in outline, was the budget of a typical member of 'the patient, struggling, loyal, middle-class backbone of Britain'. He felt himself usually rather badly done by, as the pre-war social and financial chasms—the kind of disparity that in 1909 had put the £200 a year village schoolmaster into a different world from the £70–£100 a year miners around him—had by now appreciably shrunk. But in fact he was still in many ways the most favoured member of the community. The new, higher tax burdens, which one way and another took 11·9 per cent out of the income of a £100 a year family (two adults, three children), 11 per cent from a £1,000 a year household, and a full 31·2 per cent at £10,000 a year, left his £500 a year

group almost untouched, at a mere 6·2 per cent. And with virtually
guaranteed job security, it was possible to scrape by quite adequately
at this level—the level of the middle manager in industry, the chief
cashier in the bank, or the established university lecturer. The conventional wish, to the person who took the last slice of bread-and-
butter at middle-class tea-tables in the twenties and thirties, was 'a
thousand a year and a handsome wife'. It was a pleasant aspiration.
But meanwhile £500 a year would do very well.

It would buy, for instance, the occasional bottle of whisky at
12s. 6d., even though this now carried the 'enormous tax' of 8s. 6d.
And most of the other pleasures and appurtenances of life were
priced on a similar scale. Players No. 3 cigarettes were 8d. for 10,
while you could buy Rothman's Cork Tipped at 5s. 10d. the hundred
(or 4s. if you ordered wholesale). A Harris Tweed sports suit from
Austin Reed cost £6 16s. 6d., and there was a great row in the spring
over complaints that golf club lunches had sometimes been charged
as high as 4s.–5s. (the investigating committee concluded their probe
by sampling the 1s. 6d. menu at Mitcham, which gave them Scotch
broth, choice of roast beef and steak and kidney pudding, and apple
pie, suet pudding or treacle tart). A single room at the Kensington
Palace Hotel cost 7s. 6d. a night (12s. double). You could hire a punt
or a skiff on the Thames for 10s. a day. And if you wished to go
abroad the Church Travellers' Club ('Economical Travel for the
Educated Classes. Pres. The Archbishop of Canterbury') would give
you a fortnight in Lugano for £12 7s. inclusive, or The Holy Land
(with extensions to Egypt) for 49 guineas.

For the home, whether bought or rented—house rental was much
more common between the wars, with offers like '2½ guineas a week
for six-room, centrally-heated bungalow at Chichester harbour
(yacht and pony by arrangement)'—furnishing, outside the luxury
range, remained very reasonable. A typical three-piece chesterfield
suite 'in antique effect rexine, with brown velveteen cushions' would
cost around £17 10s. in Tottenham Court Road, or £21 in rexine and
velvet with adjustable backs. Heal's Patent Box Spring Mattress
was 5 guineas for the three-foot size and £8 5s. for the five-footer.
And Hampton's were always advertising their seamless Axminster
Carpets at prices which worked out at just under 14s. a square yard.

Gas, at 8d. a therm (against today's level of about 1s. 5d.) and
electricity at 2d. a unit (now 1·9d. in London, and 0·9d. off-peak)
were both relatively expensive. Gas was still well in the lead for most
domestic purposes—the big London-based Gas Light & Coke Co.
claimed in 1925 to be selling on its own more heat-equivalent than
the amount generated by the whole British electricity industry—but
the electricity marketing people were doing their best. The GEC

group that spring were offering a Complete Domestic Outfit, comprising electric kettle, electric toaster, electric bowl heater and electric iron, for five guineas the lot.

Neither of them, however, were really making much impact yet on the traditional coal fire-place. Best coal in London averaged 29s. 6d. a ton in 1925, against 17s. 6d. in 1909 and 15s. in 1896, which was a good deal less than the general rise in the cost of living. For anything over four hours, it was calculated, coal fires were cheaper than any rival, by a progressively growing margin the longer you kept them going. And as long as there were plenty of willing hands around to lay them, light them, stoke them, and clean out the grate every morning, they comfortably held the field.

By the middle twenties the hands were still almost as numerous as before the war, though probably a good deal less willing. There were over 1·3 million domestic servants in the country at the time of the 1921 census, as hundreds of thousands of girls who had flooded into the munitions factories found there were no jobs left for them once the men had returned. Few women between the wars whose husbands earned £5 a week or more found it necessary actually to touch a scrubbing-brush, or get on their hands and knees. But gradually the whole economic and social basis of personal service was starting to fray. As an irate St Pancras housewife put it to the *New Survey of London Life & Labour* in 1928: 'Physically defective and girls of less than normal mentality apply for housework at wages 70 per cent higher than efficient trained maids before the war.' And this was one area where the lower middle classes in the £5 to £10 a week area found themselves increasingly at a disadvantage. Competent living-in maids were getting rarer, older and more expensive—the *Survey* reckoned that in the last quarter of a century their average wages had gone up by 143 per cent, to £46 a year, while their numbers had dropped by half. Even then, the figures were only kept up by the number of over forty-five-year-old women who went back into service after Churchill's 1925 Budget, in order to qualify for the new contributory Old Age Pension. The less well-off household, which could hardly afford such well-trained paragons at the best of times, normally fell back on the sixteen- and seventeen-year-olds who had just left school. But their average pay was rising, relatively, even faster than the twenty- and thirty-year-olds. In Booth's day, back in the 1890s, girls were happy (or at any rate prepared) to work all hours of the day and night for £8 10s. a year. Now the figure was more like £24, and the conditions were increasingly set by enlightened employers like the Willesden woman who told the *Survey*: 'In 1922 we allowed our maid to become non-resident, with excellent results. She has regular hours, 8-2, 5-8, good holidays (one month a year) and every other week-end off.' Even the humble daily woman, by the late twenties, was demanding and getting 11d. an hour, which was twice the rate which had been laid down by that splendid Victorian organization, The Association of Trained Charwomen, in 1898 and universally derided as 'a counsel of perfection'.

However, even at these extraordinary wage levels, it was still possible to screen oneself fairly effectively from the harsher realities. The readers of *Queen* magazine, which then, as now, addressed itself largely to the flying,* skiing, hunting and night-clubbing sector of society, were treated, just before Mr Churchill's gold announcement, to an uplifting account of how a rural household, consisting of one lady, two gentlemen and their modest complement of three maids managed to subsist on a weekly housekeeping budget of 12s. per head per week. With the aid of a large garden, which provided virtually all their fruit and vegetables, and such devices as baking much of their own bread, and buying 500 eggs wholesale at 1d. each to preserve them in waterglass, they managed to keep expenditure down to £1 3s. for meat ('One joint of English meat a week, and make up the rest with Canterbury lamb, or foreign beefsteak and kidney'), 8s. for fish, 12s. for milk, flour and bread, 11s. for butter, lard, cheese and margarine and 12s. for other groceries. Occasionally it was possible to supplement the diet with rabbits at 1s. or 1s. 6d. each. And as the authors truly wrote: 'To housekeep on so small a "fixed sum" teaches one a lot, and especially an immense sympathy and admiration for the wife of a country labourer.' The average farm hand's pay at the time was around 32s. a week, including an allowance of 3s., taken to represent the use of a 'free' cottage. And it was in such a district, South Stonham in Suffolk, that the rate collector for the local Board of Guardians that spring had resigned his £300 a year job on the grounds that the villagers were 'utterly unable to meet demands made upon them without causing a considerable amount of distress to the children of the agricultural labourers. . . . I cannot

* Commercial flying was still an expensive and somewhat erratic method of travel. British Imperial Airways, the government-supported fore-runner of BEA and BOAC, had just been formed (1924) out of a hasty amalgam of private companies which had been trying since the war to establish a viable London–Paris service. As their early single fares, of 20 guineas, and then 15 guineas, had to compete with the already State-subsidized 6 guineas of Air France and the £3 8s. 5d. rail-and-boat ticket, their efforts had not been strikingly successful. But the pilots, who in the early days had worn frock-coats at the controls to give an air of solid respectability to the enterprise, began as they intended to go on. They flatly rejected British Imperial's first pay offer of £100 a year plus flying pay, and finally settled for £450 plus 10s. for every hour in the air. And at 1925 tax rates that compared very reasonably with 1970's BEA average of £6,000 a year.

conscientiously go on forcing money out of the people who have but a bare subsistence.' The Board duly accepted his resignation, and re-advertised the job at the more economical rate of £250.

In fairness to *Queen*, though, they did run on their back pages (but in very small print) a column under the rather breathless title of 'Queen's Helping Hand and The Friends of The Poor' which offered a rather more direct glimpse into the social abyss. Every week it was full of small, specific appeals—for £3 to dispatch an old lady of seventy-four (Old Age Pension and 6s. a week for son killed in the war) to a convalescent home 'for a week or two', or for '15s. a week which will enable a deserving man to hire a barrel organ'. And just occasionally it produced one of those tiny, but fully etched, vignettes, which bring alive a whole mode of life. 'A middle-aged couple are deserving of help. The man has been out of work spasmodically for four years. They have taken the last penny out of the bank. The husband is a commercial traveller working on commission. Trade is very slack and when he is working his earnings run from 3s. 6d. to 13s. a week. They have one lodger who lives in the house and pays 11s. a week. Of course, it is necessary that the husband should present a good appearance and his last suit is almost worn out. He could have obtained a job as a salesman in a shop in the North at a special week's sale, but of course his clothes were far too shabby. He has no unemployment pay because being a salesman he has never contributed to the Unemployment Insurance. It is so dreadful that the couple are almost destitute. Please send £10.'

That, tucked away among the Bond Street advertisements for 'fully fitted dressing cases, from £25 to £500', and the chirpy announcement that 'the aggregate length of London's shop windows is now greater than that of any two other cities in the world' carries the authentic whiff of the twenties. It is the same quietly desperate world as that of the waitresses described that year by Ellen Wilkinson, later to become a Labour cabinet minister. In a Midland picture-house café, she found, the manageress was working a 95½ hour week for £1, and the other girls, after deductions for breakage and the 11d. a week insurance stamp, got the equivalent of 1d. an hour. In the main shopping street of Liverpool the normal take-home pay was 9s. 6d. a week. And she urged the victims to follow the example of Manchester and Leicester, where, after strikes, the wages in the leading restaurants had gone up to between 18s. and 25s. a week, with meals thrown in, 'valued by the union at 15s. a week'.

The pound in which these wages were paid had depreciated by about 45 per cent in comparison with its 1913 value. Most of the other countries involved in the war had similarly suffered from inflation—some, like Germany, Austria and Hungary, to such an

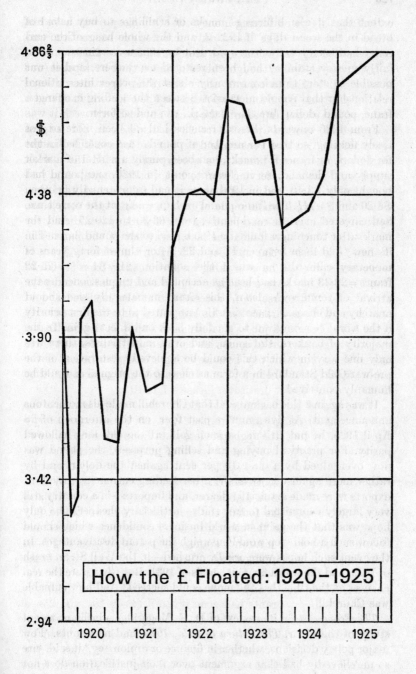

How the £ Floated: 1920–1925

extent that it cost billions of marks or schillings to buy a loaf of bread in the worst days of 1922–3, and the whole basis of the currency had been totally destroyed. But by 1925 a certain amount of fairly uneasy stability had been restored everywhere, and it was possible to start thinking seriously about the proper international relationship that should now exist between the leading exchanges, franc, pound, dollar, lira, Reichsmark, yen and so forth.

From 1920 onwards these currencies had all been more or less freely floating, so that the number of pounds that could be bought for dollars, or francs for marks, had been purely a matter of market supply and demand. At its lowest point, in 1920, the pound had bought only \$3·40, and in 1924 alone it had swung crazily between \$4·20 and \$4·74⅜. The franc-pound exchange rate, at the same time, had careered even more violently, from 63·30 to 120·25. And the mark, after touching a fantastic 19·5 billion to the pound, lurched in its new Gold form between 17 and 22. After almost forty years of monetary calm during which the equation $£1 = \$4·86\frac{31}{32} = 25·22$ francs $= 20·43$ marks had been as accepted and unquestioned as the arrival of tomorrow's dawn, this situation naturally smacked of anarchy and chaos. Full stabilization appeared to be the first priority if the world economy was to get fully back on its feet again. To the majority of bankers, statesmen, and even industrialists, there was only one way in which this could be achieved: restoration of the pre-war Gold Standard in a form as close to the original as could be humanly contrived.

It was against this background that Churchill made his momentous announcement. At five minutes past four, on the afternoon of 28 April 1925, he put Britain back on gold, at the old, long-hallowed parity. For practical buying and selling purposes, the pound was now overvalued by a clear 10 per cent against the dollar, and by rather more against most of the other leading currencies. In effect, exports were made artificially dearer, and imports—in a country still very largely committed to free trade—artificially cheaper. The only hope was that the gains in world business confidence which should follow such a bold step would outweigh the patent disadvantages. In the event such hopes were cruelly crushed—in the Wall Street crash of 1929, and the world financial crisis of 1931. But what were the real chances at the time that the move could succeed? And how culpable was Churchill?

The Economist, in its review of D. E. Moggridge's brilliant recent study of the affair, *The Return to Gold, 1925*, had no doubts. 'Few major policy decisions, whether in finance or diplomacy,' it said, 'are so unrelievedly bad that argument over their justification does not sway back and forth as documents accumulate and memories fade.

Britain's decision in 1925 to restore the pre-1914 gold parity of sterling is a striking exception.' And it is hard, despite one or two more charitable interpretations, notably by Professor R. S. Sayers,* to find any fundamental reason to disagree.

The history of the decision went back to 1919, when the Government-appointed Cunliffe Committee on Currency and Foreign Exchanges unanimously agreed that: 'In our opinion it is imperative that after the war the conditions necessary to the maintenance of an effective gold standard should be restored without delay.' Although in the chaotic conditions of demobilization, the 'homes fit for heroes' débâcle, and the atmosphere of hysterical speculation which caused a quarter of Britain's farmlands and cotton mills to change hands in 1919–20, it was not thought prudent to act on this, it was firmly enshrined as official policy. And by 1922, after a savage dose of deflation had brought the economy back 'under control', the Treasury and the Governor of the Bank of England, Montagu Norman, were ready to start moving towards the Cunliffe target.

In a sense, they cannot be said to have ignored or misunderstood the implications of what they were doing. Sir Otto Niemeyer at the Treasury wrote at an early stage: 'If we are to get back to an effective Gold Standard . . . it is certain that there must be some deflation, some fall in the proportion borne between spending power on the one hand measured in terms of pounds sterling . . . and on the other the output of goods and services. . . . If we recognize this and remember that though the war has made us poorer it has also won for us our freedom to go forward on our traditional lines of development to new successes, we need not feel unduly depressed.' But although the words appear to express some appreciation of the situation he was helping to bring about, they lack any real feeling for what his 'falling proportions' would mean to a coal miner working a thin seam at wages that had barely kept up with the cost of living, or for the extent to which 'our traditional lines of development' were now diverging from reality. Steel exports by 1924 were only 77·5 per cent of 1913, cotton 64·8 per cent, coal, even when the Ruhr mines were closed, could only reach 80 per cent, and shipbuilding, responsible for two-fifths of all overseas sales immediately before the war, was down to a disastrous 35·2 per cent; with the result that our balance-of-payments surplus on current account (before providing anything for our still very substantial overseas capital investment programme) had been slashed from nearly £200 million in 1913 to just over £70 million. Even that low figure owed a good deal to the fact that the terms of trade—the amount of imports that could be bought with a

* In *Studies in the Industrial Revolution*, ed. L. S. Pressnell (Athlone Press, 1960).

pound's worth of exports—had turned sharply in our favour. And it would have looked substantially worse if allowance had been made for the general rise in prices.

Despite these ominous figures, Norman, early in 1924, decided that it was time to move, and on 19 March he asked his Committee of Treasury at the Bank of England to empanel a group of experts—Niemeyer and Sir John Bradbury (of the 1914 pound notes) from the Treasury, Sir Austen Chamberlain, as an ex-Chancellor, Gaspard Farrer from the City and Professor Pigou, the eminent author of *The Economics of Welfare*—to decide among other things a date for the export of gold to begin. Norman, as first witness, said that although he did not think a return to gold would have 'quasi-catastrophic' effects on industry, he agreed that it implied 'an element of sacrifice' which he believed that businessmen should make 'for stability', for the good of their business and for future success. Most of the other witnesses supported a return, the only exceptions being John Maynard Keynes, the economist, and Reginald McKenna, another ex-Chancellor. Keynes, who later published some of the most damning criticisms of the move (notably in the savage *Economic Consequences of Mr Churchill*), foresaw at this point a necessary fall in costs, chiefly wages, of around 12 per cent, and McKenna, in an impassioned and only too prophetic deposition, hammered the point home. 'You can only get back to a gold standard by a rise in prices in the US relative to our price level. There is no other means of getting back. The notion that you can force down prices here until you get to the level of the United States, if they remain constant, is a dream. . . . The attempt to force prices down when you have a million unemployed is unthinkable. . . . You cannot get on the Gold Standard by any action of the Chancellor of the Exchequer. . . . He could cause infinite trouble, unlimited unemployment, immense losses and ruin, but he could not balance his Budget while he was doing it, and he would have to begin again to borrow . . .'

The Committee, partially convinced by this line of thought, decided that the best policy would be for the Government to postpone their decision till the autumn of 1925 to see if the widely expected rise in US prices actually took place. But before they could accept this relatively cautious approach, the Labour Government, headed by Ramsay MacDonald, fell, over other issues, and was replaced by the Conservatives, with Churchill as Chancellor. At that point the pound was trading at only $4·50, and the gap, if it had continued at that level, would probably have been so wide as to frighten even Norman away from the irrevocable plunge. But with the Tory victory came a landslide of speculation, pushing the exchange up to $4·74, or within touching distance of the goal, and as Moggridge drily says, 'the wagon was ready to roll'.

The irony is that Churchill, despite his protestations of financial innocence, was nobody's fool. In a terse and extremely pertinent memorandum to the Treasury at the beginning of 1925, he asked almost all the right questions about the strategy he was being advised to pursue. But unfortunately he then failed to press for any real answers, and went ahead, on the basis of cotton wool, double talk and unwarranted hope.

The six points raised in what the Treasury called 'Mr Churchill's Exercise' were as follows:

1. 'A Gold Reserve and a Gold Standard are in fact survivals of rudimentary and transitional phases in the evolution of finance and credit.' Could not Britain's international credit be upheld rather through financial policy and healthy trade?

2. 'We are now invited to restore the Gold Standard. The US seems singularly anxious to help us do this.' Are the UK and US interests really parallel? Especially as the cost of supporting the gold price would now have to be shared by Britain?

3. What about forgetting the Gold Standard and shipping £100 million worth of gold off to New York, to pay our war debts and 'congest the US with gold'? (This refers back to an earlier plan, ultimately vetoed by Norman, to push up US prices by deliberately boosting their already embarrassingly high gold stocks.)

4. 'The merchant, the manufacturer, the workman and the consumer have interests which, though largely common, do not by any means exactly coincide, either with each other or with the financial and commercial interests.' A rise in Bank Rate, which would be an essential part of the deflationary package, would be a 'very serious check' and would leave the Government open to accusations that 'it favoured the special interests of finance at the expense of the special interests of production'. Such a risk would have to be offset by 'very plain and solid advantages'.

5. What was the urgency? Legislation was renewable, and the prospect, after three elections, four governments, five chancellors, and 'the advent of a Socialist administration for the first time' was now for four years of political stability. Why upset it?

6. Could not the US be persuaded to offer better terms, especially if restoration was to mean a decline in the position of London?

To all these questions, he ended, he expected to receive 'good and effective answers'. But they were not forthcoming, and in the end he went ahead without.

In any case, even Churchill's list omitted one very important area of inquiry. Everyone's eyes, including Keynes's, were fixed almost hypnotically on New York and Washington, and the shifting balance of trade and financial strength between Britain and America. But events in Europe, which were to turn out of at least equal importance, were virtually ignored. Norman was prepared, as Europe's most eminent central banker, to offer lordly assistance in clearing up the fantastic post-war financial mess in Germany and Austria, and to a lesser extent in France and Belgium. But the notion that the terms on which they finally stabilized their errant exchange rates might have some relevance to British performance seems hardly to have crossed his mind. Yet Germany, whose relatively modest post-war cost rise (despite the disastrous inflation) was already giving her at least a 12 per cent advantage against the UK, had chosen to stabilize the mark in 1924 at a rate which fully preserved this favourable competitive position, and it was hardly conceivable that France and Belgium would fail to follow suit. In fact, both of them deliberately undervalued their currencies when they returned to gold in 1927, and left Britain's 'unsheltered' export trades wide open to the icy blast.

Moggridge quotes a whole variety of estimates about just how chill the wind turned out to be, and agrees that there is no clear consensus. But after considering the trend of British and American unemployment and wage costs from 1920 to 1925, and the relative deterioration and flowering of the two countries' financial positions, he takes the position that 'any exchange rate which did not undervalue sterling *vis-à-vis* the dollar was probably too high. As even the most optimistic indices . . . hardly did that, and as the most pessimistic indices suggested an overvaluation by as much as 10 per cent, one must incline towards the view that given official policy goals ("full employment" at the pre-war level of 95·3 per cent, enough surplus to support unrestricted foreign lending, and maintenance of free trade with minimal exceptions) sterling was significantly overvalued . . . an exchange rate perhaps 10 per cent lower than $4·86 would probably have been somewhat more appropriate for sterling.'

In the event, the rate chosen triggered off every kind of undesirable development. Not only were there direct effects on exports, imports and unemployment (the out-of-work figures, as firms grimly set about trimming costs, moved up from 925,000 on 25 May to 1,009,000 on 8 June and 1,034,000 on 22 June, and never dropped below that until the aftermath of Dunkirk), but it also brought losses on the invisible side of the account, on shipping, interest and commissions, reparation receipts, insurance, tourism, foreign investment incomes and even items like remittances from Britons who had emigrated abroad. And as Keynes was to demonstrate in the

Scotch Whisky: Born 1820 – Still Going Up

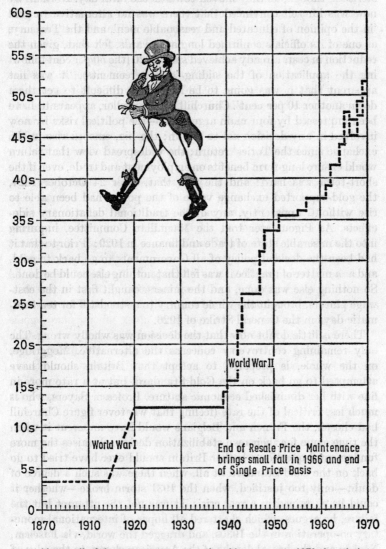

Prices supplied by the Distillers Company Ltd.

World War I

World War II

End of Resale Price Maintenance
brings small fall in 1966 and end
of Single Price Basis

60s
55s
50s
45s
40s
35s
30s
25s
20s
15s
10s
5s
0

1870   1910   1920   1930   1940   1950   1960   1970

Almost all of these increases are attributable to tax—in 1970 the wholesale price of the Scotch in a bottle of Scotch was still less than 5s.

1930s, all this had a multiplier effect, spreading depression, over-caution, pessimism, and removing any remaining buoyancy from the country which was still the world's biggest importer, and whose fortunes affected not only itself but every primary producer on the globe.

Such considerations were far from the minds of Churchill and his advisers, though, as they moved towards the fatal day. Norman by now was himself convinced that there was no alternative to gold 'in the opinion of educated and reasonable men', and the Treasury, as one of its officials confirmed long afterwards, felt that, given the reduction in costs already achieved since 1920 (the 50 per cent following the application of the sliding-scale agreements), 'it was not apparent that it was going to be frightfully difficult to get them down another 10 per cent'. Churchill, as Chancellor, appears to have been impressed by four main arguments—the political risks by now involved in any decision *not* to return; the big, smooth rise in the exchange since the Tories' return; the widespread view that return would ensure long-term benefits on employment and trade, even if the short-term was hard; and the fact that, after 24 October 1924, the gold-supported exchange value of the pound had been able to rise without, apparently, any of the traditional deflationary side-effects. As Pigou later told the Macmillan Committee, inquiring into the miserable state of trade and finance in 1929: 'Prior to that it had been the decided policy of all Governments to go back to gold, and as a matter of practice it was felt that nothing else could be done.' So nothing else was done, and the miners, caught first in the cost-wage pincers, brought the whole country to a standstill for ten traumatic days in the General Strike of 1926.

There is little doubt now that the decision was wholly wrong. The only remaining controversy concerns the alternative. Moggridge, on the whole, is prepared to accept that Britain should have attempted to go back on the Gold Standard, but at a rate more in line with her diminished economic stature. Professor Sayers, who is much less critical of the rate (feeling that whatever figure Churchill had chosen, the French and Belgians would have undercut it when the time came for their own stabilization decisions), raises the more fundamental question whether Britain should ever have tried to go back on the Gold Standard at all, when there was such a degree of doubt—only too justified, when the 1931 storm broke—whether it could be sustained in a real crisis. It was not the attempt but the failure, he argues, which shattered all hopes of international monetary co-operation in the 1930s, and dragged the world, via Fascism, Nazism and the brutal depths of the American slump, to the edge of a second world war. The men who chose gold in 1925 did so because they had failed to realize the extent, or to assess the consequences, of London's weakened financial muscle after the 1914–18 holocaust. 'And the reason for this omission is quite simple. In the years between 1918 and 1925 people had too often said that London's financial strength before 1914 was due to the Gold Standard. The truth was that the strength of the Gold Standard was due to London's international financial position.' It was an error with many unpleasant consequences.

The Pound in 1931

was worth £4 3s. in 1970 money

Do you think it a paradox that we can continue to increase our capital wealth by adding both to our foreign investments and to our equipment at home, that we can continue to live (most of us) much as usual or better, and support at the same time a vast body of persons in idleness with a dole greater than the income of a man in full employment in most parts of the world—and yet do this with one-quarter of our industrial plant closed down and one-quarter of our industrial workers unemployed?

John Maynard Keynes, in the
New Statesman & Nation (March 1931)

In January 1931, Keynes, now much more formidable after the publication of his *Treatise on Money* and the only-too-obvious fulfilment of many of his gloomier 1925 forecasts, spoke on the now-firmly-established and immensely influential BBC radio to the worried, thrifty, penny-pinching families of Britain. 'The best guess I can make', he told them, 'is that whenever you save five shillings, you put a man out of work for a day. Your saving that five shillings adds to unemployment to the extent of one man for one day and so in proportion. On the other hand, whenever you buy goods you increase employment—though they must be British, home-produced goods if you are to increase employment in this country. . . . Therefore, oh patriotic housewives of Britain, sally out tomorrow early into the streets and go to the wonderful sales that are everywhere advertised. You will do yourselves good—for never were things so cheap, cheap beyond your dreams. Lay in stock of household linen, of sheets and blankets to supply all your needs. And have the added joy that you are increasing employment, adding to the wealth of your country, because you are setting on foot useful activities, bringing a chance and hope to Lancashire, Yorkshire and Belfast.'

It was probably the most remarkable commercial ever to emerge from the austere loudspeakers of Portland Place. But even Keynes's eloquent salesmanship failed to persuade many people to open their purses in that truly awful year. Government policy, as the world's rickety financial system lurched progressively towards collapse, tended all the other way—retrenchment, stringent economy, ruthless paring of wages and costs, wherever practicable (which normally meant attacking either the weakest, the poorest or the most patriotic). And in September, after a currency blizzard of unprecedented intensity, sterling was forced once more off gold, and effectively devalued by around 30 per cent.

The whole year is packed with paradox, to an extent only touched on in the passage quoted at the head of this chapter, and with the kind of crypto-analysis, religio-economic exhortation and politico-economic gobbledegook, whose echoes continue to reverberate through every post-war monetary crisis, down to the present day. Then, as in 1949, and again in 1967, the trusting public were assured on all hands that the defence of the pound was of overriding importance to its physical, moral and international well-being. Then, as later, a picture of unexampled and indescribable chaos, anarchy and disaster was painted as the inevitable consequence of any slight weakening. In the event, on each occasion, the authorities swung round, once the deed was done, to proclaim the excellence and benevolence of the whole affair. Meanwhile life continued much the same as before.

It is a somewhat depressing repetition. If it could be explained as merely a matter of straightforward cynicism—the creation of an essential smokescreen, while carefully thought-out but politically unattractive policies were being prepared and carried through—then one would merely dismiss it as one of the inescapable concomitants of democracy. But unfortunately there is ample evidence that in each case the men in power at the time believed a substantial part of what they were saying, right up to the final moment of truth. With the result that the action taken was almost without exception ill timed, based on inadequate assessments of the situation, panic-stricken to a degree, and carrying with it all sorts of unwanted side-effects which nobody had bothered to consider in the earlier, almost mystical urge to 'save the pound'.

In 1931, the main thing it needed to be saved from, as Keynes was pointing out in his sales talk, was its stagnation in people's pockets. It was the only year between the wars—and almost the only year in the past century—when real consumer spending in Britain actually dropped below the level of the previous twelve months. Even in 1932, when unemployment reached its all-time official peak of 2,829,000 (which with families, dependants and various categories of workless who slipped through the statistics, probably meant between 6 and 7 million people living on the dole), it managed to stage a modest recovery. And that was after the British people, in an access of self-doubt and self-punishment, had not only awarded themselves swingeing wage-cuts and extra taxes but actually queued up at the Inland Revenue offices to pay early. *The Times* ran a lengthy correspondence on the question whether or not it was in the national interest for the rich to indulge in conspicuous expenditure, and such was the moral tangle people had got into that scarcely any contributor—not even Keynes—was prepared to say flatly that, with two men in three idle on the Clyde and the Tyne, the building of luxury yachts, for anyone who could afford them, was practically a national duty. Certainly, there is little sign that the heirs of the nineteen millionaires who died in the fiscal year 1930–1 were bold enough to spend much of the £24·4 million they received (after estate duty) on such an eminently good cause.

They would have got a bargain. Keynes was right, and prices right across the board were as low as anyone now under sixty-five has seen in his lifetime. The bookshops were full of learned monographs like John Todd's *The Fall of Prices: A Brief Account of the Probable Causes and Possible Cures*. And announcements such as that for Ponting's Spring Sale put the matter with commercial succinctness. 'Prices 30 per cent Lower than 1930!—Values Which Put the Clock Back 17 Years—to the Levels of 1914!' Artificial silk frocks were

10s. So were welted shoes. A spring tweed coat was £1. An outsize winceyette nightdress, 3s. 11d. And so on down the line. Whiteley's had reduced men's 14s. 6d. macs to 10s. D. H. Evans's big bath towels were 5s. 11d., with Witney blankets at 14s. 9d. Selfridge's cotton sheets were 10s. a pair in cotton (single-bed size) and 18s. 9d. in linen. And Hampton's Axminster carpets, which had been 14s. a square yard in 1925, were now selling at a rock-bottom 10s. 6d.

'Prices were never so advantageous where the essentials of living are concerned than they are now, nor were facilities for making a little go a long way ever greater,' wrote a lady named Lucy H. Yates in a slim volume *Marriage on Small Means*, published that year by Country Life. And although that was small comfort to the one person in every six who was without work, or dependent on someone without work, it made life unprecedentedly easier for the other five.

Some of the price falls were of quite staggering dimensions. Wheat in Liverpool in January 1931 was said to be changing hands at the lowest level since Charles II was on the throne, and the average price for the year, of 5s. 9d. a quarter, compares with 12s. 2d. in 1925 and 46s. 11d. in 1870, where our investigations in this book began. Other declines made even this look sedate. Rubber, which had traded at 8s. 9d. a pound in 1910, was now 3 ³⁄₁₆ pence. Silver, which had been 7s. 7½d. an ounce in 1920, and 1s. 9½d. at its previous twentieth-century low point in 1902, touched 1s. in February 1931. And sugar, tobacco, cotton, hemp, jute, silk, wool, copper, tea and lead were all at levels which sent the producing countries—usually poor enough to start with—close to despair.

By and large, though, they were good for English customers, and good for English trade. And this is the point about the thirties which it is important not to lose sight of: that although things were so bad in Britain, particularly in the industrial North, and Scotland and Wales, that they often seem to have left a permanent scar, they were far, far worse elsewhere.

To take specific items: between 1929 and 1933, Britain's national income declined by one-tenth in money terms while America's was down by over a half. In real terms, allowing for the fall in world prices, the US was down by a third, while the UK was actually up by 6·4 per cent. In sector after sector—industrial production, coal output, factory building, manufacture, consumption of domestic and capital goods, even employment, the drop in Britain was only somewhere between a half and a third of that experienced in North America. And in items like electric power, where the US suffered a net reduction, and residential house construction, where the whole industry virtually collapsed, Britain roared ahead with increases of over 40 per cent. As Joseph Schumpeter, the historian of trade cycles and business fluctuations, put it: 'The outstanding fact about the English depression is its mildness, which makes it doubtful whether that term is applicable at all.'

Naturally, that is not how things looked in Sheffield, where a group of investigators* found in the latter part of 1931 that some two-fifths of the working population were living at or near the (fairly stringently defined) poverty level and more than half the town was only kept going by one or other form of social relief. But 1931 raises, in even more than usually acute form, the inescapable dilemma facing a study like this. Are we interested in the pound which, in the pocket of the Sheffield worker living on the standard diet listed below, was supposed to provide food for one man for three and a half weeks? Or the pound in the hands of the visitor to the 1931 Motor Show at Olympia (not Earls Court till 1936) who would find there a 20–25 horse-power, seven-seat limousine, designed 'for those who desire to purchase a Rolls-Royce at a moderate price' at an all-in £1,695? Or of more general relevance, the pound in the savings account of the man who is able, for the first time, to consider buying a motor car, when Rover with an £85 'pup' are vying with Morris's 'baby' at £100? It is not without significance, for a country supposedly sunk in hopeless slump, that the only industrial sector which grew continuously every single year from 1929 to 1937 was motor-car repairing.

In order not to give too optimistic a picture of the time, let us take first the situation in the industrial North and West, where there is a wealth of statistical and descriptive material to illustrate the realities of life on the basic 15s. dole for a single man, or 29s. 3d. for a couple with three dependent children (if the universally hated Means Test, introduced to help cut the soaring benefit bill in autumn 1931, allowed them to keep even so much).

The Sheffield survey took, as its starting point, a basic standard diet, calculated, at the prices ruling in the city in November and December 1931, to provide the minimum physiological needs of an adult male engaged in medium-heavy manual work. The results came out like this:

	d.		d.
Bread 5·25 lb. @ 1¾d.	9·19	Butter 0·11 lb. @ 1s. 2d.	1·54
Flour 2·06 lb. @ 1¼d.	2·575	Margarine 0·35 lb. @ 6d.	2·1
Rolled oats 0·83 lb. @ 3d.	2·49	Fresh milk 2·01 pts @ 3d.	6·03
Rice 0·30 lb. @ 3d.	0·9	Condensed milk 0·33 lb. @ 3½d.	1·155
Dried peas 1 lb. @ 3½d.	3·5	Cheese 0·183 lb. @ 8d.	1·456
Biscuits 0·69 lb. @ 7d.	4·83	Sugar 1·28 lb. @ 2½d.	3·2
Bacon 0·26 lb. @ 7d.	1·82	Fresh egg, one @ 1¼d.	1·25

* A Survey of the Standard of Living in Sheffield, ed. A. D. K. Owen, 1933.

	d.		d.
Beef 0·98 lb. @ 7d.	6·86	Tea 0·15 lb. @ 10d.	1·5
Mutton 0·5 lb. @ 8d.	4·0	Potatoes 3·4 lb. @ 1d.	3·4
Beef sausage 0·9 lb. @ 7d.	6·3	Carrots 1 lb. @ 1½d.	1·5
Lard 0·224 lb. @ 6½d.	1·456	Cabbage 1 lb. @ 1½d.	1·5

The total, correct to three places of decimals, thus came out at 5s. 8·552d., to which the Owen team added an extra 7d., if the man was engaged in really heavy work; 3d. a week for cleaning materials (2½d. for children); 11½d. for clothing (1s. 3½d. for a woman and 9½d. for a child); and a series of adjustments to meet the assumed lower needs of the non-working members of the family, to produce an overall minimum standard running as follows:

		s.	d.
Man or woman over 65		4	5½
Man,	16–64	6	11½
Woman,	16–64	6	1½
Youth,	14–15	5	10½
Girl,	14–15	5	7
Schoolchild,	5–13	3	10⅓
Child,	0–4	2	11

After allowing 2s. 1d. for fuel (coal in Sheffield was 1s. 5d.–1s. 6d. a cwt. that winter) this meant that the smallest sum on which it was possible for a man, wife and two schoolchildren to keep going without physical deterioration was 22s. 10d. plus rent. As the median rents in the various quarters of the city were currently running between 7s. 6d. in the central district and 10s. 2d. in the south, with an average of 9s., it is clear that not many such families managed to grow fat on their 29s. 3d. unemployment benefit.

In fact, the report reckoned that, during the week in which the survey was conducted, one in five of the working-class population was on or below the subsistence line, another one in five only slightly above (less than 50 per cent) and more than one in twenty was living in very serious poverty indeed, at less than two-thirds of the minimum rate. But, of course, even on those figures, three out of five were comfortably clear of the abyss. And even that only includes, in effect, manual workers and their families. The whole middle class, broadly defined as members of any family where the main income exceeded £5 a week, was deliberately left out. And as this group was taken to include not only steel magnates, but all the city's clerks, draughts-men, managers, wholesale agents, commercial travellers, insurance officials and shopkeepers whose takings averaged over £5 a week, this probably left nearly 350,000 out of the City's 511,000 inhabitants virtually untouched by the storms and tribulation of the year.

Where it struck, though, the unemployment blight was lethal, and not only to the immediate victims. The exclusion of those under £5 a week shopkeepers from the middle-class fold represented a very real distinction. Fenner Brockway, in his documentary account *Hungry Britain* (1932), described a tailor and outfitter in one of the poorer parts of Birmingham (relatively unscathed by unemployment) whose takings came to precisely 4s. 6d. in one desperate week. He cannot have been alone. The local authorities in Thornaby, North Yorkshire, dispatched a petition to the North Riding County Council that autumn asking for restoration of the school meal service, which had been cut in one of the many economy moves at the time, and gave details derived from the records of a charity called the Mayor's Boot Fund. One community in the town, they reported, consisted of 460 households, containing 859 parents, 361 infants, 173 girls and youths and 1,100 schoolchildren. Their total weekly income was £742 11s. 8d., out of which they paid rent of £166 16s. 7½d., and that, after allowing 2s. 6d. per household for fuel, and £491 2s. 10d. for minimum subsistence food, left precisely 2½d. per head per week to cover every other human need. The Mayor (who was a Conservative, not a Socialist) commented: 'From these figures, which are based upon the lowest accepted standard . . . it is dreadfully evident that a huge proportion of the 2,493 persons cannot be obtaining the barest necessities of life, and they prove that all clothes purchased, every pair of boots purchased or repaired, the soap with which they wash themselves and the clothes they dirty, are all bought at the expense of the food which is required to keep body and soul together.' And his food standards were really low— applying the Sheffield level would have left his families with nothing at all.

In practice, of course, people in this plight never got anywhere near the nutritional standards laid down by the anxious investigators. The typical weekly budget was something like the one detailed to Brockway by a woman in Great Harwood, Lancashire, who was keeping herself, her out-of-work mill-hand husband and four children on 31s. 9½d. a week (the Means Test allowance of 31s. 3d., augmented by sale or pawning of the few remaining family possessions—the number of pawnbrokers was down to 4,321 by the 1931 census, against the 1901 peak of 13,000, but they were doing boom business). Her shopping list, after allowing 8s. 8d. for rent, 3s. 6d. for coal, 2s. 6d. for gas and water, 3s. 2d. for insurance and union subscriptions, 1s. for the Co-op Club (13s. worth of goods paid off at 1s. a week) and 6d. for the children's often-kicked-off clog irons, read starkly:

	s.	d.
Meat	2	0
Milk	2	6½
Bread	4	8
Mayco (margarine)	2	0
Jam		9

The meat, normally around 9d. a lb., could be augmented, at a pinch, by delaying purchases till just before the butcher closed on Saturday evening, at which point he might be prepared to sacrifice his remaining bits and pieces for 3d. a pound. And the interminable bread and marge and jam was occasionally varied by a windfall, such as the time the husband was paid 45s. by the union for picketing, and they splurged on a meal of bacon and eggs. On that memorable day, the wife spent 1s. on a new broom and 1s. each for two pairs of knickers. Otherwise clothes were hand-me-downs or patched, though, as she said, if you could afford anything for home dressmaking, 'It's wonderful how cheap stuff is nowadays.'

Often conditions like this were made even worse by would-be generous efforts elsewhere. There was a big slum clearance scheme going on in Stockton-on-Tees in 1931, as the result of which the whole population of one condemned district was moved to a spick and span new housing estate. That was fine, and all the new tenants—despite the nasty remarks about coal in the bathtubs which were current at the time—strained every nerve to live up to their new surroundings. But unfortunately the rents, which had been about 2s. 6d. a week in the slum, were now 8s. 10d. and the difference came straight out of the family food bill. Malnutrition and death rates leaped, and the local doctors reported that 66 per cent of the children were now unfit, as against only 26 per cent in the rat-ridden tenements they had left. One family, with a father and three working-age sons, was down to ¾d. per head per meal. And such slender pickings were not improved when some local Public Assistance Committee, in the interests of 'economy', decided not only to make a small cut in their average grant, but to hand it out in the form of goods rather than cash. It was bad enough being told that you were to get 10s. a week instead of 10s. 6d. But when margarine was put into the parcel at the 'Committee price' of 8d. a pound, instead of the 5d. at which it was obtainable in the shops, and eggs at 2d. against a normal 1d. each, the victims' sense of baffled fury naturally knew no bounds.

It was, however, the Means Test, introduced as the final inept and heartless move in a game over which the country seemed to have totally lost control, that set the bitter seal on 1931 as far as the unemployed were concerned. Two 'National Economy Orders' were introduced in October, under the first of which benefits were reduced (from 17s. to 15s. 3d. for a single man) and contributions increased; and under the second, all 'transitional payments', made when insurance benefit ran out, usually after six months, were to be reduced according to the total amount of money, from savings or from other members' earnings, which was coming into the household. All this was policed through regular inquisitorial visits from 'the means test man', sent by the local Public Assistance Committee. And the net effect was to drive honest families apart and put the maximum premium on evasion and low cunning.

The kind of case which scarred people's memories, and still makes any kind of 'wage-related benefit' anathema to many British working families even after twenty-five years of full employment, is summed up by the autobiographical sketch by 'A Skilled Engineer', which appeared in a volume called *Memoirs of the Unemployment*, collected by R. S. Lambert and H. L. Neales in the mid-thirties. The man in question, when he lost his job in 1929, had been working for ten years for a large firm in the North Midlands. During that time, 'I had lived the life of an ordinary respectable artisan. I earned the standard rate of wages, round about £3 a week, and maintained a decent house at a rent of 15s. 3d.' He had been happily married for twenty years, was devoted to his wife and child, had been active in the union and held most possible jobs in his branch, but his company went bust and he was out. By 1931 he was getting pretty desperate. No jobs at all had appeared in his own trade, and occasional scraps of work, like door-to-door canvassing, had been a miserable flop. The whole family was very down, thanks to the constant lack of good food, and while the wife was in hospital with gastric trouble, debts to tradesmen started to build up. Then came the Means Test. The wife had managed to earn a little as a saleswoman for a house agent, during the extraordinary building boom which was going on at this time, even in the stricken North, and for obvious reasons she hoped to continue. The husband was sent the Means Test form, and, knowing that a true statement of the family earnings would stop his benefit, he was afraid to send it in, with the result that benefit was suspended for six weeks anyway. At this point relations, which had been steadily deteriorating, broke up completely, and his wife, backed up by the son, who was now earning a few shillings, 'told me to get out as I was living on them and taking the food they needed'. So he took himself off to an unfurnished bedroom, at 4s. 6d. a week out of his 15s. 3d. a week dole, which was now unaffected by the other family income, and concentrated mainly on trying to feed himself on 8s. a week, without cooking facilities. During this period of semi-starvation he was summoned as 'head of the family' by the shopkeepers who had given credit during the wife's illness. But, as he ruefully records, 'the judge had a sense of humour and suspended judgment'.

The system was riddled with inconsistencies and loopholes. Income used to pay life insurance premiums was eliminated from the calculation of disqualification from benefit, but not endowment payments, so many families lost the policies they had thriftily taken out for their children's coming of age. And the treatment of savings caused endless friction. A man with £80 in something like the Co-op Bank was supposed to spend £30 of it on subsistence, at a rate laid down by the authorities, before he was allowed to draw any help. But many naturally just transferred the £30 to another bank, and trusted that no overworked official (nor, more likely, a prying and jealous neighbour) would catch them at it.

Ironically, though, these forced economies—the total outlay on benefit dropped from £110 million in 1931–2 to £104 million in 1932–3, despite a rise of almost a million in the number of people out of work—probably did as much as anything to realize Keynes's prescription at the beginning of the year. Fiddling apart, the Means Test destroyed any incentive to thrift among those likely to fall into its net. So families split up, as soon as the children came to an age when they could earn anything at all, and spent every penny.

As Orwell says in *The Road to Wigan Pier*, still the most evocative account of this whole grisly era: 'You can't get much meat for three-pence, but you can get a lot of fish-and-chips. Milk costs threepence a pint, and even "mild" beer costs fourpence, but aspirins are seven a penny and you can wring forty cups of tea out of a quarter-pound packet. And above all there is gambling, the cheapest of all luxuries. Even people on the verge of starvation can buy a few days' hope ("Something to live for" as they call it) by having a penny on a sweepstake. . . .' And so, slowly, turgidly, the money started to circulate once more. The whole 'love on the dole' tendency, so deplored by the respectable classes,* helped to melt the frozen economy, as pitiful and desperate young couples tried to set up some kind of home life for themselves ('Complete house furnishing for 26 guineas —stored free till required', as Cox's Depositories, Wandsworth, advertised each day in the *Daily Herald*). And gradually the multiplier effect of such spending, which had been properly analysed for the first time that summer by a young economist named Richard Kahn, in the *Economics Journal*, started to re-stoke the fires in the

---

* One survey showed that one-third of the unemployed in Liverpool between eighteen and twenty-five had married while they were out of work.

potteries, and the brickyards, and the factories which made saucepans and scouring powder and bicycle wheels. It was at this time that social phenomena like the widely deplored football pools started to build up towards their formidable post-war stature. The rewards were modest by today's standards—Littlewoods were proudly offering prizes of £750 for 1s. and £1,233 for 2s. when the spring 1931 football season closed. But even £750 looked like a fortune beyond the dreams of avarice to a Suffolk farmworker who had just heard (on 3 March) that the County Wages Board had agreed a cut from 30s. to 28s. in his weekly wage.* And Emilio Scala, the Battersea café owner who won £177,272 on the Irish Sweepstake that spring, was driven close to a nervous breakdown by those fellow-citizens who felt they had a right to share his good fortune. Such fairy-tale windfalls, even if bought at the sacrifice of two-thirds of a cup of nourishing rolled oats and half a cabbage, seemed to offer a good deal more in the way of hope than the increasingly incomprehensible cavortings of the politicians and the international money-men.

The intensely complex situation with which these people were trying to cope, and which blew up in their faces in the weeks between July and September 1931, had its origins far back. Versailles, the intense French suspicion of any move which appeared to reduce the burden of German reparations, the unresolved struggle for power between the New York banks and the still-evolving Federal Reserve Board, and the rigid, but only very partially accepted, Gold Standard discipline to which Churchill and Norman had committed not only Britain, but effectively the world in 1925, all played their part in stoking up the sullen flames of economic depression which by now had spread to all the major industrial and primary producing countries. And in fact, as we noted above, Britain was by no means the most obviously stricken. Already, by the end of 1930, Germany, with a roughly similar population, had over four million men unemployed. And the US had seen 608 banks fail during November and December, including the powerful Bank of the United States, which, although its name rather overstated its importance, still represented over $200 million in deposits, and was at that time by far the

---

* The Transport & General Workers Union collected a wide sample of budgets to show what this would mean (including a meticulously-kept one from a couple in Stowmarket, who listed everything, down to the 1d. they put in the church bag each Sunday, and the two 1½d. poppies they bought for Armistice Day) and came to the conclusion that for the average labourer's wife this would mean making 140 meals for less than 12s. At the meeting where this was announced, one labourer, Ben Ford, who had spent his whole life on East Anglian farms, growled: 'A penny for a meal—ah, it's a godsend to get home and know that the missus can spare a penny for a meal.'

biggest commercial bank ever allowed to go smash without the US authorities coming to the rescue.

The last period at which sterling had been relatively strong and the leading world economies (including Britain's) relatively healthy had been in mid-1928. But even then the calm was deceptive. It followed three years of chronic unease, during which the tight money and generally deflationary policies required to protect the Bank of England's gold stocks were continually at odds with the crying need for expansion in the domestic economy. France and Germany, with their undervalued currencies, were running large balance-of-payments surpluses, and insisting that they be settled in gold, to an extent that either of them could easily swallow the whole of South Africa's current production in any given year. The Bank of France had large sterling holdings which it was maintaining with growing reluctance, and both the Bank of England and the Reichsbank had short-term liabilities to foreigners many times as big as their reserves. Norman, in his conversations and correspondence with overseas bankers was frequently using phrases like 'queer street' to describe Britain's economic performance, and brandishing the threat to sever the connection between sterling and gold as a negotiating instrument; while at the same time leaving the Cabinet and even the Chancellor of the Exchequer totally in the dark about various key items in the country's monetary arrangements, like the $200 million which the Bank held in New York on its own account. Even the temporary strength of the pound depended on a particularly strong flow of American capital into the UK, which could be reversed any time. And the efforts to reach this moderate degree of equilibrium had engendered so much bitterness and acrimony among the central bankers and finance officials concerned that it sharply lowered the chances of mutual aid when the next real crisis blew up.

The wind-up to the crisis had in fact already begun, with the opening of the fantastic sixteen-month-long bull market on Wall Street which preceded the Great Crash of October 1929. During that time New York money rates reached record heights as everyone tried to get their hands on speculative cash, and the American gold outflow, which had totalled $500 million in the year to June 1928, went sharply into reverse. Some $300 million went back to the US during the stock market lunacy, and at the same time the Bank of France raised its gold reserves by a formidable $434 million. Between them, the two countries thus pre-empted something like three years' worth of new gold production, and the resulting pressure was felt throughout the world. The strain was particularly acute in Germany, which had been most heavily dependent on the US loans which had

now dried up. But London was heavily embarrassed also, first by the
foreign borrowing demands switched from New York, and then, when
Bank Rate had been raised sufficiently to discourage them, by the
cashing-in of sterling balances which immediately threw the pound,
and its whole relation to gold, into danger. Pleas from Norman for
an alleviating rise in US discount rates caused a sharp rift between
the internationally minded New York Reserve Bank, which duly
suggested a jump to 6 per cent, and the domestically orientated
Federal Reserve Board in Washington, which unprecedentedly turned
it down. In the three summer months of 1928, Britain lost $133
million of gold, before the Hatry scandal provided a suitable excuse
for Norman to push the British Bank Rate up to the near-crisis
level of 6½ per cent on 26 September 1929. Almost simultaneously the
bottom dropped out of Wall Street. The result, as far as the exchanges
were concerned, was an abrupt reversal of the trend: capital and gold
flowed out of New York again, the major currencies recovered, and
for a brief moment it appeared that the whole episode might be
regarded as a blessing in disguise. But the final conflagration was not
far away.

During 1930, the brief US recovery petered out. France, hitherto
relatively buoyant, joined Britain and Germany in deepening unemployment. Hitler's Nazi party emerged for the first time as a
major electoral force. Demand for raw materials slumped, prices
collapsed, and the primary producing countries, drained of their
meagre gold stocks in a desperate attempt to stay solvent, started to
default on their foreign loans, to devalue their currencies, and, in
South America and Eastern Europe, to dispatch their governments
in a series of increasingly bloody political coups. Gold piled up in the
US and in the Bank of France—Britain alone shipped nearly £60
million, or rather more than South Africa's total annual output,
across the Channel during the eleven months up to July 1931—
but did nothing to boost confidence or activity, and the pound and
the German Reichsmark remained under heavy pressure. Pictures
of bankers sailing—and even occasionally now flying—hither and
thither in search of some long-term method of easing the strain
became commonplace components of the, since 1929, all-talking
news-reels. The faces of Montagu Norman, Harrison of the New
York Federal Reserve, Luther, who had succeeded Schacht at the
Reichsbank, and Moret of the Bank of France, were as familiar
in Jarrow, where 7,000 out of the town's 9,600 workers were now
unemployed and the top price in the biggest local cinema was 9d.,
as they were in London, where the Dominion, Tottenham Court
Road, felt confident enough to advertise Charlie Chaplin in *City
Lights*, with all seats bookable from 2s. 4d. to 10s. But they achieved

nothing. And on 11 May 1931, the monetary dry-rot reached the industrial heart of Europe.

Austria's largest commercial bank, the Credit-Anstalt, was heavily committed with loans to depression-struck firms, and on that day its directors announced that they were in serious trouble. They owed some £20 million in short-term liabilities, largely to British, US and German banks, and all the ingredients were ready for a chain of panic withdrawals, as depositors rushed to protect their funds. In all three countries, Austria, Germany and Britain, such short-term liabilities, many of them payable almost on demand, were several times as big as the total national gold and currency reserves, which in any case were largely committed, under the Gold Standard, to backing the domestic note issue, and the threat to exchange stability was immediate and immense.

In fairness to the men concerned it is important to remember that this was a crisis of a magnitude no one had ever experienced before, and, at the start, they were groping even for basic information on what they were up against. It was over a week before Norman and Harrison acquired full data on the extent of their countries' commitments in Austria, and the magnitude of London's involvement in Germany did not emerge until July, with the belated report of the Macmillan Committee on Finance and Industry, which had been set up in 1929, to assess the effect of Britain's return to gold. In the event, the Report, which revealed for the first time that short-term foreign deposits were more than three times as big as the Bank of England's total reserves, was a not insignificant factor in pushing us off gold again. But in the meantime, the responsible officials, and behind them the increasingly desperate politicians, were groping virtually in the dark. And they were not helped by the latest bitterness between France and Germany, which effectively blocked any major co-operative rescue effort before it could begin.

Germany, where industrial production had dropped by a third in two years, and almost 40 per cent of the labour force was unemployed, was now making desperate efforts to obtain relief from the much-modified but still huge burden of war reparations. Their case was largely accepted in London and Washington, but Paris was dead set against. After the US President, Hoover, made the would-be generous offer of a one-year reparations moratorium in July, the French, who had not been consulted, and stood to lose around £20 million by this action, made it clear that their big gold stocks would only be made available for currency support purposes on condition that reparations were fully resumed. This was, naturally, quite unacceptable to Berlin, and the crisis lurched onwards. All efforts at concerted action—by central bankers, by governments,

and finally, in despair, by a 'committee of international experts'—
came to nothing. And the only move that was agreed, involving a
'standstill' on Austrian payments, merely made the situation worse,
as depositors started to worry about the solvency of Austria's
creditors, Germany and the UK.

In Britain itself, matters were further complicated by a furious
row in the Labour Cabinet between the 'sound finance' men, led by
the Chancellor, Philip Snowden, who stood firm on the need for rigid
economy and a balanced Budget, and a group headed by Arthur
Henderson, the Foreign Secretary, who were determined to oppose
any scheme which necessitated cutting back on the social services
and particularly on unemployment benefit.

The real attack on the pound began on Monday, 13 July, with the
failure of the big Danat Bank in Germany on the same day that the
Macmillan Report showed the full extent of London's vulnerability
to the withdrawal of short-term foreign assets. At that time these
liabilities stood at between £600 and £700 million, four or five times
as large as the Bank of England's gold reserves. When the Berlin
banks closed, thus effectively freezing over £60 million of British
cash in Germany, every kind of panicky fear and rumour swept the
foreign exchange markets. British banks were on the point of sus-
pending payment! The Government would impose a swingeing
capital levy! Belgian, Swiss, Dutch, French and Swedish banks pulled
out their London deposits immediately, in an effort to protect their
own liquidity, and they were joined by at least some Britons, fleeing
the expected wrath to come. In two weeks the Bank of England lost
over £40 million in gold and dollars, a quarter of its reserves. But for
some reason—possibly sheer exhaustion: Norman, after a year of non-
stop negotiation and conferences, collapsed on 29 July and did not
recover till gold was finally abandoned—no strong move was made
to stem the flow. Bank Rate, which on Norman's own admission
should have been at least 6 or 7 per cent on any traditional assessment of the situation, rose only hesitantly, from 2½ per cent in June
to 4½ per cent at the beginning of August, and then stuck. Two more
bankers' conferences, in Basle and then in London, ended in deadlock,
and Parliament, after hearing a Government promise that every
possible step would be taken 'to ensure that the proud and sound
position of British credit shall be in no way impaired', adjourned
until, it thought, October.

While they sunned themselves at the seaside or embarked on one
of that year's popular sea cruises ('126 Days Afloat for 126 Guineas
with the Blue Funnel Line'), more efforts were being made to
scramble together some sort of Franco-American support for sterling.
In the end a fairly substantial package of loans was put together.

But as Stephen V. O. Clarke puts it, in the excellent New York Federal Reserve Bank account, *Central Bank Co-operation 1924–31*: 'The program that actually was adopted was definitely a second best, even by the standards of mid-1931.' It came in two parts, with no dramatic fanfare to impress the speculators; its first instalment was totally unsupported by any measures to solve the pound's weaknesses; and its second instalment, not granted till everyone knew that the first was virtually exhausted, was immediately entangled in the bitter and still reverberating controversy over the 'Bankers' Ramp'.

The intial £50 million credit, raised by the Federal Reserve and the Bank of France, could in fact have hardly arrived at a worse time. The transfer was made on 1 August, the day after the May Committee (named after its chairman, Sir George May, head of the Prudential Insurance Company) had presented its report on Britain's domestic finances, which produced the then-shattering news that, in the absence of major policy changes, Snowden's Budget deficit for 1932–3 would be £120 million, and even bigger the following year. The market opened very weak the day after the Bank Holiday, 4 August, and collapsed calamitously when the Bank of England, which was engaged in a complex and disastrous effort to put pressure on the British Government and at the same time to bamboozle the Paris speculators, failed to use its new support funds anyway. When it did come in it was too late, and the exchanges grew progressively more hectic and panicky ('Have the French withdrawn support? Are they insisting that Norman must go?') right up to the day the Labour Government resigned, on 24 August.

The immediate cause of the resignation, naturally, was the composition of Snowden's promised 'retrenchment' Budget, now brought hastily forward from the October date originally planned. The inner cabinet members had now been informed that the May Committee's estimate of the deficit was far too low—the figure, unless drastic action was taken, would be nearer £180 million than £120 million—and everyone agreed that this meant higher taxes and a sharp cutback in spending. But Snowden insisted, despite Henderson's obviously immovable opposition, that it must also include the highly controversial 10 per cent cut in the dole. He refused to consider any of the possible alternatives—an import tariff, which even Keynes was now advocating; a reduction in the huge sinking fund accumulated in the wake of the 1914–18 borrowing programme; or a review of the Gold Standard—and announced: 'We believe firmly that if sterling collapses . . . you will have chaos and ruin in this country. You will have unemployment rising not merely to five million, but to ten million.'

For long afterwards the air was thick with accusations that it was the French and American bankers who had insisted on the dole cut, as a condition of advancing the second half of the loan support package, ultimately amounting to some £80 million. This was furiously denied at the time, and the truth seems to be that all they asked for was the assurance, from people in a position to know, and particularly from the oracular lips of Montagu Norman, that the proposed measures would be sufficient to restore Britain's financial health. As Norman appears to have been expressing his doubts fairly freely, particularly to Harrison of the New York Federal Reserve, it is hardly surprising that there was some hesitation. In the end, though, the loans went through, and, after a Monday of anguish and fission in the Labour Cabinet, Snowden and the Prime Minister, Ramsay MacDonald, emerged at the head of a 'National' coalition, pledged to deal with the crisis, to balance the Budget, and 'to restore sterling to its reputation for reliability'. Thanks to the National government, MacDonald told Parliament, 'this House meets . . . with the pound worth 20s.'. And one has a sneaking suspicion, based on a long study of politicians' utterances on such occasions, that he actually thought the phrase had some meaning.

Snowden duly presented his Budget on 10 September—three days after an announcement from King George V that he desired 'personally to participate in the movement for the reduction of national expenditure' and had therefore decided to cut the Civil List, under which royal monies are provided, by £50,000 'while the emergency lasts'. Following this eminent example, the Budget was as savage as could be wished: income tax up 6d. to 5s., with changes in allowances which effectively doubled its bite on smaller salaries and wage packets; higher taxes on beer, petrol and cigarettes ('On every 6d. packet of cigarettes approximately 3d. now goes to the Exchequer.'); the dole reductions, from 17s. a week to 15s. 3d. for men and from 15s. to 13s. 6d. for women; and a wide range of salary cuts, affecting virtually everyone within the ambit of the public service. Police constables, by then earning between 70s. and 95s. a week, were docked by 5s. Doctors operating the health insurance 'panels' were cut back from 9s. a patient to 8s. Government ministers and judges gave up 20 per cent of their salaries if they were over £5,000, 15 per cent from £2,000 to £5,000, and 10 per cent—the same as teachers, MPs, and almost all civil servants—if they were below the £40 a week mark. A first-class General in the Army was unceremoniously reduced from £9 4s. a day to £8 5s. 8d. And even the Chaplain of the Fleet was not immune—his pay dropped overnight from £1,500 a year to £1,335.

It was, in fact, from the Navy, rather than from the dole queues, that the trouble came which finally sent the pound over the edge. Cutting an Admiral of the Fleet from a daily allowance of £8 to £6 12s. 6d. was something that an officer was expected to accept in the normal spirit of sacrifice for King and Currency. But a long-service chief petty officer who had entered into substantial mortgage and particularly hire-purchase commitments, on the basis of a 'statutory' 8s. 6d. a day, took a very poor view of the new scale offering 7s. 6d. (which in any case was rather worse than the 10 per cent cut imposed on other civil servants). And the long-serving able seamen, whose rate dropped from 4s. a day to 3s., and still more the ordinary seaman, down from 2s. 9d. to 2s., were naturally very put out indeed. It was only the very senior men who were concerned— new entrant rates had already come down sharply from the levels set in the inflation of 1920—and the resulting protests, though heartfelt, were extremely orderly. But they were sufficient to cause the cancellation of that month's North Atlantic manœuvres, and such an event, when cheerfully blown up by the world's (non-British) press into 'The Invergordon Mutiny', set the final seal on the impression that Britain was heading for hell in a long-boat.

The rest of Snowden's victims had in fact accepted, and even welcomed, the bitter Budget medicine. They listened solemnly to the Chancellor's lurid radio description of the horrors of the German 1923 inflation and accepted his assurance that 'that is what going off the Gold Standard means, and that is the menace to which British money has been alarmingly exposed in recent weeks'. From the Army, who had been quite as savagely treated as the Navy, there was not a whimper, and the teachers, who stopped all school football in South London as a protest, were sternly rebuked by their fellow citizens. After all, had not Mr Snowden told them that 'the choice is between the Budget, with its unpleasant economies and heavy taxation, or a paper currency with no stable value and more or less the ruin of everybody'? And had not the widow of Admiral of the Fleet Sir Henry Bradwardine Jackson gone far towards refurbishing the honour of the Navy by relinquishing her £300 a year pension 'during the present financial state of the country'. But stoicism alone was not enough.

Big headlines on 'The Mutiny', which appeared in New York, Paris, Berlin, Zurich, Amsterdam and most other important financial capitals on 15 September, precipitated the final onslaught, and by midday Saturday, 19 September, when the foreign exchange markets closed, the Bank of England's books showed a loss of £200 million in gold and foreign exchange in just over two months. Its net reserves, after allowing for outstanding commitments and the French and US loans, were down to a nominal £5 million, and the end was only a matter of hours. Panic withdrawals by the Dutch and Swiss banks, ambiguous dealings by the French, and the Bank's own strange action in using the loans to support the pound, not at the low price at which gold exports became automatic, but half a cent above, which gave every encouragement to the speculators and thus maximized the potential loss, all conspired to send sterling down the last slippery slope. At 6.30 on Saturday afternoon Sir Ernest Harvey, the deputy Governor, who was standing in for the sick Norman, telephoned Harrison in New York to say that, in the absence of any alternative, the British government would suspend gold sales as from the opening of business on Monday, 21 September.

Snowden returned to the microphone on the Monday night, and discussed the affair with the, by now, justifiably bewildered British public, in a discourse which still rates as a masterpiece of the word-swallower's art. 'When about a fortnight ago I spoke of the inflation and of a great depreciation of sterling,' he told them, 'I was referring to what might happen if we did not balance the Budget and at the same time had to abandon the gold standard. It would have been a very different thing if the pound had started to go a month or so ago when we had a huge deficit in our national Budget and when our capacity to set our house in order was viewed with suspicion. I should have been very alarmed as to the consequences then, for in that case the Government would have had to borrow to meet current expenditure. With confidence destroyed it would very soon have found it impossible to borrow and it would have been driven to inflate the currency—that is to say, to print more and more paper money in order to make ends meet. In that way the vicious circle of inflation would have been started which it might have been almost impossible to check. That was a real danger. As things are now there is no such danger. The British Budget is the most securely balanced Budget in the world. There is no longer any risk of an internal inflation—that is to say, printing of paper notes to pay our way. There is no longer any reason for doubting the essential soundness of our financial position.'

As an essay in half-truths, misconceptions and *non sequiturs* this takes several prizes. There was a 'great depreciation' of the pound—it was down to 17s. 6d. against the dollar on the first day of free trading, and 14s. by the end of the year. There were still grave doubts whether Britain could balance her Budget—under pressure, many of the more slashing cuts in the armed services' pay had already been restored—and thus 'put her house in order'. Borrowing was already impossible, as the Treasury had found three days before when it tried to raise further franc and dollar loans. And 'the essential sound-ness of our financial position' depended essentially on abandoning our traditional position as world banker, and open, free-trade market, and shutting ourself away for eight years to work out our own economic salvation. But still, in its twisted, accidental, illogical way, the formula thus arrived at did achieve its desired effect—Britain's slump was hell while it lasted, but it did not last long, in its most virulent form; its intensity was a great deal lower than most other people's; and even at its worst, large parts of the country were able to shrug off its impact almost *in toto*.

Already, at the height of the panic, important events were going forward against the general gloomy trend. Ford's were building their huge new plant at Dagenham, employing, right from the start, over 15,000 men. The electricity grid, set in train during the twenties to rationalize a then thoroughly backward and fragmented industry, provided over 100,000 jobs through the depths of the depression. And the housebuilders, though not yet hitting the 360,000 a year peak achieved during the boom of the mid-thirties, were already averaging well over 200,000 throughout the dark years of 1929–32, and a very respectable 219,000 in 1931 itself. The furnishing, decorating, fitting-out and filling the garages of 'The Little Mansions of Edgware' (£775 cash or £25 down and 25s. 6d. a week) or of Richard Costain's Greenford Estate (three bedrooms, two living-rooms, bath, kitchen and car space for £730) went a long way to encourage the demand which Snowden's topsyturvy budget was overtly and masochistically designed to stifle.

Some people, in fact, were now ready and willing to spend their way out of depression; even though it was another five years before Keynes's *General Theory of Employment, Interest and Money* made such a bizarre notion intellectually respectable. And even those who practised thrift at the Government's behest fortunately chose to practise it largely through the building societies, which experienced a huge and fructifying growth in their funds at this time. Official policy, however, continued to erect the maximum amount of obstruction in everyone's path.

Certainly the Budget, whatever its defects, had gone a long way to restore the confidence of those businessmen who thought, in the words of Professor Pigou, that 'the country was going to the dogs on account of extravagant consumption'. But initially, any resulting expansion in activity was effectively squashed by crisis-level interest rates. Bank Rate went to 6 per cent on 21 September, and stayed there for five months. Foreign capital flowed back to London, pushing up the now-freely-floating rate of sterling exchange and threatening to erode the competitive advantages that devaluation had given to the country's still groggy exporters. Overseas sales, which had collapsed from £729 million in 1929 to £391 million in 1931, dropped a further £26 million in 1932. Many people began to share the view of Sir Ralph Hawtrey, always one of the more outspoken economic critics of those years, that all the gold suspension had done was slightly slow down the depression. By February, when Bank Rate started to drop, Hawtrey was convinced that it was already too late and that deflation of the worst kind had once more set in.

As it turned out, he was wrong. The Abnormal Importations Act of the previous November, which finally put up the tariff walls round Britain's economy, had already started foreign companies, like Hoover, looking very hard at the attractions of setting up in the UK.* And the era of cheap two per cent money, which lasted, apart from a slight hiccup in September 1939, for almost twenty years, was just around the corner. This was brought in, not as a direct stimulus to trade, but as part of the mechanics of lowering the crippling interest burden of the State's Great War borrowing,† but its effects were none the less beneficial for that. And by the end of 1933, the Treasury and the Bank were fighting, not to keep the pound from falling, but from rising far too far. In the end, by the expedient of the Bank's Exchange Equalization Account and the expenditure of some £550 million, the rate was effectively pegged in a narrow band around $5, or 3 per cent above the figure abandoned in 1931. And there it stayed till the approach of war brought it down to the fixed 1939–49 level of $4·03.

Looking back, it is clear from the figures that Britain's industrial recession had already touched bottom in 1931. It was the exaggerated response to the purely monetary crisis, stemming in turn from the distortions of the post-1925 Gold Standard system, which stretched out the worst of the agony till the first quarter of 1933, when the unemployment figures finally started to subside. Recovery after that was fast and, by world standards at the time, spectacular. According to H. W. Richardson's detailed study, *Economic Recovery*

---

* In 1930 only 37,550 vacuum cleaners were made in Britain, and 140,130 imported. Hoover, who had been manufacturing in Canada, arrived in Perivale on London's Western Avenue, in 1931, built up a formidable door-to-door sales force, largely from men who had been on the dole, and by 1934, domestic production was up to 318,039 and imports had slumped to 11,205 machines.

† This conversion was an urgent need. The cost of servicing the National Debt, which had leaped from £706 million in 1914 to £7,582 million in 1931, was now eating up no less than 8·3 per cent of the national income. A large part of this was the interest on £2,086 million worth of 5 per cent War Loan. After Bank Rate had been brought down, in several steps, from 6 per cent in February to 2 per cent in June, it became possible to convert this mass of stock to a reduced 3½ per cent coupon, in the biggest operation of its kind ever handled in Britain. The saving was an immediate £55·5 million a year, and by 1936 the total debt charge was down to a more reasonable 4·6 per cent of the nation's earnings.

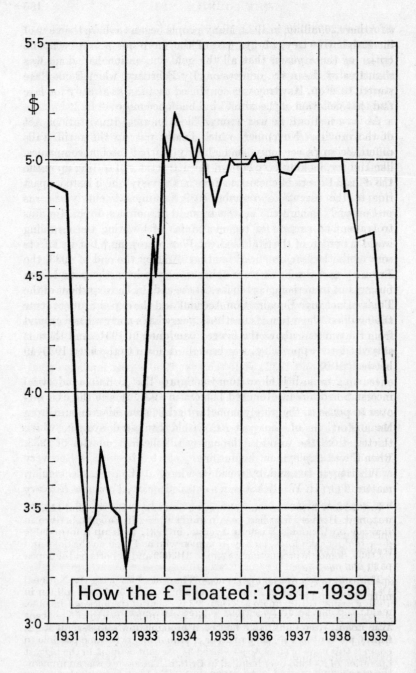

How the £ Floated: 1931-1939

in Britain, 1932–39, real national income in the five years to 1937 increased by 20 per cent, income per head by 18 per cent, production by 46 per cent and car sales and electricity output, the two leading measures of domestic improvement, more than doubled over the period 1929–37. As Professor R. S. Sayers puts it in his *Economic Change 1880–1939,* a family lucky enough to keep its breadwinner in a job saw food which had cost perhaps £8 a month in 1927 come down to £6 11s. by 1931 and to £6 two years after that. They used the difference to power 'the demand for more and better houses, the demand for buses to go to the shops that used motor delivery vans, the demand for radios, electric light in the bedroom, a motor-coach ride to the seaside, and rayon stockings to shimmer along the promenade'. Behind the tariff walls and the foreign exchange controls set up to insulate the pound and its owners from the continuing world trade storm (Detroit's car production in 1932 was only 25 per cent of the 1929 figure, and even in 1937 it was barely 85 per cent), Britain—or the four-fifths of it in employment—got down to the business of smartening up the material standards of everyday life. This was not just the comfortable middle-classes either, in fact rather the reverse. Wage earners and the lower-paid salary earners (apart from the unfortunate civil servants, with their 10 per cent 1931 cut) saw the real value of their personal income rise appreciably, even between 1929 and 1932, while the over £250 a year families experienced on average an almost 30 per cent fall. The proportion of lower-income borrowers from building societies rose in many cases to well over 50 per cent. And this, coupled with the fact that, even under the Means Test, 'the unemployed man with a family was better off in the thirties than the unskilled labourer in full work in 1913',[*] kept Britain well this side of revolution.

Whether it benefited the country in the longer run is another matter. The export industries, which had employed one man in every five in the 1880s and one in every four at the outbreak of the 1914 war, now occupied less than one in every eight. The boom of the mid-thirties was almost entirely a matter of the new, consumer-oriented trades—major re-investment and re-equipment played only a tiny part, and even when it came, it was almost entirely taken up with the specialized needs of arming for war. There was no government commitment to full employment; no belief in the virtues of public investment; and as a result no serious attempt to find useful outlets for the million man-years annually wasted in the dole queues even after the 'recovery' was complete. This was a tragedy, not only for the men pathetically idling their time away, answering advertisements like the ones which invited 'send 2s. 6d. for a kit for making shoe polish to

[*] C. L. Mowat, *Britain Between the Wars* (Methuen, 1956).

sell to your friends', but for the country, which might have used their skill and energy in repairing some of the old industrial ravages. With war, and its aftermath, these remained in many cases an eyesore and a clog to efficiency for another twenty or thirty years. And the resulting human bitterness has survived to the present day.

For Britain the whole episode of the inter-war gold gamble was a classic example of the way that monetary myth and half-digested economics can bring a nation to its knees. Equally ill-understood remedies, with results often diametrically at variance with the expectations of the physicians who prescribed them, then brought the patient back on its feet again, ready—or more or less ready—to embark on the most titanic military struggle in history. Ramsay MacDonald's dubious promise of 23 August 1931 was more than fulfilled—by 1933–4, when the domestic purchasing power of the pound reached its post-1914 peak, it was worth, not 20s. of Gold Standard money, but 21s. 5½d., and in foreign-exchange terms it looked the dollar more firmly in the face than at any time in the last hundred years. These results were some kind of landmark. But the world, sensibly, was too concerned about real problems by then to worry about such patently fictitious triumphs. They had been bought at too high a price—in complacency, in insularity, in resistance to change and in too great an attachment to a not particularly inspiring *status quo*. From then on, the steady attrition of sterling set in—through the remaining uneasy years of peace, through the second war to end war, and on into the new world power pattern beyond. It has now continued, without noticeable remission, for the last thirty-six years.

The Pound in 1949

was worth £2 4s. in 1970 money

> The purpose of this debate is to discover whether there is a chance left, however small, to save sterling from a collapse.
>
> David Eccles MP: Speech in the House of Commons (14 July 1949)

> For, as to the base, swindling execrable plan of *lowering the standard*; as to that cruel design, which could have been suggested by nobody but the Devil himself in person, it will not, it cannot, it must not, be adopted, nor attempted.
>
> William Cobbett on Devaluation, in the *Political Register* (22 May 1821)

O n 18 September 1949, after a summer of denials that such a step could be regarded as necessary, possible, tolerable, honourable or desirable, Sir Stafford Cripps, then Chancellor of the Exchequer, briefly announced that the dollar exchange value of the pound had been devalued, by approximately 30·5 per cent, from its 1939–49 rate of $4·03 to $2·80. With some relief and alacrity, Holland, Greece, and most of the countries of the Commonwealth, Scandinavia and the Middle East followed suit; France, Belgium, Canada, Portugal and, after a little hesitation, Germany went part of the way in the same direction; and only Switzerland, among the major financial nations, remained firm. Globally, some such movement, at some time, was probably almost inevitable as an adjustment to the massive post-war economic dominance of the United States, and to the emergence of 'the dollar gap', where the world's most desirable goods, from nylons to petrol, were obtainable only in a currency which most countries were quite incapable of generating in sufficient quantities for their needs. But whether it was necessary, at that moment, for Britain to move so fast and so far has been a matter of doubt and controversy ever since.

More immediately and reprehensibly though, it raised the whole question, brusquely put by *The Economist* the following weekend, whether such violent upheavals did not stem from the fact that 'the British people have voted themselves, in cash and in kind, larger incomes than they earn'. That argument—'Does Britain pay her way? Are her foreign exchange troubles in some way an expression of deep moral malaise? Is she the greedy grasshopper in a world of economic ants?'—has been raging one way and another ever since. It has run through, by my count, ten major sterling crises* and a further devaluation; and judging by the speeches in the run-up to the 1970 General Election it shows every sign of surviving into the twenty-first century.

To the British people in 1949, however, such accusations appeared to have little relation to the drab realities of everyday life and everyday shopping. Certainly they had the Welfare State, of which other countries seemed so vociferously envious; but they also had rationing and Utility furniture and universal overtime, to the extent that on average everyone was working two hours more than they were in 1938. And those official statistics which seemed pertinent to the situation—industrial production up by 50 per cent; exports up by a massive 75 per cent; unemployment down to a marginal 350,000, almost all of it very temporary—failed to offset the prevailing

---

* 1951–2, 1955, 1956, 1957, 1961, 1964, 1965, 1966, 1967, 1968.

impression that 'we ended the war poorer than we started it and we have been growing poorer ever since'.*

For most people, admittedly, this was not strictly true. The average national income per head, after adjusting for the virtual doubling of prices, was almost exactly the same in 1949 as it had been in 1938. And for the average wage earner—the man who had been getting under £5 a week in 1938, and was now getting its equivalent of up to £10 a week in 1949—who made up five-sixths of the population, the purchasing power of his pay packet had improved by some 25 per cent. The big losers were the top sixth, hard hit by high taxes and the big price increases in 'luxury goods'. These had risen sharply in comparison with the basic necessities of food, clothing and accommodation, which by and large had been controlled and often subsidized as part of the wartime economy. On average, salaries, rents and dividends had depreciated by a clear 30 per cent over the period, and the sufferers felt no necessity to keep quiet about the fact. As Seers says, in seeking explanations for the widespread feelings of post-war poverty: 'One reason is that the minority who are definitely poorer are on the whole the most vocal section of the community; a second is that many who are actually better off tend to compare their present position with what it might have been before the war if they had been successful; thirdly, a number repeat the opinions of the strata above them; and finally extremists of the Right and the Left have wanted, for various reasons, to disparage such improvements as have occurred.'

Comparisons were complicated also, of course, by the fact that, at this period, the pound in your pocket was not the only criterion of buying power; you needed a ration book as well. Rationing, by this time, was largely done on the 'points' system—in effect, a second currency under which you could only acquire goods if you were in a position to hand over cash and points at the same time. It was, in Peter Wiles's phrase, 'a beautiful economist's toy' and one of them, George Worswick, in an elegant essay called 'Points, Prices and Consumer's Choice' demonstrated, with the aid of indifference curves and disequilibrium analysis, the complex intuitive process which had to go on in the mind of the normal housewife if she was to discover the 'point of maximum satisfaction' without going raving mad.

The practical hazards of the system were neatly illustrated in the 1947 case of Lord Trent's overcoat. Lord Trent, the multi-millionaire chairman of the huge Boots Cash Chemist chain, could normally buy all the crombies, Burberrys and tweed ulsters in London without a twitch of his cheque-book, but in the coldest winter of the century,

* Dudley Seers in *The British Economy 1945–50*, ed. G. D. N. Worswick & P. H. Ady (Oxford, 1952).

in the middle of the worst fuel crisis in Britain's history, his coat was stolen. The police, having caught the thief almost immediately, naturally wished to keep the coat as evidence until the trial. And Lord Trent, who had rashly expended too many of his current clothing coupons, was forced to petition the court to release his coat between hearings, to save himself from freezing to death. That was the kind of thing that brought reality to the post-war rich.

Clothes were off the ration by 1949 (though devaluation brought rumours of reimposition and a big rush to stock up on Selfridge's 70s. all-wool tweed jackets and C & A's 89s. 11d. bargain cloth coats). But there were plenty of other irritating rules and frustrations. One man was fined £6 at Luton in July for putting real milk in his ice-cream. Londoners, offered a 6d. bonus on their 1s. 4d. a week meat ration to cover a temporary breakdown in the milk rationing scheme, then lost it because the £6 6s. a week Smithfield men would not move the extra loads without a bonus. Football pools coupons, now offering 'amazing dividends' of £50,382 for 6d., could only be obtained after sending a 2s. deposit 'under the paper control'. A woman in Sunderland, who had borrowed some coal from a neighbour to warm a bedroom for her sick sister and asked the coal man to deliver her ration to the neighbour in repayment, was hauled to court for 'offences under the coal distribution order' and told, before the case was dismissed, that the maximum penalties she could have incurred ran to £500. And the whole British nation was roused to fury by the news that sweet rationing had ended in Germany, just as ours, thanks to the dollar shortage, had had to be reimposed.

Among the entertaining classes, the 5s. upper limit on the permitted cost of restaurant meals produced endless grouses and counter-grouses, and frequently invoked the full majesty (not to say ingenuity) of the law. In July the Member of Parliament for Twickenham raised the collective wrath of the House of Commons (now paying its MPs £1,000 a head) by listing the additional charges which one restaurant had succeeded in adding to his basic 5s. bill—6s. house charge, 4s. for oysters, 10s. for flowers on the table, 7s. 6d. for 'liquor in food' (a dash of maraschino on the strawberries), 2s. 6d. for dancing, 2s. for coffee and 3s. service. Some hotels, it was alleged, were getting round the 'illegal fourth course' rule, then in force, by serving lobster in guests' rooms—a 'separate meal'—before they went down to the dining-room for the main attack. And in September, one such establishment was fined £20 for the sin of serving asparagus to two Ministry of Food inspectors 'as a separate dish' rather than on the same plate as their meat 'as a vegetable'.

However, these were minor blemishes on the social surface (like the pub notice observed by one of Seebohm Rowntree's investigators:

'Beer 1s. 2d. a pint. Half pints only. If the chap next to you has a pint, don't grumble. He's a regular.'). The real source of discontent was the burden of post-war taxation, which, to anyone who remembered the twenties and thirties—let alone the large number of people who could recall the world before 1914—seemed a crushing and intolerable incubus. And by any previous standards, they were absolutely right. It was in 1845 that John R. McCulloch wrote of taxation, in his *Treatise on the Principles and Practical Influence of Taxation and the Funding Systems*: 'The severity of its pressure in England is but too apparent . . . the evil is one of a very marked character; and . . . till it be materially mitigated, it will furnish matter for perennial agitation and discontent, and be a formidable obstacle to our progress.' By 1949 the net real income of the country was roughly six times as great as in McCulloch's day, which suggested that the obstacle had not been wholly insurmountable. But the tax revenues had multiplied by no fewer than 150 times.

The total bite imposed by Cripps's 1948 'austerity' budget, which was the one chiefly affecting life in 1949, came to £4,073 million out of national earnings which, after removing the distorting effects of taxes and subsidies, worked out at just over £10,000 million. Direct taxes—income tax, now 9s. in the pound, profits tax and national insurance contributions—represented just over half. Indirect taxes, which added £83 16s. 6d. to the basic £229 cost of a Morris Minor car and had pushed the price of Johnnie Walker whisky to 33s. 4d. a bottle, brought in another £1,684 million. The rest came from death-duties (£180 million) and Cripps's one-year 'special contribution', which abstracted an additional £112 million from those fortunate or unfortunate enough to have both an income exceeding £2,000 a year, and unearned rents, dividends or interest payments of more than £250. Those two together added up to an overall capital tax of about 1 per cent on the country's accumulated private wealth; and to something over 4 per cent for those 10,700 families with incomes of over £10,000 a year, whose holdings still represented the most concentrated part of it.

Income tax was by now virtually universal among those in any kind of regular work. Some 92·2 per cent of the population made more, one way and another, than the exemption limit of £135 a year (it had been £125 in 1938 when the cost of living was approximately half). Most of the 2,793,000 below this mark were reckoned to be either young, unskilled workers just starting out, or old people living on small accumulations of capital who for some reason did not qualify for, or had not sufficient additional means to augment, the 24s. a week Old Age Pension (only raised in 1947 from the 10s. at which it was set in 1918). And at the other end of the scale there were roughly 215,000 individuals or couples in the surtax bracket, which till the mid-1950s started at £2,000, irrespective of whether the money was earned or unearned.

Getting into the surtax bracket, however, was one thing: living up to it quite another. The impact of high war and post-war taxes on large incomes had been (and indeed still is) quite confiscatory, as the following table shows. The first column gives various levels of net, personal, take-home income, and the other two the gross amounts that would have been needed to provide them, in 1938 and in 1949.

Net personal income	Equivalent gross income	
	1938	1948–9
£500	£570	£640
£1,000	£1,203	£1,450
£5,000	£7,790	£47,500
£10,000	£19,000	£247,000
£25,000	£60,000	£847,500
£100,000	£278,000	£3,847,500

As is clear, all these pay levels were a practical proposition before the war. But afterwards it became virtually impossible, except by the adroit manipulation of gifts, business expenses and windfall capital gains, to carry home very much more than £10,000 a year. That still remains more or less the situation today, but in 1949 it had all the freshness and horror of novelty. The victims were not slow to make themselves heard.

In fact, though, the real victims were probably a good deal further down the pyramid. Cutting a £50,000 a year property income to a quarter of its post-tax 1938 value, and to less than a tenth of its 1938 real value, which is what Seers* calculated to be the combined fiscal and inflationary effects of the changes, was all very sad. But there were big untaxed gains on land and shares to offset it, in most cases. And it hardly compared with the horrid things that had been happening to the living standards of the salaried classes, especially when the Government was in a position to impose 'economies'. The £950–£1,250 a year salary range for a principal in the higher civil service in 1949 was roughly equivalent to the £415–£505 which in 1938 had been the level of that very lowly creature, the higher clerical officer. Additionally, the £300 worth of annual increments standing between the bottom and the top of the range, which was unchanged since before the war, was worth less than one-third of its former value. And the promotional jump from assistant principal to principal, though now, on paper, £200 as against £175, was in fact worth only £70 in hard, pre-war cash.

* *The Levelling of Incomes since 1938* (Oxford, 1951).

This was only one example of a general phenomenon. Differentials for skill and experience had been shrunk during the war and its aftermath right across the spectrum of working activity. This was true in teaching, where the bonus for possessing a university degree was now worth less than half its 1938 value (and probably more like a third if you tried to spend it in the traditional manner on foreign travel). In offices, like those on the railways, senior, experienced women clerks, Grade W2, were now getting only 12s. more than the young, flibbertygibbet twenty-eight-year-olds of Grade W1, where in the thirties the gap had been 17s. 6d., in money with twice the buying value. And even on the shop floor or the housing site, the same erosion was evident. The bricklayer, who had collected a skill premium of 18s. 3d. more than his mate in 1939, had seen it cut by rate and price changes to the equivalent of only 13s. 3d. ten years later. And in engineering and on the railways the figures looked even worse—an effective drop of 45 per cent in the first case, and 54 per cent, from 21s. to 9s. 8d., in the second. In practical terms, as Seers remarked, the engineering premium would have bought nearly three times as much beer in 1938 (allowing for the diminished post-war strength) as it would in 1949, and a full four times as many cigarettes. Wills' Three Castles were now 3s. 10d. for twenty; standard brands, like Player's Navy Cut, were 3s. 6d.; and even the working man's Woodbines were 2s. 9d. after the depredations of several wartime Chancellors. There was considerable approval (till people tasted the results) for the tobacco companies' September announcement that, because of the dollar shortage, they proposed to introduce cigarettes with a nine-sixteenths of an inch cardboard filter tip, which would effectively save the country large quantities of foreign exchange and the customer 7d. a packet.

Still, the vocal and often bitter woes of those who had suffered financially in the introduction of the country's huge post-war welfare programme form only part of the picture. A massive redistribution of the national income had taken place, affecting, for better or worse, every individual and family in Britain, and even among people in the same street or doing the same job in the same factory the range of possible experience was enormous. Taking extreme cases, the effect of tax and price changes between 1938 and 1949 would have been to treble the cost of living of a man dividing his income between wines and spirits, pipe tobacco and potatoes and vegetables. But if he spent his money instead on butter, margarine, meat and bacon and lived in an all-electric house at a controlled rent his expenses would hardly have increased by 10 per cent.

Allowing for such oddities, though, it is still possible to get some idea of the overall impact and significance of the tax-benefit shift.

Seers's way of expressing it was to say that, at 1938 prices, it represented a transfer of £450 million from property owners and £150 million from the salaried and self-employed (apart from farmers). With a growth of £100 million in total personal income over the period, this provided about £50 million for the farmers (virtually doubling their annual earnings compared with the depressed levels of the thirties) and some £650 million for the working classes—a real increase of about a quarter.

An American economist, Allan Murray Cartter, in his *Redistribution of Incomes in Post-War Britain* tried, with some success, to establish a more precise cross-over point between the gainers and the losers, and came to the conclusion that, in 1948–9, it fell somewhere around the £650 a year mark. This depended, however, on various assumptions about the proper way to allocate the 'benefits' from such things as defence spending and the interest on the national debt. As far as the crude balance between taxes paid and welfare cash received was concerned, break-even came a good deal lower—around £225 a year. The average person in the £250–£500 bracket handed the Treasury £48 2s. that year, and only got £28 18s. back in assorted social services. And above £500, of course, people did a great deal worse.

Below £250, though, the combination of full employment and the Welfare State had transformed the scene. When Rowntree, in 1950, did his third survey of York he found that the number of people in 'primary' or 'abject' poverty, which had been 15½ per cent of the population in 1899 and 7 per cent in 1936, was now down to only 0·37 per cent—just 81 families. And in not one of these households, nor among the 765 (2·77 per cent) in 'secondary' poverty, was the continued low income due to the main breadwinner being out of a job.

To show the kind of changes that had been taking place in the High Street, here is Rowntree's post-war subsistence diet (opposite), costed at the prices current in late 1949. In overall nutritional value it is as close as possible to the version used by pre-war researchers, like the Sheffield team whose work I discussed in the last chapter. The main differences were to substitute white flour and fresh milk, now heavily subsidized, for wholemeal and condensed, and to add and subtract suitable oddments of sugar, cheese, bacon and cooking fat to accord with ration book quantities. Also the schoolchildren, of whom there are supposed to be three, plus mother and father, living on the Rowntree shopping list, now get one-third of a pint of free milk for 180 days of the year.

Broken down, this allowed 12s. 6½d. for a man, against the 1931 figure of 6s. 11½d.; 10s. 5d. for the wife, against 6s. 1½d.; and 8s. 1½d.

The 1949 Grocery Bill

	s. d.		s. d.
		2 lb. Oatmeal @ 6d.	1 0
2¼ lb. Breast of mutton @ 8d.	1 8	1 lb. Jam @ 1s. 2d.	1 2
2 lb. Minced beef @ 1s. 4d.	2 8	1 lb. Treacle @ 10d.	10
1½ lb. Shin of beef @ 1s. 6d.	2 3	¼ lb. Cocoa @ 8½d. a qr.	8½
1 lb. Liver @ 1s. 6d.	1 6	10 oz. Rice @ 9d.	5½
1 lb. Beef sausage @ 1s. 3d.	1 3	¼ lb. Sago @ 9d.	2¼
1¼ lb. Bacon @ 1s. 11d.	2 4¾	2 oz. Barley @ 9d.	1
10 oz. Cheese @ 1s. 2d.	8¾	½ lb. Peas @ 10½d.	5¼
14 pts Milk @ 5d.	5 10	¾ lb. Lentils @ 10½d.	8
1½ lb. Herrings @ 8d.	1 0	½ lb. Stoned dates @ 10½d.	5¼
1 lb. Kippers @ 1s.	1 0	6 lb. Swedes @ 2½d.	1 3
3 lb. 2 oz. Sugar @ 5d.	1 3½	4½ lb. Onions @ 5d.	1 10½
14 lb. Potatoes @ 9 lb. for 1s.	1 6½	4 lb. Apples @ 5d.	1 8
13½ Loaves (23½ lb.) @ 5½d.	6 2¼	1 Egg @ 3½d.	3½
2½ lb. Margarine @ 10d.	2 1	Extra vegetables & fruit	1 6
10 oz. Cooking Fat @ 1s.	7½	½ lb. Tea @ 3s. 4d.	1 8
1¼ lb. Flour @ 9½d. a 3 lb. bag	4	Salt, Oxo cubes, etc.	9
		Total	47 4

each for the children, against 3s. 10½d. And although it was no doubt possible to pay more for the individual items if you shopped at Harrods or Fortnum & Mason, while rationing lasted that list approximated to the diet and more or less the food expenditure of most families in Britain.*

In 1917, the rather rudimentary rationing system of the first World War enabled the majority of the population, for the first time in history, to enjoy a Christmas dinner. In 1949 the success of the vastly more sophisticated second World War version caused Professor James Spence, head of the Child Health department at Newcastle Royal Infirmary, to inform the British Association annual meeting that serious rickets was now so rare in his city that it had become impossible to find a case to show to medical students.

Such a desirable outcome naturally depended not only on making the ration available, but ensuring that everyone had the money to

* My wife priced a precisely similar shopping list in London in February 1970, and the bill came to a total of 130s. 9d.—two and three-quarter times that of 1949, which is slightly more than the general rise in the official cost-of-living index over the period, where the ratio is about 2·3 times. There were very big discrepancies, though, in the individual items. The smallest change was in mutton, which the 1970 butcher quoted at exactly the same price as his 1949 colleague, but added that nobody bought mutton nowadays, only for the cat. The dates, the egg, the sago, the cocoa, the milk, the jam, the treacle, the margarine, the sugar, the peas and the barley had no more than doubled. And at the top end of the spectrum, the liver, the bread, the bacon and the potatoes showed a near-fourfold increase. Biggest rise of all was in the apples—four and a half times more expensive, at 2s. a lb.—but that probably had a good deal to do with the time of year. And one must also allow for the fact that London suburban prices, at both times, were almost certainly rather higher than those in the working-class districts of Rowntree's York.

M

take it up, and it is here that the new welfare provisions really justified themselves. Full employment was certainly of major importance but, as Rowntree shows, there would still have been large-scale distress in the immediately post-war period if benefits had remained only on the scale available in the thirties. The comparison for York came out like this:

	Percentage in primary poverty	Percentage in primary & secondary poverty
Actual 1950 figure	0·37	2·77
If 1950 welfare same as 1936	4·72	22·18
If no food subsidies in 1950	2·42	13·74
If no family allowances in 1950	0·79	5·97
If unemployment at 1936 level	2·38	14·25

This was the measure of the welfare revolution. In the glum and miserable thirties, the support of the socially deprived had been financed to a large extent (because of the self-balancing rules imposed on the unemployment fund) by the contributions of those lucky enough to be in work. Now in the drab and 'Utility' forties this was reinforced by a major tax switch from high incomes to low. And the general greyness of the Crippsian 'age of austerity' could be offset by the reflection that, for the first time in, say, three hundred years, the percentage of Britain's population primarily preoccupied with food and subsistence was now well down into single figures. Whether this afforded full compensation for losing an empire and failing to look the dollar in the face is always arguable. But it certainly represented an achievement of a fairly substantial order.

Clothes probably marked the change as clearly as anything. Even in 1931 the *New Survey of London Life and Labour* was observing that Kensington housemaids on their days off were virtually indistinguishable from their mistresses, but it certainly was not true of working-class wives in the industrial north, where clogs and head-scarves and overalls continued to set as rigid a demarcation line as they had in the nineteenth century. By 1949 the frontier was already fading fast (though it was probably only in the 1950s, when austerity gave way to the Age of Marks & Spencer, that it finally vanished altogether) and the mass-circulation women's magazines were instantly transmitting fashion's marching orders from Land's End farm cottage to John o'Groats hunting lodge. Rowntree, who had set his poverty-line budget for women's clothes at 1s. 9d. a week in 1936, had to treble it, to 5s. 2d.—well ahead of actual price changes—to meet the higher standards of 1949–50. And in fact the average expenditure of the wives, even in his sample of under £6 a week families, came out at 11s. 6d.

This is how one thirty-eight-year-old mother, with three children, managed to keep her spending down to the bare minimum, and what she got for her money:

	Per annum		
	£	s.	d.
Dress @ £2 2s. 0d., once every three years		14	0
Coat and skirt (second hand)		12	6
Odd skirt (second hand)		2	6
Overcoat @ £6 6s. 0d., once in three years	2	2	0
Raincoat (second hand)		12	6
Jumper		3	6
Hat @ 17s. 6d., once in three years		5	10
Shoes @ £1 10s. 0d., once in two years		15	0
Stockings, twelve pairs a year @ 3s.	1	16	0
Under slip		7	6
Vest, two a year @ 5s. 6d.		11	0
Knickers, four pairs a year @ 6s. 6d.	1	6	0
Corset	1	1	0
Nightdress, one in two years @ £1 10s. 0d.		15	0
Apron, three a year @ 4s.		12	0
Wool for gloves		2	0
Handkerchiefs, two a year @ 1s.		2	0
Shoes repaired every three months @ 10s. 6d.	2	2	0
Total	14	2	4

Naturally, even while the government's fixed-price, fixed-quality, minimum-choice Utility scheme still applied to the great mass of clothing, it was perfectly possible to pay much more. This was the great age when nylon stockings could be confidently relied on to purchase the affections of anything female from Nottingham to Novaya Zemlya, and the British Customs were kept busy during 1949's dollar crisis tracking down the illicit import of nylons, at 16s. 6d. a pair, as part of a highly organized traffic in 'unsolicited US food parcels'. And even in a solid provincial store like Binns in Newcastle upon Tyne, there were advertisements for python shoes at £6 6s. 3d., which would have eaten up half Rowntree's minimum annual budget in one swoop. That appeared in the same edition of the local evening paper that offered a rail excursion from Newcastle to London for 30s. return (against today's normal second-class price of £8 6s.) and reported a heated controversy as to whether Hebburn Council would ever be able to let its latest five-roomed maisonettes, described as 'expensive dream houses', for the inflated sum of 23s. 9d. a week which they proposed to charge.

One of the great commercial dilemmas of the period concerned the need to rechristen the Fifty-Shilling Tailors. This was a massive chain of men's clothing shops which, with Montague Burton, had pioneered the sale of cheap, custom-made suits in pre-war Britain. Its proud name, in its heyday, had proclaimed the ultimate in value for money. But now, with even Rowntree's £6 a week families expecting to spend £7 10s. on a decent blue-serge Sunday best, and Austin Reed's charging an average of £15 off the peg, it was beginning to look like a rather poor joke. The question was whether to try for another figure and hope that prices would stabilize (The Two-Hundred-Shilling Tailors?) or accept the inevitability of inflation and look for something completely neutral. Caution won, and the name changed to John Collier, which was just as well—even after valiant recent efforts by the group, which kept prices level for more than a decade, they would now need to be somewhere between the Three-Hundred-Shilling and the Four-Hundred-Shilling Tailors.

As it turned out, this progression was just one part of a trend which has, to a greater or less extent, affected the whole world, developed and undeveloped, since the war. A selective list of anti-inflationary measures between 1953 and 1960 alone, prepared by the Organisation of European Economic Co-operation for their study, *The Problem of Rising Prices*, covers thirteen countries and occupies 64 pages. But in 1949 the British government still felt themselves able to exercise a high degree of control, particularly over those areas such as clothing, furnishing, rent and food, where wartime powers remained in full operation. In fact, as the devaluation crisis developed, the Board of Trade, under its president, Mr Harold Wilson, made a vigorous effort to reverse the tide, and laid down that, as from 1 September, the prices of all Utility clothing should be cut by 1s. in the pound (with the shopkeepers taking the resulting stock loss as part of their contribution to the national effort).

Such moves only accentuated the artificial distortions imposed by this sort of partial control. The marginal anomalies were bad enough, as the mothers found who complained bitterly that, even before the 1s. cut, a normal schoolgirl's Utility gym slip, free of tax, cost £3 2s. 3d., while a large schoolgirl's outsize gym slip, falling outside the Utility scheme, cost, with purchase tax, £4 0s. 9d. But

more serious and more weakening was the effect of deflecting so
much unsatisfied demand to the uncontrolled and 'luxury' end of the
market.

Keynes had been so worried about the inflationary effects of such
demand that, in his 'How to Pay for the War' proposals, he strongly
advocated a capital levy to remove some of the overburden of
accumulated wartime savings. This was rejected by the Labour
government, and up to a point they were right—there were sufficient
checks and controls available to save Britain from the kind of frenzied
spiral which destroyed the German currency system after both World
Wars. But the problem was still there: people did have a lot of money
in their pockets, and one way or another they were going to spend
it, whatever the Government said. So they gambled an estimated
£200 million in 1949 on greyhounds, staked some £450 million on
horse-racing, paid £5 a time (till the police stepped in) for places in the
queue to attend the trial of John Haigh, the acid-bath murderer,
and provided a ready outlet for any non-standard, non-rationed,
non-controlled item that manufacturers could manage to trundle to
market. These were the years when 'Export or Die' was supposed to
be the national slogan, and everything saleable for dollars—whisky,
cars, china, woolly jumpers—was automatically forbidden to the
home consumer. But home demand was so profitable and so lacking
in competition that it was worth going to any lengths—including the
deliberate manufacture of sub-standard articles, so that they could
earn the coveted label, 'export reject'—to capture a share. And it is
hardly coincidence that, once the booming seller's market of the late
forties was over, the British firms which had indulged themselves
in this way found it very difficult to recapture their competitive
edge, against the re-emergent hard men of Germany and Japan.

It is easy to forget, even for those who lived through those years,
just how high many prices had already risen, and how relatively
small have been the increases in the last two decades, among those
products which have managed to stay afloat and move from a luxury
to a mass market. Dry Fly sherry was selling at £1 a bottle in 1949
against today's 27s. 6d.; GEC's vacuum cleaners were £14 14s. plus
£3 13s. 6d. purchase tax and £3 3s. for attachments; Summit shirts
were 38s. 6d.; portable radios were £15 16s. 6d., with all the bother of
valves and clumsy batteries; a fifteen-day coach tour to the Dolomites
and Venice was 59 guineas a head. The new, sensational ball-point
pens were selling at figures anything between 4s. 6d. and 13s. 9d.,
with refills at 1s. 10d.; and the Radiolympia exhibition opened almost
on Devaluation Day with the introduction of a nine-inch black and
white television set which, at £36 15s., was a clear £10 cheaper than
anything previously available. All this at a time when the average

weekly earnings for men in manufacturing industry was £6 19s. 11d., according to the *Ministry of Labour Gazette*, and the increase from 1d. to 1½d. in the price of a cup of tea in the British Overseas Airways maintenance shops at Croydon was sufficient to bring the whole staff out in a canteen boycott.

Demand, even at astronomical prices and profit margins, seemed insatiable—new cars at this time had to be sold with a warranty declaring that the lucky customer, who had often had to wait up to two or three years in the queue for his Morris Oxford (£546 7s. 3d. with tax) or his Rover '75' (£1,106), would not immediately resell at a substantial profit to those with more money and less forethought.* And the easy lure of the home market was compounded—to the lasting detriment of British design, quality standards, and cost-efficiency—by the almost equally easy and undiscriminating demand overseas (apart, of course, from those hard currency areas of North America, whose approval and support really mattered). Europe, at that time, was prepared to take virtually anything we cared to send them, and still bitterly recalls the performance of some of the results. And the Commonwealth, now largely subsumed in the Overseas Sterling Area, provided, for the moment, an even more attractive market.

During and immediately after the war, Britain's vast credit purchases from the Commonwealth had the effect of building up massive sterling reserves in London for the countries concerned. The total, which stood at £2,352 million at the end of 1949, represented a

---

* *The Economist*, on 15 October 1949, expressed grave misgivings as to whether British cars at such levels were not pricing themselves off British roads. Before the war, they observed, there were two million cars registered, of which the cheapest cost about £125, and there were two million people with net incomes of £550 a year. Applying the same relationship—motorists are those whose annual after-tax earnings exceed four times the price of the cheapest car—to the post-war minimum price of £300-plus (with purchase tax), it appeared that only 400,000 families now had the £1,250 a year take-home pay required to sit behind the wheel. 'To say that the domestic market has been reduced by 80 per cent would be wildly pessimistic. But whatever the answer is, it is nothing like two million. Unless the present relationship between costs (including purchase tax) and incomes is very radically altered, the permanent domestic market for the British motor car industry—which in the long run is the backbone of its business—will only be a fraction of what it was.' Fortunately for the manufacturers it did change, though not perhaps in the direction *The Economist* hoped. Prices continued to rise—the cheapest car on the road in the late 1960s cost well over £500, implying a minimum motoring income of £2,000, which, even after twenty-five years of wage inflation, is only enjoyed by some 620,000 taxpayers. There were, however, by 1967 already over ten million private cars. If there is any factor linking incomes and car prices it is probably more like one and a half now than the pre-war four.

sum four and a half times the liabilities outstanding when the
Sterling Area came into official existence as a wartime exchange
control measure in 1939. Many of these countries, notably India,
which had achieved its independence in 1947, were able to make use
of these paper receipts in London as an easy way of paying for goods
and services, without having to produce a counterflow of exports of
their own. The greater the scarcity of dollars, the greater became the
pressure for these 'unrequited' sterling sales, and the greater the
premium they were able to command. 'For this reason,' as one contemporary comment put it, 'the continuing ability of Sterling Area
countries to command a surplus of sterling available for current
expenditure in Britain has become not only one of the main props
of the excessive level of British prices and costs, but also a lever which
is constantly widening the gap between that level and the level of
dollar prices.'

This was probably a trifle exaggerated—if only because £930
million worth of the cash, including a large slice of the Indian and
Pakistani share, was 'blocked' and only released for use in relatively
small packets—but the general tendency was right enough. And
certainly argument is nothing unusual here. The whole existence of
the Sterling Area, and the precise status and function of these sterling
balances, has generated endless discussion throughout the post-war
period. As early as 1945, Keynes, in his last public speech, was
scathing in his denunciation, describing the Area as consisting of
'countries to whom we already owe more than we can pay, on the
basis of their agreement to lend us money which they have not got,
and buy only from us and one another goods which we are unable to
supply'. But the subtle and pervasive nature of the arrangements,
not to mention the sheer amount of money involved—one is, after
all, talking about a large part of the non-Euro-American world's
total currency reserves—make it impossible to dismiss the matter
with a terse phrase. The Sterling Area—which effectively came into
being in the nineteenth century when sterling and gold were synony-
mous—has remained in existence during the last fifty troubled years
because, despite all the drawbacks and rigidities, a sufficiency of
countries, by no means always including Britain, have always thought
there was more advantage in keeping it than in abandoning it.
Although the immense weight of the resulting liabilities has frequently limited Britain's freedom of monetary manoeuvre—giving
General de Gaulle in 1967 the excuse for his second Common Market
veto, and in 1968 triggering off its own massive run on the pound, in
the disenchanted aftermath of the second post-war devaluation—
there have always been offsetting factors. In the form of stability,
or financial insulation from the dollar world, or contributions,

desirable or otherwise, to the underpinning of Britain's remaining relations with both the old and the developing Commonwealth, these have always seemed sufficient—though frequently only just sufficient —to keep the somewhat rickety, not to say mystical, structure in being. Even now the highly ambiguous Basle Agreement, concluded in the wake of the 1968 crisis to protect other Area members against any further British currency depreciation, leaves it deeply unclear whether official policy is now to run down the balances, or to rebuild them into some less vulnerable and more productive form.

However, in the summer of 1949, the Sterling Area was only one of the far-reaching new wartime and post-war financial arrangements interacting to help push the pound over the $4·03 precipice. The thirties had been a time of beggar-my-neighbour and go-it-alone when all attempts at international co-operation foundered in in-effectual bitterness. But now the proliferation of institutions—the International Monetary Fund, the World Bank, the Marshall Aid Administration, the General Agreement on Tariffs and Trade, the European Payments Union and a dozen lesser lights whose initials flickered in the background of economic life—were all helping to set new limits and directions to national policy. Not all of these, by any means, were necessarily in tune with the real needs of the time (or even with their own designers' intentions). And in particular they conspired that September to help the United States force on Britain what seems in retrospect to have been a singularly unhelpful and ill-timed parity adjustment, which went a long way towards perpetua-ting the economic weaknesses from which we have been suffering intermittently ever since.

This was the third important post-war occasion on which the short-term domestic interests of the US took forceful precedence over those of her recent transatlantic ally (and arguably, over the rest of the world at the same time). For the first two, the victory of the narrow, cautious US view at the Bretton Woods monetary conference in 1945, and the onerous, self-defeating terms of the Anglo-American Loan Agreement which brought on the 1947 'convertibility' crisis, both sides were probably equally to blame. In any case, ungrateful thoughts there could be regarded as being wiped out by the extra-ordinarily generous Marshall Aid gesture of 1948, which finally put Europe back on the high road to prosperity. But in 1949 the positive impetus was all on one side. Throughout the spring and summer Americans, in all sorts of private and official shapes and sizes, announced that in their opinion it was time that sterling was de-valued. In the autumn their views were flatly and unequivocally restated in no less a publication than the annual report of the Inter-national Monetary Fund (then, however, a much more circumscribed

body than it is now, and under almost total US domination).
And by the time the annual IMF meeting took place in Washington
in late September, there seemed, in the virtually unanimous minds
of the world's bankers, finance ministers and currency speculators,
to be nowhere for the pound to go but down. So down it duly went.

To decide whether it should have gone down at that particular
moment, or by the particular amount chosen by Stafford Cripps,
requires a slightly more detailed look at the situation in which
Britain found herself in the immediate aftermath of VE Day, and
the unexpectedly early VJ Day, which followed Truman's decision
to drop nuclear bombs on Hiroshima and Nagasaki. And it is always
necessary to bear in mind that it took the British government and
people a very long time to appreciate just how seriously their traditional power and strength had been sapped between 1939 and 1945.
Obligations imposed on Britain's negotiators—even on Keynes
himself—by a Congress and a State Department deeply suspicious
of all machinations involving the Bank of England and the British
Empire were accepted as natural and tolerable (though often highly
insulting) by men who in their hearts shared the US view that these
institutions were basically still as rich and formidable as in the
legendary past.

In hard figures, however, the legend had already lost an alarming
amount of its lustre. The total deficit in Britain's balance of payments
during the war came to over £4,000 million. With exports close to
vanishing point this had been met by selling valuable assets, particularly in the United States (like Courtaulds' once hugely profitable
American Viscose offshoot, which went for a mere £13·5 million
after expenses), by running down gold reserves, and by accepting a
very big jump in foreign liabilities. Probably another £500 million
worth of overseas property had vanished by default, confiscation or
physical deterioration. Major markets like South America had been
permanently taken over by other suppliers. Net overseas income—
our receipts less dividends and interest payments to foreigners—
dropped from £175 million in 1938 to only £73 million in 1946,
and barely got back to £120 million by 1951. With import prices up
four times on 1938, this meant that the purchasing power of our
overseas earnings had dropped by almost five-sixths. Even the very
big increase registered in home production as unemployment disappeared and output per head advanced was hardly enough to bridge
that sort of gap. But notwithstanding this, the Government went
ahead with a full-scale programme of military spending, administration, relief grants, loans and debt cancellations overseas, which
averaged over £400 million a year during the late forties. And, just
as seriously, they used up scarce items like petrol and shipping,

which could have been sold for dollars, of which the shortage quickly started to strangle all hopes of smooth recovery, not only in Britain but virtually world wide.

Naturally, some parts of the vast problem facing Britain were recognized. In their 1945 White Paper, setting out the background to the Bretton Woods talks, the Labour Government estimated that 'a full restoration of a reliable equilibrium which can persist without measures of restrictions or the other defensive mechanisms of the type with which it is hoped to dispense, may require a volume of exports nearer 75 per cent than 50 per cent in excess of the pre-war level'. But it failed to allow anything for the effect which all this extra activity could be expected to have on the terms under which we exchanged our products for other peoples' (in fact these 'terms of trade' deteriorated by about 10 per cent in 1945–50, during which this ambitious export target was triumphantly met and exceeded). And it assumed, with what looks now to be sublime self-confidence, that such a programme could co-exist with the assumption of military, diplomatic, banking and aid responsibilities on the most opulent great-power scale.

For the immediate moment, in 1945, however, there was one large obstacle—an expected balance-of-payments deficit of £750 million immediately, and another £250 million in each of the two succeeding years. America's 'Lend Lease' programme had already come to an abrupt halt, with a curt bill for $650 million to cover war goods which still happened to be in the pipeline, and this alone was enough to cancel out a full third of the country's diminished gold and currency reserves. So a large injection of dollars was required before any programme of reconstruction could even begin.

Keynes had already spent two years watching his sweeping, imaginative plans for international central banking, international currency, international trade and the generous creation of international liquidity whittled down to the worthy but rather plodding constitutions under which the IMF and the World Bank still, by and large, operate today. Now, in his last great economic task, he set about negotiation of the payment which could, if all went well, break up the immediate post-war cash jam, and clear the way for Britain's recovery.

The initial hope was for $5,000 million—just a little more than the expected 1946–8 deficits—to be given as a free grant-in-aid, in recognition of Britain's relatively bigger wartime sacrifices. That met very deaf ears, as did the more modest request for an interest-free loan, and in the end the best the British team could achieve, without breaking off talks altogether, and throwing not only recovery but the fate of the Bretton Woods agreement back into the melting

pot, was $3,750 million, 30 per cent below expected requirements—
to be repaid at 2 per cent a year over fifty years, starting in 1951.
Even that rather sour offering was hung around with conditions.
And the most important of these—the guarantee that Britain would
make sterling freely convertible into dollars as from 15 July 1947—
duly precipitated the pound into the first of its chronic series of post-
war crises.

The underlying thought was clear enough. The USA wanted to get
away as fast and as far as possible from the 1930s when what international trade was done at all tended to occur only between two
countries who had cooked up a specific deal. Under such 'bilateral'
arrangements trade had naturally stagnated, and there was every
reason to go for a 'multilateral' set-up, where countries could buy
where they liked, sell where they liked and settle up the resulting
bills, in some universally acceptable currency, at the end of the day.
Inside the Sterling Area, the pound was just such a currency; but
where the world wanted to buy was in North America, where only
dollars would do. Hence the 'convertibility' provision in the Washington Loan Agreement. And hence, thanks to the total blindness of
both the British and the Americans to the forces they were handling,
too the 'convertibility' débâcle of July–August 1947. From the
granting of the loan, in early 1946, pressure built up only gradually,
and the authorities were so lulled by the appearance of peace that in
July 1947 Hugh Dalton, then Chancellor of the Exchequer, was
announcing that 'the world had already discounted convertibility'.
No one could have been more wholly misinformed. From 1 July to
15 August, when the responsible clause was abruptly suspended,
every private and official holder of sterling on earth tried to change it
into dollars while the going was good. The net gold and dollar deficit
of the Sterling Area jumped from £226 million in 1946 to £1,024
million in 1947—most of it in those six hectic weeks—and by the
time the shutters came down all but £77 million of the US loan,
and £49 million of the £167 million Canadian loan which had been
granted on roughly the same terms, for the same purpose, had gone
with the wind. In September, when Cripps took over the Chancellor-
ship, the begging bowl was as good as empty. Only the £64 million
a year repayments of capital and interest remain, till the year
2001.

Such a disaster could have plunged the whole non-American world
back into economic chaos. But, of course, at this point Marshall Aid
made its appearance, and most of the more jagged broken bits could
be swept under the carpet. Under the Marshall Plan, more than
$20,000 million was ultimately pumped into the international
monetary system—against the mere $800 million which was all that

the niggardly charter of the much-vaunted IMF allowed it to provide in its first five years of existence—and the nastiest post-war economic corner had been safely negotiated.

Britain was by no means left behind, either on the giving or the receiving end. She was allocated more Marshall funds than any other country—$1,239 million in 1948–9 against $704 million for France, $407 million for Italy and $348 million for Germany—but in return she had put her house in order again with what looks now like breathtaking speed. The huge external deficit of the immediate post-war period had disappeared to produce a current account absolutely in balance (to within a statistically insignificant £1 million, which was in fact on the plus side). Domestic investment was booming, financed by the Marshall money. Delivery dates were long, and vacancies in the labour market sharply ahead of men to fill them. Both the cost of living and the index of wholesale prices in Britain, though well up on 1937–8, showed an appreciably smaller rise than those recorded in the US, as indeed also did wages per unit of output. Even on the crucial question of export prices, the British index (taking 1938 at 100) had risen only to 251, against the United States' 237. As Sir Roy Harrod said in his 'Policy Against Inflation', these various figures 'are inconsistent with the idea that prices had so soared up in Britain as to be out of relation with the dollar level and to require a 31 per cent devaluation of sterling against the dollar'. Even if devaluation had been the right prescription for a booming, fully employed economy, with its balance-of-payments problems— apart from the dollar gap—in reasonably good shape, it is hard to see the argument for a drop of more than about 6 per cent. Certainly none at all for the 'heroic' 31 per cent announced by Cripps—and which, of course, if passed on completely would have made Britain's imports, not 31 per cent more expensive, but more like 44 per cent.*

Twenty years away, the outcome looks like a tragedy of stubbornness and highmindedness. Already in December 1948, various highly placed American commentators were beginning to ask nastily what Britain would do to avoid bankruptcy (whatever that may mean in national terms) when Marshall Aid came to an end. And such questions were pointed up by the tendency of people in the City and Fleet Street to suggest quite falsely that the US aid money was being dissipated on an orgy of wigs, National Health spectacles and imported American films. By the spring it was clear that a heavy groundswell was building up in the foreign exchange markets, and a modest devaluation—something around 10 per cent—could well have halted speculation in its tracks. Or alternatively, some official

* If $4·03 worth of US goods cost you £1 at the old parity, their new price is £(4·03/2·80), which comes to £1·44.

deflationary action to clear the export pipelines, whose clogged delivery dates cost Britain several huge orders in early 1949, could surely have been devised to reinforce Cripps's increasingly hollow-sounding devaluation denials. But nothing was done, and six months later the floods of 'no confidence' overwhelmed the dam.

On the figures, though, it would appear that the floods were more verbal than physical. From John Snyder, head of the US Treasury, telling the Senate Foreign Relations Committee in February that devaluation should be 'explored' (though not specifically mentioning the pound), through June's reports in the London *Banker* that the City reported devaluation to be 'inevitable', up to the IMF's September recommendation of 'exchange adjustments' for countries in dollar difficulties, the moral pressure was intense. But the actual dollar deficits, as J. C. R. Dow says in his *Management of the British Economy, 1945–60*, were 'moderate rather than spectacular'. Quarter by quarter, they varied during 1948 down from £147 million, to £107 million, to £76 million and then up to £93 million. In the first two quarters of 1949 they were £82 million and £157 million respectively, with probably another £150 million in the two and a half months before Cripps capitulated. This is not the stuff of which great currency panics are composed, and indeed most of the fluctuation can be explained without bringing in speculation at all, by the fact that the mild US recession of early 1949 had reduced Sterling Area dollar exports, at a time when most of the countries involved had slightly eased their rigid control on dollar imports. That was rapidly put into reverse at a Commonwealth Finance Ministers' meeting in July, where it was agreed to follow the UK decision already announced and cut dollar purchases by 25 per cent, which in Britain's case meant about £100 million a year. With the US economy already on the rebound, this alone should have been enough to cure most of the trouble. But it was too late; the momentum of events was running too fast, and with Cripps out of action in a Swiss sanatorium for six weeks during July and August, they appear (though none of the memoirs and autobiographies of the period so far published throw any real light on the episode) to have passed beyond control. On 18 September, after a further series of strenuous denials (Mr R. H. S. Crossman was unlucky enough to be enunciating one of them in his column in the *Sunday Pictorial* published on the day of the announcement) the inevitable was duly bowed to.

The exact depth of the bow required was clearly a matter of considerable argument inside the Treasury. There was one school of thought even at that time (it became much stronger during the early 1950s and again during the franc-deutschmark confrontations of

1969) which held that the dollar value of the pound should not be altered to some new fixed value, but allowed, for a period at any rate, to 'float', as it had in the thirties, and find its own proper level. Cripps rejected this—'we could not possibly think of such a course'—and decided that if there had to be devaluation, then it must be a large one. To put British export firms 'in a fairly competitive position in the North American markets' it was necessary, he calculated, 'to go at very least as low as three dollars to the pound'. And at the same time it was essential, to end adverse speculation, 'to make it absolutely plain that this was not a tentative first step but . . . that we had without doubt gone far enough'.

The general tone of his devaluation speech in the House of Commons was fairly cheerful, especially from a man who had earlier said, with some considerable accuracy, that 'when you are at the limit of exports and already rigidly control your imports, you do not get any better control by monkeying about with your currency'. Now the Chancellor, as Anthony Eden pointed out rather acidly on behalf of the Opposition, spoke in the manner of a conjuror who has 'brought off a clever trick and expects everyone to join rapturously in the applause'. David Eccles, whose somewhat apocalyptic remarks about the state of sterling in July, quoted at the head of this chapter, had no doubt done their own small bit towards undermining confidence, came in with a new broadside, demanding savage cuts in government spending and a programme to 'unfreeze the factors of production'. Should this fail, he warned, 'and the degraded pound be again degraded then gone is the last chance to restore London as a financial centre. The Socialists will then have reduced the status of sterling to that of one of the untrustworthy currencies of Europe or South America.'

In fact most of the world's non-dollar currencies, trustworthy or untrustworthy, took the opportunity to follow suit, and at the end of the day Britain's effective devaluation against the rest of the world probably worked out at something like 15 per cent—which, of course, meant an increase of around 18 per cent in the cost of imports, which in turn acted in such a way as to push Britain's costs up, fairly directly and fairly quickly, by about 3 per cent.

This is the main criticism of the Cripps devaluation. His earlier analysis had been only too accurate. Britain's exporters were already working full tilt, even if their customers wanted to pay in the wrong sort of currency, and devaluation alone produced no new flood of goods available for dollar markets. Imports were already held to the bare minimum by government controls, so there was little scope for the new, higher prices to cut down their volume. Costs, despite all the Cassandra cries about work-shy, feather-bedded Britain,

had been held down with extraordinary success, by a combination of
rationing, subsidies and Cripps's evangelical appeals to the trade
unions, which had induced a virtually total wage freeze for the past
two years. Such a fragile equilibrium required very little to shatter.
And the effects of devaluation—starting with an immediate rise
from 4½d. to 5½d. in the price of the standard loaf—gave Britain a
large and almost certainly unnecessary push into chronic inflation.
Up to 1949, most of the rise in the cost of living could be ascribed
directly to the effects of war, and it looked, for a brief moment, as if
the curve might be flattening off. Devaluation killed that faint
chance, and the starting whistle blew on the wage-price leapfrog
game we have been playing ever since.

Even in the short term, it is doubtful if the Cripps parity change
had any particular relevance to events. Certainly the dollar value of
British exports to North America in 1950 was 15 per cent up on 1948,
but a great deal of that could be put down to the end of the US
recession and the intensive post-war selling effort that had already
been mounted in the dollar area. There was a big drop in dollar
imports, but that had more to do with the Commonwealth Finance
Ministers' restrictive agreement before devaluation than to any
price effects after. And meanwhile the cost-effects of the change were
beginning to seep slowly and insidiously through the system.

Immediately, as Cripps told the British public in his broadcast,
they would be pretty small. School meals went up by 1d. to 6d. for
the first child, and 5d. for the second. A shilling prescription charge
was introduced into the hitherto free National Health Service,
precipitating a bitter split in the Labour Party. Petrol went up by
2½d. a gallon to 2s. 3d. Mayfair baby-sitting agencies raised their
charges to 3s. 6d. an hour. West End prostitutes, according to a
current survey of life and leisure, demanded five guineas for a
twenty-minute encounter (particularly from visiting Americans?).
Copper jumped from £107 10s. a ton to £140. And gold sovereigns
reached a new high in the collectors' market at 58s. Apart from that,
there was little to record. But devaluation works pretty slowly,
especially in a world of quotas and controls. Import prices, which
were only 14 per cent above 1949 levels in 1950, were 52 per cent up
by 1951; and although this was largely a freak effect of the extraordinary Korean rearmament boom, they were still 34 per cent ahead
when things settled down in 1953–5. The cost of living followed some
way behind. British producers on the whole did not put their prices
up immediately but waited for the higher costs to come through.
But after a mere 2·7 per cent rise in the retail index in 1950, the
pace quickened; by the mid-fifties the figures were 34·2 per cent up
on 1949; wage rates had crept slightly ahead, at 38·9 per cent; and

wage earnings, the real yardstick, had scored a 52·7 per cent gain. As Harrod dryly remarks, the 1949 devaluation can only be said to have finally worked itself out when, in 1957, it reached the General Post Office. The price of sending a letter in Britain, which had been ½d. in the 1880s, went up from 2½d. to 3d. 'in face of ever rising costs'.

The Pound in

was worth £1 10s. in 1970 money

A general loss of confidence in the future of currency starts slowly like a snowball, and then builds up very quickly. That in the summer of 1957 it should have produced a balance of payments crisis in spite of a comfortable surplus in the balance of payments on current account is not an indication that it was a 'phoney' crisis, but rather that it was a peculiarly grave one. It was a real crisis of confidence in the future of sterling, originating in this country.

R. F. Henderson: *Not Unanimous*,
ed. Arthur Seldon (1960)
(Institute of Economic Affairs, 1960)

Let's be frank about it—most people have never had it so good.

Harold Macmillan: Speech at Bedford (1957)

Nineteen fifty-seven, when the effects of the 1949 devaluation reached postage stamps, was a complicated year for the pound, as for the people who tried to pay their bills with it. The sick aftertaste of the Suez fiasco; the signing of the Treaty of Rome and the setting up of the Common Market; the first outpouring of those later so drearily familiar league tables showing the slippage in Britain's post-war economic performance; all these helped add to the general sense of failure, moral bankruptcy and national drop-out. Over £70 million of sterling capital fled through the 'Kuwait Gap' in the six months before the Treasury got around to closing that most famous (but probably not largest) of exchange-control loop-holes. A Chancellor of the Exchequer, for the first time in history, made a speech in the City of London openly questioning the soundness of investing in gilt-edged and fixed-interest securities. A quarter of his gold reserves promptly disappeared in a bout of speculation triggered off by a partial and inadequate French devaluation. And to stop the resulting rot, Bank Rate in September was hoisted to its highest level since 1920 (7 per cent) amid scenes of gloom and panic which, as described in the report of the subsequent Bank Rate Tribunal, sound as though Throgmorton Street and Threadneedle Street had temporarily returned to the financial dark ages.

Yet Macmillan, despite the boomerang insouciance of his Bedford phrase, was probably a good deal closer to the truth about Britain's 1957 situation than Peter Thorneycroft, his Chancellor, and the darker prophets of City doom. The pound was certainly under pressure; and continued inflation was certainly eroding confidence in the attraction of fixed-interest savings (though saving at large hit a post-war peak that year—9 per cent of national income was thriftily set aside). But it is not difficult to argue, as Samuel Brittan eloquently shows in his recent account, *Steering the Economy*, that the underlying strength of both the currency and the economy were much greater that summer than the don't-just-stand-there-do-something school were prepared to allow. And as a result the precise measures chosen in September to 'save the pound' from being rocked off its $2·80 parity were such as to ensure that its final slither—though delayed in the event until November 1967—would be as painful and humiliating as possible.

That aspect of the 1957 experience will be discussed more fully later in this chapter. But what about Macmillan's immediate contention? How far did the summer of 1957 represent some kind of golden age in Britain's post-war living standard? The best witness in such matters is always the most potentially hostile witness, and perhaps one can start by quoting an extremely Left-wing commentator, Kurt Map, whose *British Economy and the Working*

Class covered precisely the relevant years, from 1946 to 1958.

Map's main concern in his pamphlet was to warn that things were too good to last, and that the British proletariat should not relax its militant vigilance in the face of unaccustomed Macmillanite luxury. But that merely reinforces the weight of his testimony to how good they had actually become. 'There can be no doubt', he wrote, 'that British workers improved their standards both absolutely, as compared to the past, and relatively, i.e. compared with other classes in capitalist society. . . . The advance of the workers was truly remarkable.' And his estimate of the division of personal income between the social classes underlines the point.

(£m)	Working Class	Salaried Employees	Petit Bourgeois	Capitalist	Total
1938	2,299	992	650	1,131	5,072
1949	5,547	2,397	1,400	1,216	10,560
1957	9,637	4,487	1,794	2,044	17,962

The picture comes out even more clearly when you reduce these figures to index form, and to percentage shares:

	WC	%	SE	%	PB	%	C	%	Total	%
1938	100	45·3	100	19·6	100	12·8	100	22·3	100	100
1949	241·3	52·5	241·6	22·7	215·4	13·3	107·5	11·5	208·2	100
1957	419·2	53·2	452·3	25	276·0	10	108·7	11·8	354·1	100

The point that Map fastened on in this was that, in his terminology, the workers' share had peaked at 54 per cent in 1955, and was now infinitesimally starting to slide; while the capitalists had just begun to edge forward again after their long wartime retreat. (Actually, he got his turning point just about right—the capitalists have continued to claw back a tiny fraction of their old heritage, and the wage earners to lose out. But the trend is very marginal and quite swamped in the really big change, already becoming visible in the table, away from wages and in favour of salaries.)

For our immediate purpose, however, it is the figures on what had been happening to real income which are the more interesting. By 1957, the average wage earner was collecting some £506 a year and the average salaried employee £764. Allowing for a 40 per cent increase in the retail price index since our last chapter, this meant that in real terms the factory-floor man was around 27 per cent better off than he had been in 1949, and the office worker about 10 per cent. It was not quite the doubling of the standard of living in twenty-five years which Mr R. A. Butler had put forward in 1955 as the Conservative Party's overall economic target, but at least it was comfortably in the right direction.

Not only were wages rising handily ahead of prices—Macmillan said twice as fast over the previous six years, and there were plenty, like the Coventry toolmakers, whose hourly earnings moved from 5s. 5d. to 8s. 1d. over that period, who had done substantially better than that—but the whole tax structure was being progressively lightened. The standard rate of income tax reached its peace-time high point of 9s. 6d. in the Korean alarums of 1951, and then came down, first to 9s. in 1953 in Butler's 'incentive' budget and then to 8s. 6d. in the 'classic purity and simplicity' of the run-up to the 1955 General Election (producing, in quick succession, a thumping Tory victory and a roaring balance-of-payments crisis). And in 1957 itself Thorneycroft, the new Chancellor, improved matters still further by dramatically raising the ceiling below which it was possible to claim the earned income allowance (to £1,550, from the previously very skimpy £450). He also marginally tempered the wind to the country's 300,000-odd surtax payers (who were then paying the extra tax, it must be remembered, on everything, earned or unearned, over £2,000 a year). Harold Wilson, already well known as the Tory Chancellor's scourge, called his Budget 'an assignment with inflation'. But Thorneycroft, at least equally validly, could report that 'since 1951 almost every income had received some benefit'.

The net result was a very striking shift in the pattern of Britain's after-tax incomes, which, between 1949 and 1957, moved like this:

After-Tax Incomes ('000s)

	1949	1957
Under £250	13,040	6,070
£250–£500	10,140	8,070
£500–£750	2,020	7,430
£750–£1,000	442	3,120
£1,000–£2,000	368	1,220
£2,000–£4,000	84·4	173
£4,000–£6,000	5·1	16
Over £6,000	0·1	0·8

Even making full allowance for the fact that £1 in 1957 would buy little more than 13s. 4d. worth of goods at 1949 prices, the upward surge is clear and unambiguous. Its effects, as one would expect, were spread all over the economic scene.

This was the springtime for television; the commercial channels had opened up in 1955, and the customers were still falling over each other to acquire the new toy. The seven-millionth licence was taken out in April, only eight months after the six-millionth, and the eight-millionth followed almost within weeks. The prices of sets, for those who actually bought them, as opposed to erecting an aerial to impress the neighbours, ranged around 69 guineas for a 17-inch screen and 88 guineas for the more prestigious 21-inch models. Hire-purchase figures, which only began to be collected in the mid-1950s, showed that the nation's outstanding debt on cars, furniture and consumer durables now amounted to some £448 million, much of it tied up for the moment in sales of the square-eyed monster. And although this 'reckless mortgaging of an uncertain future' occasionally brought forth its ration of moral condemnation, most people now shrugged their shoulders, as good inflationists should, and got on with the business of living now and paying later. Even the Church of Scotland's Committee on Church and Nation, after wrestling agonizingly with its granite conscience, was prepared by 1957 to pronounce in print that 'hire-purchase is often condemned as veiled money-lending, but it should be recognized that in many cases it is generally beneficial to society. Homes and holidays, motor cars and washing machines . . . have been brought within the reach of almost all.'

Not everyone, of course, went quite so far in their praise of the beneficence of affluence, and it is no coincidence that 1957 saw the birth of the Consumers' Association, and its magazine, *Which?*, which within six months had acquired 50,000 members and readers (ten years later it was 500,000) dedicated to the task of getting best value for their steadily depreciating currency. One of the first things they did was to look at the operations of the credit industry, and they were able to announce in their third issue that it was only too easy to pay £5 more than you need on the hire-purchase of a £70 television set. Bicycles, though Gamages, the London store, would give you nine months' credit for nothing, were discovered by eager consumer-investigators to be attracting interest rates of up to 59 per cent in some of the cheerier 'cut-price' outlets, and someone hard up enough to sign an HP agreement for a £3 0s. 3d. electric fire found himself paying £1 6s. 0d. a year in finance charges.

The early numbers of *Which?* give a fascinating picture of the kind of goods and prices which the British middle classes were worried about in 1957–8. But they also provide a vivid warning of the dangers inherent in the attempt to compare purchasing power over time in a complex, highly fragmented, taste-and-fashion-ridden market economy. To take the product which *Which?* chose for its first comparative study—the humble aspirin. They briskly pointed out in autumn 1957 that plain, unbranded, unadvertised Aspirin BP from Boots cost a mere 4d. for 25 tablets, as against 1s. 11½d. for 26 tablets of the most expensive, soluble, nationally promoted competitor, and that for headache-curing purposes there was little to choose between them. Now in the early spring of 1970 both these items are still available. Boots no longer bother with 4d. bottles and offer instead a minimum of 50 tablets for 9d.—a relative rise of 12½ per cent. The more expensive competitor, after a series of elaborate reformulations and re-packagings, now gives 25 tablets at a recommended price of 2s. 11d., so that there has been there an effective rise of 55 per cent. So what has happened to the cost of living or to the value of money? The official retail price index figures of the period look like coming out somewhere over 45 per cent (the 1970 index was not yet available at the time of writing). But are such indices based on *Which?*'s idea of the Best Buy? Or on some kind of average for each group of commodities? And more generally has the pound in the really careful shopper's pocket been eroded less than the one dispensed by the normal citizen? Or by just the same amount? Or perhaps by even more, if you looked at the whole range of purchases and services? Such questions, unfortunately, remain either unanswered in the official publications or unanswerable within the scope of this book. But they need answering if we are to get any grip on the problems posed by the chronic, gentle, but now accelerating inflation we (and most of the world) have been suffering since the mid-1930s. According to the text-book picture, the manufacturer who holds down his prices most effectively will quickly be rewarded by taking the business away from the man who lets them go. But in the case of the aspirins, and in many similar instances, it just is not so. Over more than a decade, during which the voters, the house-wives, the Government, the unions, and every kind of official and near-official agency has grumbled continuously about rising prices, the discrepancy between these two virtually identical products, which was already huge, is now almost half as much again. If that is marginal price sensitivity at work, then we can expect inflation to be with us for a long, long time.

The Consumers' Association tried, and still tries, very hard to sharpen up this sensitivity, but it is a thankless, uphill task. In 1957 the Chief Inspector of Weights and Measures for Nottingham reported that 'there is no doubt that petty and sometimes gross overcharging, not only in butchers' meat, but in other goods sold in bulk or by the piece, adds materially to the rapidly rising cost of living'. He instanced the case of the steak labelled 3s. 11d. for 'a little over ½ lb'. Entirely true as far as it went—the slice weighed just on 8½ oz. But the price worked out at 7s. 4½d. a lb., which was between 1s. 4½d. and 1s. 10½d. a lb. more than nearby butchers were quoting for the same quality. In other words, he was overcharging by a clear 25 per cent. But who, except on the rarest occasions, would ever notice such a thing?

That, of course, was crude, dishonest practice, liable to lead its perpetrators into court. But by 1957 much subtler methods of shading the edges of the cost-of-living index were spreading through the shops. The great days of the trading stamp and gifts-with-everything were still in the future, but all the complex promotional panoply of '3d. Off' coupons, loss-leadership and the give-away plastic daffodil was already moving into place. In the winter of 1957–8 *Which?* carried out a survey of cut-price grocery shops where, even before the outlawing of Resale Price Maintenance, Nescafé was offered at 6d. less than the official price of 3s. 6d. a tin, Typhoo Tea at 2d. less than standard at 1s. 9d. a quarter, and Bird's Custard down from 1s. 8½d. to 1s. 6½d. Those were the sensational price-slashing, never-to-be-repeated bargains displayed with lavish use of red ink in the windows; but to get some idea of what all this really meant to the housekeeping bills, the investigators set out to buy a list of fifty standard items at five shops. The fully priced basket resulting would have cost 33s. 5½d. on the manufacturers' official figures, and the respective savings available, after fighting through the crowds, were respectively 1s. 4d., 11½d., 7d., 5d. and the princely sum of 2½d.

Such were the small victories which the careful, and the hard pressed, were able to achieve against the encroaching inflationary tide. And some were indeed hard pressed. As Colin Clark, the Oxford economist, said in his 1957 study, *The Cost of Living*: 'An increase in prices of 60 per cent in a peace-time decade—something which has never happened to us before, and only in very few other countries—involves the most outrageous injustice to all those receiving incomes or other payments fixed by contract for a long period. It means the wholesale plundering of the savings of the poor.... We make a lot of silly statements about our so-called Welfare State in which poverty has been abolished and provision made for everyone. But the number of people on Poor Relief (we now call it National Assistance, but this is only a change of name) now number 1,700,000, nearly as high as the figure for the worst depression years, and very much higher than it was before 1941.... Not a record to be proud of.'

Old Age Pensions stood out as the most striking case for lack of pride. The rate had been steadily rising—the 24s. a week fixed in 1947 as an improvement on the pre-war 10s. went up to 32s. 6d. for a single person in 1953 (after its effective additional purchasing power had been totally wiped out by rising prices) and then again to 40s. in 1955, and 50s. in January 1958. Even after that final improvement, the real value of the pension, allowing for the relevant price changes, was still worth less than twice the minuscule 1938 figure. And the 40s. available in the never-had-it-so-good summer of 1957 would buy only something like 15s. 2d. worth of pre-war-priced goods and services—an improvement of a bare 50 per cent over those two socially climacteric decades.

Admittedly, the National Assistance Board, about which Clark was so scathing, stood ready in 1957 to supplement the modest 40s. with an additional payment of up to 37s. 6d., plus a rent allowance averaging perhaps 12s. 6d. But even together this amounted to barely one-third of the average earnings of a manual labourer, which that spring was calculated by the Ministry of Labour at £12 2s. 11d. a week. Similarly, married couples received a joint pension of 65s., and this too, unless they were willing to sink their pride and go to 'the Assistance', meant a very sharp drop below the working-class norm. Whatever the evidence of the calory-subsistence tests—and old ladies dying of starvation were by now rare enough to provide an excuse for large, shocked headlines in the national press whenever such unhappy events occurred—it must have been true, as Peter Townsend recorded in his 1957 study, *The Family Life of Old People*, that 'among those interviewed a fall in income of over a half and often as much as two-thirds was certainly *felt* as poverty'. No doubt it was such households who could have made maximum use of the Consumers' Association's brisk advice, including the fact that the best current buy in single bed-sheets was to be found in the Government surplus stores, where a pair could be bought in the winter of 1957 for 37s. 6d., clearly marked with broad arrow, catalogue number, initials of maker and year of supply. But they probably could not afford the necessary subscription of £1 a year.

However, while the old were only too frequently condemned to live from hand to mouth, there is plenty of evidence that the children and young people of 1957 were more than fulfilling the Macmillan assessment. This was the time when the first mouth-watering reports from the market researchers indicated the existence of Teen-Age Buying Power, and the manufacturers of clothes, films, cosmetics, gramophone records and motor-cycles set off on a breathless pursuit of Youth which still continues with, some think, obsessive, and possibly socially disruptive, fury. Already boys under twenty-one were averaging £5 11s. a week and girls £4 3s. 11d.; the cash being largely free of tax and, apart from often nominal home contributions, available for free spending. The hourly pay rates for juveniles, starting from a base date in 1947, had outpaced grown-up women by 13 points and grown-up men by a clear 20 points, and thus firmly established the pattern of shrinking age-differentials which has continued to this day.

Perhaps even more striking, though, was the increasing affluence at the nursery and school end of the spectrum. A somewhat ill-

informed poll of preparatory school headmasters in 1957 suggested
that 4d. to 6d. should be regarded as adequate weekly pocket money
for the normal schoolboy. As this was the benchmark figure adopted
by the majority of parents as far back as the middle 1920s, when
sweetshop prices were little more than one-third of their post-war
level, this looked a bit mean even by academic standards. And it
was certainly wildly out of touch with reality. Spending on sweets
alone averaged out at 2s. 3d. a week for every chewing and sucking
infant in Britain, and easy-going parental generosity far more than
compensated for the brand of inflation which had multiplied the
going rate on liquorice bootlaces from ½d. to 1½d., and escalated the
halfpenny ice-cream cornet, which was the standard weekend treat
of my 1930s childhood, to a minimum of 3d. In any case, not all
under-fourteen commodities had increased in that sort of ratio.
Comics like *Beano* and *Dandy* were no more than they had been when
Hitler remilitarized the Rhineland, and their more sophisticated
competitors, *Eagle* and *Girl*, at 4½d. were little more than twice as
much as the pre-war equivalent. Fizzy drinks were still available for
1d., and new technological wonders, like iced lollies at 2d., had
arrived to vary the tedium of half-holiday choice. Books like *Little
Women* were selling in standard editions for 10s. 6d., against the
5s. of twenty years before. After allowing for the £60 million spent
on children's luxuries at Christmas, the £40 million for birthdays,
and the £100 million spread one way and another over the rest of the
year, it was possible to reckon the average child's incomings of
cash, goods and services at around 4s. a week. This represented a rise
of at least one-third in juvenile living standards between 1938 and
1957, where the normal adult had been hard put to it to achieve
better than 10–15 per cent.

The difference could hardly be ascribed to the advent of children's
allowances. These had come in in 1946, as part of the Welfare State
package, and when they were first introduced it was calculated that
the payment, set at 5s. for the second and subsequent children,
would meet about two-fifths of the cost (estimated to be 13s. a
week) of actually keeping a second child. Raising the figure to 8s.,
which was done in 1953, did little more than restore the purchasing
power eroded by inflation. And by 1957, when the cost of keeping
boys and girls in bread and beans and boots had risen to something
like 25s. a week, the 8s. was beginning to look increasingly irrelevant.
Even the 1956 concession, which raised the allowance to 10s. for the
third child and beyond, went only a tiny way to closing the gap, and
it took another twelve years, of steadily rising prices, before there
was any further revision. Both for well-off families, where mother
collected the cash and father paid the income and surtax on it, and

for the really needy, the allowance looked—and indeed still looks—
like an increasingly ill-thought-out joke.

Still, such matters, though irritating, are hardly the stuff of which
social revolutions are made, and in 1957 the tide of affluence was
running pleasantly strong for most families outside the obvious
social-problem belts. Such things are almost entirely a matter of the
point of view, and it so happened that for a variety of reasons (and
despite the humiliation of Suez) all the factors happened for a brief
moment to be running more or less right. It was perfectly correct
for economists like S. G. Sturmey to point out (in his *Income and
Economic Welfare*) that the real net income of the British people,
after allowing for everything in the way of taxes, benefits, subsidies
and so forth, and revaluing the whole lot at constant 1948 prices,
had only moved a matter of 10 per cent, from the equivalent of £199
a head in 1938 to the equivalent of £226 in 1957. But the explanation
why people *felt* richer than pre-war in 1957, whereas they had *felt*
so much poorer in 1949, lies in the precise way in which this relatively
small improvement had taken place. To start with, almost all of it
had effectively been crammed into the past eight years—real
national income in 1949, as we saw in the last chapter, was almost
unchanged in gross terms from 1938. But also the 1938–49 period
had seen a massive redistribution of this income from the top to the
bottom of the social pyramid. This process had virtually ceased
during the early 1950s, so that the improvement was now really
general—almost everyone (except for the old age pensioners and the
children in large, poor families) had felt some share of its warming
breath.

The warmest breath of all, perhaps, wafted over Mr M. Robson, a
Liverpool dock labourer, who, in September 1957, was proudly
paraded by the proprietors of Vernons Football Pools as the first
man to win £75,000 for a stake of 2d. But even those relying on their
own taxed earnings were not doing too badly. Coal miners, still the
aristocrats of the labour market—coal remained technically on
ration until 1958, and no one had yet grasped how swiftly the post-
war fuel shortages were about to turn into a fuel glut—were averaging £12 19s. 7d. a week, more than half as much again as in 1948–9.
And their progress was positively lethargic against groups like the
chemical, steel and engineering workers, all at least 70 per cent ahead,
or the printers and paper workers, with a clear 86 per cent jump from
1949 to their 1957 level of £10 13s. 7d. a week.

Those were industry-wide averages, of course, and in each group
there were plenty of families who by now had jumped over the car-
buying threshold, which, at this time, probably stood roughly at
£850 a year before tax, or £750 after the Inland Revenue had taken

its share. Four million private motorists now formed one of the most
vocal groups expressing mutual interest, and although it would be
three or four years yet before the parking meter and the traffic
warden provided a natural focus for their enmities and aggressions,
there was still plenty for them to grouse about together. Most of it
is summed up in this table, which shows how the cost of taking the
wheel had escalated over the past few years.

	1947			*1957*		
	£	s.	d.	£	s.	d.
12 horse-power car (Austin)	597	0	0	820	0	0
Road tax	10	0	0	12	10	0
Insurance (comprehensive, London)	15	10	6	34	0	0
Petrol (gallon)		1	11½		4	11½
Battery (12 volt)	9	10	7	10	18	0
Labour charges (per hour)		10	0		15	0
Tyres (each)	3	4	0	6	8	6

Insurance went up by a further one-third on 1 July 1957, and the
British motorist, not for the last time, felt that the cup of bitterness
was running over—especially as petrol was still on ration, as part of
the Suez retreat, during a substantial part of the year. The only comfort was that, after drowning one's sorrows (Black & White whisky
was now 36s. a bottle), it was once again possible to write at full
length to the newspapers, which had had the last restrictions lifted
on the number of pages they could print, as from 1 January 1957.
For the first few months news and views were cheaper than they
have ever been since the war—the *Daily Express*, in several issues,
offered almost 1,000 column-inches of editorial text for each 1d.,
where today, even with the vast increase in the number of pages,
one is lucky to get more than 300. But such bargains were short-lived.
The Economist, which had been 1s. since 1920, went up to 1s. 6d. in
September, and the rest of the press quickly followed suit (including
the *Sunday Times*, then at the beginning of its explosive recent
growth period, which very quietly announced the proposed increase
from 4d. to 5d. in an issue whose lead story carried the hopeful
headline 'New Measures to Halt Inflation').

Much of the resulting correspondence, when not chronicling the
plight of the car-owner, concerned itself with that perennially
fascinating subject, the decay of the middle-class way of life. But
this, like some other aspects of social mythology, can easily be
exaggerated, and it is in fact possible to identify, on the basis of the
Inland Revenue's sample survey figures, just exactly where in the
income scale the family of the late 1950s started to become actually

worse off, in real terms, than its equivalent in the high Edwardian summer of 1911–12. Guy Routh does the sums in his *Occupation and Pay in Great Britain, 1906–1960*, and the answer turns out surprisingly high—only the top 60,000 'income units' (the tax-men unfortunately do not distinguish between individuals and married couples with separate incomes) could claim to have suffered a genuine wound in the pocket-book over the period.

In interpreting that figure, however, it is important to bear in mind exactly what is being said. If all the nation's incomes are arranged in order, from smallest to largest—about 18 million of them in 1911, and around 21 million in 1958—then every income in the second set is worth more in real, after-tax terms than its opposite-number income in the first set, except for the tiny top fraction. This fraction extended, to be precise, just three-thousandths of the way down from the tip of the pyramid. In 1958 the man (or the family) three-thousandths of the way below the top had an after-tax income of £2,300, and this was precisely equivalent, in overall purchasing power terms, to the £520 a year enjoyed by the man (or family) three-thousandths of the way down from the top in 1911. Above these break-even points, everyone's position had shifted relatively for the worse. Thus the man one-thousandth of the way below the 1958 peak, with an after-tax income of £2,632, would be a full 22 per cent less well-fixed than the man one-thousandth of the way below the 1911 peak, enjoying his equivalent after-tax income of £780.

What this does not tell you anything about, of course, is what happened to individual jobs or to individual social groups. It may well be true, as one *Times* letter-writer bitterly complained in the summer of 1957, that 'all solicitors in Solihull today are far worse off than they were fifty years ago'. But whether or not these hard-pressed legal gentlemen were actually richer or poorer than their fathers, who may or may not have been solicitors, and may or may not have lived in Birmingham, remains a pretty open question. All one can say is that Cabinet ministers, judges and bishops, all of whom, as we have seen in earlier chapters, were among the most richly rewarded members of society in 1911, had all tumbled catastrophically in the income stakes by the mid-1950s, but that most other professions, despite their highly articulate complaints, had more than held their own. The Chancellor of the Exchequer's unchanged £5,000 a year was now barely sufficient to keep him in the top 60,000 at all, while the bishop's emoluments, averaging £3,200 a year in 1957–8, were actually two hundred depreciated pounds less than those enjoyed by his affluent predecessor on the eve of the Great War. This represented a savage drop—over three-quarters in terms of the soaring episcopal housekeeping bills. But bishoprics and chancellorships are not hereditary positions, any more than their attractions are wholly pecuniary, and, as Routh dryly remarks, 'there is still no shortage of candidates for these positions', from among those to whom even these reduced salaries represented a rise, rather than a fall.

In any case, there was no shortage of alternatives for those seeking a more handsome return on their time and effort. Tax and social change may have whittled away a good deal of the value of the highest incomes, but there was no capital gains tax in 1957, and it was a poor businessman who could not find some profitable way to tap the purse of the, on the whole, well-paid, un-rationed and fully employed British public. The whirligigs of fortune were by no means all one way. While the Marquess of Bath was mildly lamenting the fact that the 130,000 people who paid 2s. 6d. each year to inspect his great house at Longleat netted him, after expenses, little more than he might have got from running a small draper's shop, that newly emergent large draper, Isaac Wolfson (now Sir Isaac) was assembling, in his Great Universal Stores Group, an empire already valued in 1957 at some £80 million.

Wolfson, like Charles Clore, Jack Cotton and a thousand others who were making large personal fortunes in the 1950s, were essentially taking treble advantage of generally buoyant and inflationary trading situations. They borrowed money in the virtual certainty that it could be paid back later in sharply depreciated currency. They acquired assets—property, shoe shops, department stores, mail order houses, supermarkets, and other people's relatively moribund companies—on which it was possible to generate a spectacularly improved return. And they sold off large slices of the resulting enterprises, in the form of equity shares, to a public only too anxious to find some way of protecting its dwindling savings. And this, of course, is the classic way in which inflation operates—favouring new men at the expense of old money, and generally loosening up the dead combination of inherited wealth, compound interest, and the separation of ownership from activity, which has probably been as responsible as anything for Britain's ramshackle and unsatisfactory industrial structure over the last fifty years. As the Society for Promoting Christian Knowledge sonorously remarked in its *Easy Lessons on Money Matters for the Use of Young People* back in 1850: 'It is curious to observe how, through the wise and beneficent arrangement of Providence, men thus do the greatest service to the public when they are thinking of nothing but their own gain.' And although the gains of the 1950 take-over kings attracted more than their fair share of opprobrium at the time, one's main regret, with the benefit of hindsight, is that they restricted their activities to the relatively narrow fields of property and retailing, and did not get around to some of the more basic sectors like iron and steel and the darker recesses of electrical and mechanical engineering.

Few people in 1957, though, were thinking about the beneficent effects of inflation. In all the public utterances of that spring and summer—even in Macmillan's encomium of the affluent society—it was treated as an unmitigated and, more important, a growing evil. This, as it turned out, was way off target—both the Consumer Price Index (up 2·4 per cent) and the Index of Retail Prices (up 3·4 per cent) showed one of the smallest increases in 1957 that had been registered in the last decade. But there were plenty of ominous-looking straws floating in the economic wind which could be plaited together into a much more threatening interpretation. By grasping at all of them, the Chancellor, the Governor of the Bank of England and some of the leading men in the City, who should have known better, managed to talk the country, and the pound, into a runaway September crisis.

The trouble started in May, when there were sharp increases in coal and rail freight prices, calculated to add some £80 million a year to industrial costs. Then came the rise in Post Office charges, which appeared to mark a new departure in Government thinking by allowing not only for past inflation, but adding in a bit to take care of more cost-growth in the future. And finally figures came out showing that while industrial production in 1956 had been almost static, personal incomes had risen by a clear 7 per cent.

Mr Thorneycroft, the Chancellor, was down in the City soon afterwards, opening the new offices of the United Kingdom Provident Association, one of the smaller insurance institutions, and he chose the occasion for a full-scale attack on the nation's financial sins, as he saw them. 'How honest is our money? As honest as we choose to make it,' he thundered. And he went on, first to assure the world that a nation which paid itself 7 per cent more for doing no more work was bound to raise prices against itself, and second to pose the question, surely unique among Chancellors, whether fixed interest Government securities (of which he was currently responsible for an outstanding total of £15,000 million worth) were any longer a sound investment. Within days the *Financial Times* gilt-edged index hit its till-then all-time low, and the stage was duly set.

Already, in both 1955 and 1956, the gold and dollar reserves of the Sterling Area had made a significantly worse showing than was warranted by the actual foreign-exchange payments position—a situation which, as *The Economist* helpfully remarked, 'can be read by the ordinary man as "a flight from the pound" '. And in 1957 the British financial community did its best to turn that flight into a rout.

At this time, it must be remembered, the pound was by no means fully convertible into other currencies. After the disastrous six-week experiment of 1947, a formidable bastion of exchange-control regulations cut off sterling from the rest of the monetary world, and this was only due to be significantly dismantled in 1958. But during early 1957 large-scale advantage was taken of a loop-hole in these regulations, which allowed British speculators to buy forbidden dollar securities for sterling if they took the precaution of putting the order through the tiny, oil-rich sheikdom of Kuwait. The Bank of England was extremely reluctant, for 'technical' reasons, to attempt the closure of this notorious gap, and nearly $200 million worth of US and Canadian shares were acquired this way in the spring and early summer, before the official sentries were finally persuaded to act, in July. That only gave a few weeks' respite. In August a rather botched French devaluation, and strong rumours about the imminent revaluation of the German deutschmark, set the foreign exchange markets in turmoil again. And in the two months between the Kuwait Gap closure and the raising of Bank Rate on 19 September, a further £186 million poured out from Britain's already dangerously scanty reserves, as the world's traders, as well as the world's currency speculators, hedged against the view that the pound was about to be forced off its $2·80 perch.

That perch would have been pretty uncomfortable anyway—the thinness of the reserves, unbacked at that time by any of the vast international loans and bank support operations which have become familiar in the 1960s, made sure of that. But the precariousness of the situation might well have been mitigated if the world had known just how strong Britain's general economic performance was at that time. In the event there was a surplus of £237 million on Britain's current account in 1957, following on a £208 million surplus in 1956, and when taken together with the £344 million surplus recorded in 1958, after all the alarums, this represents far and away the most favourable showing the country's payments have put up from 1939 to 1970.

One would certainly not have guessed it, though, from the things which the eminent leaders of British financial opinion were saying to each other, and to their foreign banking friends at the time. As faithfully recorded in the evidence to the Bank Rate Tribunal* they represented a damning vote of no confidence which any currency would have had a job to withstand.

There is Mr William Keswick, for example—a director of the Bank

---

* A Government inquiry set up later to look into the, as it turned out, baseless accusation that there had been widespread leakage of the 19 September decision.

of England, and one who might reasonably be expected to know what
he was talking about—writing to the managing director of his family
firm, Jardine, Matheson, in Hong Kong on 16 September: 'But I
return to a very depressed City. I believe the trade figures are dreadful and one hears on all sides ugly rumours about devaluation. . . .
What measures the Government will take to check inflation, which is
rampant, and to protect the Pound I do not know.' As Britain's
visible exports in 1957 were at a new record peak, almost double the
figure for 1949, and also represented a higher proportion of the
import bill (99·2 per cent) than virtually any other year between
1939 and 1969, this does not really seem to qualify as a very well-
informed interpretation. But Mr Keswick was not alone. There was
Lord Kindersley, another director of the Bank of England, and also
at that time Governor of the Royal Exchange Insurance Company
and chairman of Rolls-Royce, British Match and Lazard Brothers,
the big City merchant bank. He told the Tribunal how he had
hastened back from Canada on 28 August. 'I was really worried by
the attitude of Canadian bankers towards the pound sterling in
general, towards our inability to halt the wage spiral, and our ineffec-
tive (if I may say so) Government at the time. I was really worried.
. . . I told my colleagues . . . that the whole faith in this country was
disappearing and it was a farce, and it was a critical situation and
everybody should recognise or be made to recognise that it was so,
which I did not think they did. . . .'

As Professor Ely Devons commented, in the most detailed account
so far to appear on this peculiar episode:* 'It is somewhat surprising
that not a single witness who gave evidence before the Tribunal
appeared to be aware that the underlying trading position of the
country was, for the time being anyway, surprisingly good, and that
the balance of payments on current account was expected to be substantially favourable in the second half of the year 1957. (In the
event it showed a surplus of over £140 million for those six months.)
There had, it is true, been discussion throughout the summer about
the menace of continuing inflation and fears had been expressed in
many quarters about what would happen to the balance of payments
if inflation continued at the same rate into 1958. It looks as though
when speculation against sterling started in the summer, and foreign
exchange reserves started to drain away, many people in the City
immediately jumped to the conclusion that this was because our
wage costs were getting out of hand and that the Government had
not the courage to do anything about it, and so our trade position
was deteriorating, and speculation against the pound was merely
making the position worse. One wonders, for example, whether Lord

* The *Manchester School* (September 1959).

Kindersley in his discussions with Canadian and US bankers . . .
explained, when they expressed such concern about the future of
sterling, that the trading position of this country was really very
strong, and that the pressure against sterling was almost wholly
speculative?'

Even the Governor of the Bank of England, Cameron Cobbold,
seems to have been brushed with this sense of gathering doom and
the fell forces beyond the gate. As he told the Tribunal, in his opinion
'the surprising thing was that there was not much heavier selling and
more disquiet in the City at the time'. With such authority, and
against a background of generally unsettled exchanges, even the
most sympathetic of foreigners might be forgiven for deciding that
sterling was a commodity he could well be without—at least until the
British made up their minds about their state of monetary health.
The whole affair retains a strongly self-destructive flavour.

In the event, the victim—if that is to be taken as the parity of the
pound—was saved. The strong emetic of Thorneycroft's September
measures—7 per cent Bank Rate, restriction on capital issues and
bank advances, and a heavy cut in Government spending plans—was
accepted in the best puritan tradition that nasty medicine must do
you good. The outflow of reserves went smartly into reverse, and by
November the Chancellor, for no particularly good reason, was con-
gratulating himself and the country for notching up the best set of
trade figures in the last seven years.

He should instead have been hiding his head. Those figures, and
indeed most of the other economic statistics issued that autumn,
showed just how misguided and perverse the public breast-beating of
the summer—and its policy outcome—had really been. Far from
being overheated, industry, after a three-year investment boom, had
ample capacity to spare. Labour, as shown by the unemployment and
job-vacancy reports, was appreciably less tight than it had been in
1955–6. Wage inflation had significantly slowed down. Exports were
as strong as they had ever been. And yet this was the moment chosen
to slam the machine into reverse. Of all the sins committed under the
blanket heading of 'stop-go' this looks, in retrospect, to have been
the worst.

Of course, by September, confidence was at such a low ebb that
something had to be done. It was far too late to halt the run on
reserves by merely saying in a loud voice that the pound was strong
and free (as Kennedy later did for the dollar, by the dramatic new
medium of the Telstar satellite). But if ever there was a case for at
least temporarily allowing a currency to float, it applied to the
pound in 1957. Certainly it would have floated down for a brief
period. But the export-boosting, import-curtailing effects of the

o

resultant 'devaluation', superimposed—as they certainly were not in either 1949 or 1967—on a basically strong balance of payments and an economy running well below capacity, would on any analysis have bounced it quickly back to at least the $2·80 level, and possibly even above. An unrepeatable chance was offered to establish that virtuous, export-led growth-spiral which has hoisted such countries as Germany, Japan and Italy to unprecedented success in the recent postwar period. And it was thrown away in a fit of national denigration and deflationary despair.

The mood was contagious. It even spread to the Queen, who let it be known in December that the Royal Bounty, which had run at the rate of £3 for the mothers of newly born triplets, and £4 for quads, since Queen Victoria instituted the practice in 1849, was henceforth to be suspended in favour of a letter of congratulation. The value of money, said the official statement, had deteriorated so far as to make the gift meaningless. There was no suggestion that as an alternative the amounts might have been raised. And at the other end of the scale, an ex-public schoolboy, up in court on a charge of purchasing, among other things, a suede overcoat with a lambswool lining (price £23!) with a dud cheque, was massively rebuked by the magistrate for his habit of stealing only the best. The youth humbly admitted his error, but offered the somewhat shame-faced excuse that: 'You see, the shops that sell cheaper things won't give you credit.'

Mr Thorneycroft unrepentantly continued to hammer away at his anti-inflationary drum. Already he had set up the massive, but ultimately rather inconclusive Radcliffe inquiry into the workings of the monetary system (which he saw as 'an antiquated pumping machine, creaking and groaning, leaking wildly in all the main valves, but still desperately attempting to keep down the level of water in the mine'). Even before the Bank Rate flurry, he had attempted to reinforce this with the ineffectual Council on Prices, Productivity and Incomes, a forerunner of those multifold attempts to produce and police a prices-and-incomes policy which for better or worse have characterized the past decade. And now, at the end of the year, he instituted a strongly exhortatory campaign aimed at persuading industry to reduce its prices. In a series of speeches, culminating in an address to the National Union of Manufacturers on 11 December, he thumped home the new message—that world commodity prices were falling (the highly favourable trend in the terms of trade was one of the most important economic underpinnings to the thirteen years of Tory rule) and that the big, but so far not very productive investment programme of the previous three years gave an excellent springboard for growth. The depressant effect of the September measures was not apparently regarded as relevant. But then, the whole occasion could hardly be regarded as a meeting of true minds.

The manufacturers themselves indicated their view of the state of the nation by placing before each of their guests, including the Chancellor, a reproduction of the 10,000,000,000 mark notes circulating in Germany in December 1923, at the time when, as everyone knows, it took a wheelbarrow full of them to buy a loaf of bread. Mr Thorneycroft responded with a stirring affirmation of faith that, 'I just do not believe that a combination of managerial efficiency and lower import costs cannot be reflected in lower prices. And such a lowering of any price is the biggest contribution any of you can make to the economy at the present moment.' And around the table there was presumably a certain amount of speculation about the identity of the firm mentioned in the *Manchester Guardian*'s correspondence columns that morning, which had been circularizing its trade customers to warn them that 'our product is going up on December 16th. Buy now at the old price of 1s. 2d., and sell at the new. There's an extra 4d. profit on every packet.'

No one's analysis came out particularly accurately on this occasion. Britain, despite the efforts of the 4d.-a-packet merchant, did not slide into hyper-inflation. But although a lot of manufacturers must have taken the Chancellor at his word—there is hardly an item in the William Whiteley Christmas Gift List of 1957, shown overpage, which could not be duplicated at the same or even a lower price in 1970—that did not prevent the general value of the pound continuing on its relentlessly downward path. In January 1958 Mr Thorneycroft resigned, during what Mr Macmillan, his Prime Minister, described as 'a little local difficulty' over the State spending cuts, and his voice has not been heard much in the nation's economic councils since. But one cannot leave 1957 without feeling that a very considerable opportunity had been badly muffed.

Naturally it is impossible on a list like this to get exact comparisons. Design, quality, technology, brand names, all change drastically over a thirteen-year period. But checking with a collection of 1970 mail-order catalogues it would be possible in almost every case to buy something approximating to the 1957 description at no greater price. And frequently, as with the more expensive things like radios and electric drills, the 1970 article is clearly both cheaper and technically superior. Only one or two of the smaller clothing and furniture items seem to have gone up by anything approaching the 50 per cent rise in the retail price index.

William Whiteley's Christmas Gift List 1957

	£	s.	d.		£	s.	d.
TV chair	10	10	0	Record player	13	17	6
Electric blanket	10	17	6	Crystal tankard	2	3	6
Pyrex casseroles (3)	1	8	6	Crystal ashtray	1	8	9
Linen table mats	1	5	0	Long-sleeve pullover	3	3	0
Woollen cape	2	19	6	Pure silk square	1	7	6
Lady's umbrella	3	2	6	Non-iron shirt	1	19	6
Perfume spray	3	9	6	Driving gloves	1	15	6
Electric razor	10	17	6	6' by 40" rug	4	17	6
Travel clock	5	10	6	Work box	6	12	6
Electric ¼" drill	6	12	6	Evening stole	6	15	0
Lady's toilet case	3	19	6	Delft biscuit barrel	1	0	6
Photo flash outfit	3	5	1	Brocade evening bag	1	5	0
Dress studs	1	19	11	Four lace hankies	1	3	6
Man's toilet set	2	17	6	Walnut TV table	1	9	6
Brief case	3	15	0	Crystal brandy glasses	5	17	0
Velvet housecoat	8	4	6	Man's umbrella	4	9	6
Portable radio	12	1	6	Man's dressing gown	4	9	6
Lady's evening gloves	1	19	11	Pen & Pencil set	8	3	4
Desk compendium	1	7	6	Tropical fish tank	4	4	0
Record cabinet	10	10	0	Pigskin wallet	1	19	11
Ironide suitcase	10	5	0	Brown suede slippers	2	2	11
Cashmere cardigan	10	17	6	Adjustable desk lamp	1	9	6

The Pound in

was worth £1 3s. in 1970 money

Devaluation, whether of sterling, or the dollar, or both, would be a lunatic, self-destroying operation.

Harold Wilson (3 April 1963)

From now the Pound abroad is worth 14 per cent or so less in terms of other currencies. It does not mean, of course, that the Pound here in Britain, in your pocket or your purse, or in your bank, has been devalued.

Harold Wilson (20 November 1967)

Devaluation and the defence cuts mean a reprieve for the unique animal species on Aldabra Island in the Indian Ocean. So biologists will be very pleased.

Sir Ashley Miles, Biological Secretary of the Royal Society (November 1967)

In March 1967 a nine-year-old Nottingham schoolgirl, Joanna Wilkinson, wrote to her Member of Parliament, Mr Michael English, to complain—as the British public then were cordially invited to do—at an untoward increase in the cost of living. On 24 February, she said, she had purchased a 6d. packet of marbles from her local sub-post-office; a week later, when she went to buy a second packet, the price had gone up to 7d.; and what did Her Majesty's Government propose to do about it?

The full investigative machine of Her Majesty's Board of Trade swung into immediate action. The sub-postmaster explained that there had been a sharp jump in the bill for his last delivery of wholesale marbles. The marble wholesalers, after intensive inquiry, discovered that there had been an error by one of their invoice clerks. No price rise had been intended. Joanna was credited with the sum of 1d., which she promptly spent in sweets (average price up 33 per cent over her short lifetime). And Mr Douglas Jay, then President of the Board of Trade, informed a duly appreciative House of Commons that the cost of this exercise to the British taxpayer had been precisely £3 10s.

This was not an isolated incident, either. In July the Ministry of Agriculture was in action on behalf of another nine-year-old, Barry Duffy, of Alloa, in Scotland, who had failed to appreciate the subtle economic forces which had added 1d. to the cost of his favourite brand of lemonade. In that case, however, his suppliers, Messrs Koolopop Ltd, were able to emerge without a stain on their commercial character. They had held their prices steady for six years, in face of mounting bills for sugar, flavourings, transport, labour, and label printing, and could not, in the Ministry's view, be faulted for submitting now to the ineluctable pressures of trade.

There were at least eight hundred similar cases that year. Whatever may or may not have happened to the pound in people's pockets on the night of Saturday, 19 November, when £1,000 million of international speculative money said it was over-priced at $2·80, the continued erosion of its domestic purchasing power in previous months had brought on what can only be described as an attack of advanced inflationary neurosis.

The general tone was admirably summed up by Mr John Boyd, the current chairman of the Labour Party, in a speech he made on 4 September. 'There is absolutely no justification', he said, 'for the way in which the ordinary people of this country are being fleeced by the present exorbitant prices of such essentials as meat, footwear, clothes, numerous household goods and furniture.' And he went on, to loud applause, to call for a 'ruthless' attack on the manufacturers and retailers operating in these sectors.

Such an attack, if anyone could have thought of an effective way to mount it, would, in fact, have been almost wholly misdirected. In the ten years since Mr Thorneycroft made the ringing appeal reported at the end of the last chapter the official index of retail prices had risen by 33 per cent—exactly the same as Joanna's sweets, and significantly less than such allegedly virtuous countries as France, Sweden and the Netherlands. Also, as luck would have it, every single one of the industries singled out by Mr Boyd's opprobrium had succeeded in holding its price increases below, and in several instances appreciably below, that figure. Consumer durables were up 11 per cent, men's, women's and children's clothes 16 per cent, shoes 20 per cent, and furniture 25 per cent. Only meat (31 per cent) and household pots and pans (32·4 per cent) were within touching distance of the average, and the real offenders were not mentioned at all.

Of these, the worst, by a large margin, was housing, where rents, maintenance and prices for owner-occupation had soared together by almost 70 per cent over the decade. Fuel and lighting were up by slightly over a half. And most of the rest of the running was made by the service sector—domestic help, hair dressing, holidays and things like postage and laundries—where overall charges were up by around 47 per cent.

Just what effect increases of this kind had on people's living standards obviously varies almost infinitely, according to tastes, spending patterns, family circumstances and success, or otherwise, in improving the income side of their accounts. But some general impression of what had been happening can be seen by comparing the budgets of the 'average households' as shown in the Ministry of Labour's first, pioneering Family Expenditure Survey in 1957, and its much more elaborate successor, covering 1967. Between the two the average income of these two somewhat notional families had increased from £830 a year (net of tax and benefits) to £1,416, and this is how they were laid out in the weeks that the investigators analysed.

| | The 1957 Family | | | The 1967 Family | | |
	£	s.	d.	£	s.	d.
Housing						
Rent & rates		19	11	2	5	2
Maintenance		4	11		8	8
Fuel & Light		17	4	1	9	3
Food	4	15	5	6	7	5
Drink		9	1		19	8
Tobacco		17	6	1	5	2

	The 1957 Family			The 1967 Family		
	£	s.	d.	£	s.	d.
Clothes	1	9	0	2	1	2
Furniture & durables	1	1	9	1	9	9
Miscellaneous	1	0	10	1	13	7
Transport						
Car purchase		4	11		18	4
Petrol, etc.		8	0	1	4	10
Bicycles, prams		1	2			11
Fares		9	3		13	11
Services	1	5	0	2	6	10
Pocket-money, etc.	1	4			1	9
Other Payments						
National Insurance		7	5		19	11
Mortgage*		8	1	1	19	2
Life assurance, pension fund		10	6		19	3
Other insurance			7			10
Xmas clubs, etc.		2	11		2	2
Savings		2	5		10	1
Betting (net)		1	11		4	0
Grand Total	15	19	3	28	1	10

In addition, the average 1957 household paid £60 a year in income tax and surtax, while its equivalent ten years later handed back something over £160 to the Inland Revenue.

Despite that, however, the difference in the two budgets represented quite a substantial improvement in the material standard of living. Allowing for the widely differing price developments in the various categories of spending, one can say that the Ministry's average family in 1967 was buying 10 per cent more food, 5 per cent more tobacco, 60 per cent more alcohol, 27 per cent more or better accommodation, 12 per cent more light and heat and 20 per cent more durables, clothes, services and assorted goods than its 1957 predecessor, and almost twice as much in the way of cars and general transportation.

Obviously comparisons of this kind are very crude. The averages are drawn over an immensely wide area—from single-person pensioner households in low-rent Glasgow to professional couples in London

* Both mortgage payments and rent appear on the 'average household' budget as there are, of course, both forms of spending included under the cost of housing.

with joint incomes up in the £10,000–£12,000 bracket (with joint tax bills to match). But as far as they go, they are not out of line with the evidence offered by the general trend of prices and incomes over the period. As the chart on page 208 shows, from 1957 to 1967, while the overall retail index went up by some 33 per cent, both average earnings and average salary earnings scored gains of almost 70 per cent. All of which helps to explain why inflation in Britain remained —and remains—a subject for chronic grumbling, but has generated surprisingly little in the way of effective counter-attack.

This is not to say there was no activity, of course—merely that it had small success. For in fact the history of the decade leading up to the 1967 devaluation is a running account of attempts, ranging from the academic to the frantic, to get to grips with the price-war spiral. Nor is it by any means clear, at the moment of writing, that 1970 sees us any closer to success. Mr William Rodgers, Minister of State at the Treasury, admitted to Parliament on 24 March that the purchasing power of the pound had dropped by 4s. 1d., or slightly over 20 per cent, since Labour took office in 1964. Even as he spoke, large sections of British industry were completing wage settlements in the region of 10 per cent a year, and others were preparing to join battle over claims for up to 20 per cent. And when the Conservatives took over, after a year when all attempts to impose an incomes policy had been abandoned, the spiral was already taking another violent upward lurch.

However, in 1967 the price-income troops were still fully mobilized if not in totally good heart. The pound's home defence forces—as opposed to the external fortifications, which we shall come to later— had developed considerably since Mr Thorneycroft first appointed the Cohen Council on Prices, Productivity and Incomes in 1957. The following brief synopsis gives the main points in the story so far.

July 1961. Selwyn Lloyd imposes eight month 'pay pause' as part of his sterling crisis measures. Income from employment rises 5·2 per cent in following year, after the nationalized Electricity Council breaks pay pause in November.

February 1962. 2½ per cent 'guiding light' announced for incomes. Actual rise: 5 per cent for employment earnings, 6 per cent overall, in next twelve months.

July 1962. Macmillan, overriding Whitehall, and in face of violent trades union opposition, sets up National Incomes Council (Nickie). Achieves little, but prepares way for Labour's Prices & Incomes Board.

December 1964. Labour persuades unions and employers to sign 'Joint Statement of Intent on Productivity, Prices & Wages'. This

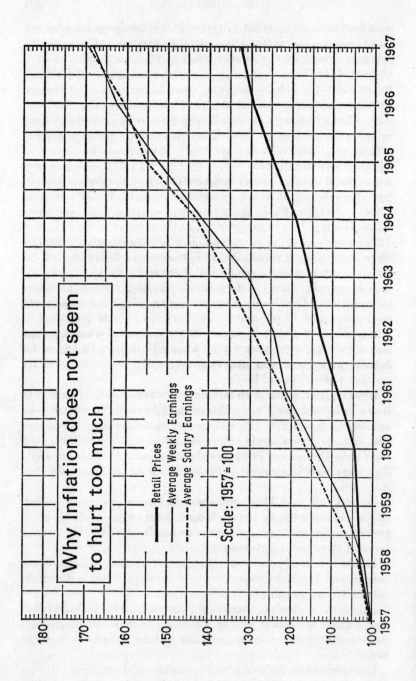

Why Inflation does not seem to hurt too much

Retail Prices
Average Weekly Earnings
Average Salary Earnings

Scale: 1957 = 100

agrees (a) to raise productivity throughout industry and commerce; (b) to keep increases in total money incomes in line with increases in real national output; (c) to maintain a stable general price level.

March 1965. Aubrey Jones appointed first chairman of National Board for Prices & Incomes (PIB). Government asks them to start by looking at proposed increase in road haulage charges.

April 1965. White Paper says money incomes per head must keep in line with underlying productivity rise of 3–3½ per cent a year.

November 1965. TUC sets up 'early warning' system to inform Government of pending pay claims. Confederation of British Industry refuses to do same for prices, but individual manufacturers 'asked' to tell appropriate ministry about proposed increases.

February 1966. Prices & Incomes Bill provides for compulsory 'early warning'.

July 1966. Sterling crisis. Government calls for complete standstill on pay and price increases and reductions in working hours till 31 December. Takes reserve powers to enforce this by law.

January 1967. Freeze moderates into six months 'period of severe restraint'. Pay and price increases only allowed in 'exceptional conditions'.

July 1967. End of pay freeze. TUC resumes pay vetting, but now with 'nil norm' instead of 3–3½ per cent. Price increases to be delayed for seven months after reference to PIB.

What was the effect of all this activity? The answer, regrettably, seems to be, 'Very little', except over the fairly brief period of freeze and 'severe restraint'. Over the twenty months before the freeze, from October 1964 to June 1966, average earnings for all employees went up at an average of 7½ per cent a year—more than twice the supposed 'norm'. During the eleven months of statutory restraint the rise was very small indeed—well under 2 per cent. But everything suggests that this merely represented a postponement of claims. Over the fifteen months from the July measures to October 1967, there was a 5·7 per cent rise in earnings, equivalent to an annual rate of 4·6 per cent. And over the twenty-one months to April 1968, when the 'nil norm' was supposed to be in operation, this rose to an average of 5 per cent a year.

Britain was by no means alone in this sort of failure. The Economic Commission for Europe, after a massive 1968 survey of all that had been done since the war in the way of 'experiment and endeavour' with incomes policies, concluded that 'such policies, as so far conceived, have not proved strikingly effective instruments of economic policy'. But the outcome was still pretty disappointing, and the big surge of pay claims that coincided with the end of 'severe restraint' undoubtedly helped to grease the slope for the pound's final Gadarene slither in November.

Where the various transmutations of policy had succeeded—contrary to accepted Labour mythology, and to most people's instinctive feelings on the subject—was in preventing more than a part of these wage increases coming through to prices. And early 1967 enjoyed the rare post-war distinction of seeing one or two actual price reductions in major areas. Esso, to the total consternation of its competitors, dropped its petrol rates by up to 4½d. a gallon (giving a range of 4s. 9d. to 5s. 6½d., which looks positively Elysian against 1970's 6s. to 6s. 9d.). Marks & Spencer's sliced 2s. off their nylon shirts. Things like foreign sewing-machines came down 13 per cent or more with the ending of the 1964–6 import surcharge. Supermarkets, for a few dramatic days, cut 5d. off a packet of twenty cigarettes, before the tobacco companies turned chicken-hearted and agreed to continue Retail Price Maintenance for a bit longer. And although the euphoric enthusiasm engendered by the discovery of large quantities of cheap natural gas in the North Sea was quickly offset by the gritty reality of an 8–15 per cent increase in domestic electricity tariffs, the general price-inflationary pressure was probably lower in 1967 than in any of the last eight years. The retail price index rise, of 2·5 per cent, compares with a best performance, of 3·3 per cent, in 1963–4 and a worst, of 5·4 per cent, in the year following devaluation.

However, the retailers of Britain continued to make it as difficult as possible to see exactly what was happening to their prices. Green Shield stamps, now going into circulation at the rate of over £20 million worth each year, were available on every kind of grocery, petrol and hardware sale, representing a discount of between 3d. and 1s. in the pound, according to the generosity or desperation of the shop manager. 'Own brand' products, where an often nationally advertised item is repacked to sell more cheaply under a store's own particular house label, were increasingly coming in to muddle the 'best buy' league tables. Often there was even double muddle, as when one supermarket operator complained bitterly in May 1967 that he could only move a famous brand of baked beans under his label at 11d., but Sainsbury's reputation was so good that they could sell the same thing under their label for 1s. 1d.

The Consumers' Association, whose subscription had (in line with most services) gone up from 1957's £1 to 30s., continued to grapple manfully with the rising tide, and also to record a few significant successes in the unending battle against what the *Daily Express* had merrily christened 'Mr Rising Price'. Their most strongly recommended twin-tub washing-machine was £69 6s. when they first investigated this sector in 1958; when they returned to the subject in 1967, they were able to find not only a by then rather old fashioned twin-tub for only £62, but a fully automatic model for £61 19s. And the same pattern applied even in products not affected by the price-cutting activities of Mr John Bloom. The best steam iron in 1967 was only a few shillings up on the best steam iron of 1957, and, thanks to the ending of RPM, most of that could be wiped out by judicious shopping round the discount stores. In 1967 people learned for the first time since the war the art of bargaining about everyday purchases—not just the trade-in prices of their motor cars.

Their wits certainly needed all the sharpening they could get. This was the year when the government, getting slightly hysterical about the economics of advertising, decided to force the detergent manufacturers to give the customers a plain, honest product where the price represented 100 per cent powder in the packet, and not some unknown proportion on gifts, TV spots, give-away competitions, and unrepeatable offers. As a result the public were faced with at least fifty permutations of price, size, content and packaging, and a whole new vocabulary and mathematics of comparative description. Which shop is the cheaper, they were encouraged to ask themselves— the one that sells Giant (meaning large) packets of Fairy Snow at 3s. 3d. and Large (meaning medium) packets at 2s. 2d.; or the one offering Giants at 2s. 10d. but Larges at 2s. 3d.; or the one full of Extra Value Tide and New Square Deal Surf somewhere in between? Predictably, most of them just closed their eyes and bought the one they first thought of, and another great experiment in inducing consumer price-consciousness bit the dust. It was all part of a consumer-cynicism, which was not exactly diminished that spring by the story of the bedroom furniture and bedding firm which started offering free holidays in Paris to encourage shop assistants to push its most expensive products. It was not so much the practice itself which worried people, though that was bad enough: it was the comment of the furniture trade paper, the *Cabinet Maker*, which was deeply concerned that 'a situation could quickly develop where the salesman's interest in obtaining gifts takes precedence over the retailers' interest in obtaining maximum profit'.

Who could afford in 1967 to buy the £200 bed which would win the helpful assistant the weekend in Paris? Since 1957 (see page 186) there had been a further significant change in the pattern of after-tax incomes shown up in the Inland Revenue statistics, and this is what it now looked like:

After-Tax Incomes ('000s)

	1957	1967
Under £250	6,070	2,338
£250–£500	8,070	5,906
£500–£750	7,430	5,418
£750–£1,000	3,120	4,882
£1,000–£1,500 }	1,220	6,466
£1,500–£2,000 }		1,832
£2,000–£3,000 }	173	730
£3,000–£4,000 }		} 224
£4,000–£5,000 }	16	
£5,000–£6,000 }		} 63
£6,000–£10,000 }	0·8	
Over £10,000 }		1

Such tables could be a good deal more informative if the various bands were more narrowly spaced. But one or two interesting developments emerge even from this. First of all there are over three million more people above the £1,000 a year mark in 1967 than there were above the equivalent £750 mark ten years earlier. And using a little extrapolation, it appears that the number above £2,000 a year —slightly more than one million—was at least double the similar figure (that is, people above £1,500 a year after tax) in 1957.

At the top end of these scales, some 357,604 people had the pleasure of paying surtax in 1967 (including, for many of them, the 10 per cent surcharge imposed in the budget of 1966). This compared with only 296,452 in 1956–7, when everything over £2,000 a year came into the net. In 1961 Selwyn Lloyd changed the rules so that earned incomes were effectively exempt up to £5,000 a year, and both the impact and the distribution had changed quite a lot.

Range of total income	No. of persons paying surtax	
	1957	1967
£2,000–£2,500	60,112	24,389
£2,500–£3,000	67,764	44,664
£3,000–£4,000	72,575	79,668
£4,000–£5,000	34,907	52,823
£5,000–£6,000	19,191	43,777
£6,000–£8,000	19,299	51,934
£8,000–£10,000	8,877	24,864
£10,000–£12,000	4,822	13,024
£12,000–£15,000	3,758	9,804
£15,000–£20,000	2,714	6,900
£20,000–£25,000	1,067	2,544

Range of total income	No. of persons paying surtax	
	1957	1967
£25,000–£30,000	505	1,229
£30,000–£40,000	449	1,014
£40,000–£50,000	165	384
£50,000–£75,000	156	366
£75,000–£100,000	46	111
Over £100,000	45	109
Total number paying surtax	296,452	357,604
Total incomes	£1,272m	£2,093m
Total surtax paid	£148m	£215m

The striking thing that emerges from a closer study of the Inland Revenue figures (annual reports for 1968 and 1958) is the big increase in the number of people in the senior management bracket—after allowing for the price changes which had reduced the value of a 1967 pound to roughly 15s. of 1957 money, there were half as many people again earning between £8,000 and £20,000 a year in 1967 as there had been in the equivalent £6,000–£15,000 slot ten years before. The number had grown from 36,000 to almost 54,000. Even above these levels another 600 people had arrived to swell the ranks of 1957's best-paid 5,000. And by and large, as far as it is possible to calculate from the statistics for these high taxpayers, they had more than held their own in purchasing power terms.

In fact the following table will probably come as a slight shock to those many and vociferous representatives of the more affluent sectors of British society who are convinced that they and their friends are being taxed off the face of the earth. It shows just how well, or badly, the effective value of a high 1957 salary was preserved over the succeeding inflationary decade. The figures concern a married couple with no children and all earned income, but they would not change all that dramatically for other possible combinations.

Earnings in 1957 £	Income & Surtax £	Take-home pay £	Equivalent @ 1967 prices £	After-tax value of same income in 1967 £
15,000	9,969	5,031	6,708	6,884
20,000	14,592	5,408	7,212	7,446
25,000	19,217	5,783	7,712	7,883
50,000	42,342	7,658	10,212	10,071
100,000	88,592	11,408	15,212	14,446

In other words, it was only at the £50,000 level that even unchanged incomes started to drift below their 1957 purchasing power.

Any increment did, despite all the tears and polemics, actually add a significant amount to the cash in the directorial pocket.

The trouble was—and is—of course, that the amount it added was proportionally so very small. The combination of inflation and progressively increasing tax rates means that it becomes increasingly more expensive each year to give anyone a decent salary rise. In 1967 the average manual worker, getting £1,087 a year, was already paying standard rate unless he had more than one child, and to give him an effective increase of 2 per cent meant giving him an actual money increase of 6·1 per cent (which probably went a long way to explain the spate of 'inflationary' wage claims which resulted after the trade unions had done a little work with their slide rules). For the typical director, however, at the £13,000 a year level, the sums involved were already getting astronomical—just offsetting the currently modest 3 per cent annual erosion in the value of money required an extra 7·32 per cent on his pay cheque, and to give him the equivalent of the manual worker's 2 per cent increase required an actual boost of 12·2 per cent.

Such figures provided the basis for A. J. Merrett and D. A. G. Monk's 1967 study, *Inflation, Taxation and Executive Remuneration*, which—possibly for the first time—set out an intellectually respectable case for easing the very high rates at the top of Britain's surtax range. Essentially their argument was that, once an able man had achieved a reasonably high income, in a job he did well, and enjoyed, there was—and indeed still is—no effective monetary means of tempting him to move on to something more risky, challenging, or time consuming, however socially desirable it might be. Hence there tends to be an excessive concentration of talent in relatively comfortable areas like the civil service, the universities, the home counties, and the boardrooms of large, solid companies, and a profound unwillingness to throw up such posts in order to help sort out some of the grimier and more intractable problems that continue to beset Britain's older industrial regions. In other words, when you can enjoy an easy life and plenty of golf at the £10,000 a year level, where the take-home pay, at 1967 rates, was £5,803, why should you uproot yourself and your wife for a chancy £20,000 in Greenock or Gateshead, when the net salary cheque at the end of the day is only £7,465—especially if it means working twenty hours a day, seven days a week, and putting your whole reputation on the line. Some do, of course, because that is their temperament. But not enough, it seems, to raise the somewhat unexciting calibre of British management at large.

Somewhere in this area—the general comfortableness of most people's lives and the pervasive lack of incentive to break new ground—obviously lies a good deal of the explanation for Britain's notoriously slow post-war growth. It is this lack of growth, rather than any mechanical effect of monetary inflation, or changes in the foreign exchange value of the currency, that has made it so difficult to shift the large residue of poverty which continues to present the main reproach to our society.

Measuring poverty is in itself a matter of enormous difficulty in a complex modern community. But taking it to include anyone whose income is so low as to qualify him or her to receive the Government's Supplementary Benefit payments (which replaced National Assistance in 1966) the best estimate* suggests that some five million people in 1967 were still below the official operational definition of the minimum level of living.

In November 1966 this level had been set at £4 10s. a week, plus rent, for a single person who had been receiving help for over two years, and it was raised to £4 15s. plus rent in October 1967. The equivalent figures for a childless married couple were £7 2s. and £7 10s. These represented the approved 'Plimsoll line' or 'safety net' below which none of the country's eight million old age pensioners were supposed to fall. In fact there is considerable evidence that a very large number of retired people—possibly as many as 700,000 'pensioner households'—were still not claiming their due benefits. Some were too proud or stubborn; others, even after a vigorous campaign advertising the benefits as 'Social Security's Best Buy', just did not know what they were entitled to.

In any case, pensioners were by no means the only category affected. Supplementary benefit levels included an allowance of between £1 7s. and £2 1s. for each child, according to age, and for many low-paid workers, with large families, the total income even when the breadwinner was in full-time employment did not reach the appropriate benefit level. While he was at work, no benefits were payable. If he was off, because of sickness or redundancy, the 'wage stop' system came into operation, which prevented the family from receiving any more cash from the state than they had while father or mother was in a job. In November 1967 the Ministry of Social Security found that 32,600 households, with 95,000 children, were subject to 'wage stop'—22,000 through unemployment and the rest through ill-health. Among those they visited, the majority of fathers were unskilled labourers normally earning between £9 10s. and £11 10s. a week, after tax, security contributions and fares to work (though most of them had not worked for over a year). Some of the larger families were living as much as £6 below the 'safety net' and

* A. B. Atkinson: *Poverty in Britain and the Reform of Social Security* (Cambridge, 1969).

P

the average was £2 10s. on the wrong side. Half of them had rent
arrears and two out of five were more or less seriously in debt elsewhere. The Ministry's investigators concluded that 'the general
impression derived from the visits was not so much one of grinding
poverty in any absolute sense as one of unrelieved dreariness with,
in some cases, little hope of improvement in the future'.

Little better could be said for the lives lived by people supposedly
a good deal higher in the social scale than these wage-stopped
labourers. The National Union of Teachers published a study
Twenty Young Teachers in 1967. The wife of one of these teachers,
Mrs Brian Farmer, wrote of the way they managed, with two
young children, and their house, financed by £200 begged from a
relative, an NUT mortgage and her own work, six nights a week, as a
barmaid. 'Although the first armchairs in our house cost 5s., we have
slowly improved on this and our home is now half-furnished. We
have had to forgo the "luxury" of a holiday for the last four years,
in order to afford the necessities of a home, such as carpets and a
cooker. My husband has one suit, which is seven years old, for school
and best wear, and I have little more. Today, my husband, in addition to his teaching and spare-time bakery job, has two night school
classes, which brings his wages to a weekly total of £20. After the
standing monthly bills are paid (mortgage and housekeeping, etc.)
the £4 left evaporates on bus fares, electricity and gas bills, and the
children's clothes. We have an old car, which is necessary for the
bakery job, and never used for any other purpose in case it needs
repair, which we cannot afford.'

This family, enjoying an income, with all the subsidiary jobs,
slightly below the average industrial worker's wage, would of course
not qualify as technically 'in poverty'—on the 1967 Supplementary
Benefit scale that only applied to households below £13 5s. a week,
if they had two young children. But it was calculated at the end of
1966 that there were at least 70,000 families, containing some 250,000
children, where the father's full-time earnings could not reach even
this bare-bones standard. If it had not been for the family allowance,
now standing at an increasingly inadequate 8s. for the second child
and 10s. for third and subsequent additions, these numbers would
have swollen to 129,000 families and over half a million children.
And even after the allowances were virtually doubled, in late 1968,
Atkinson reckoned that there were still 44 per cent of these low-
income homes, with more than 150,000 people in all, failing to achieve
the supposed national minimum.

Pensioners got their rise, from £4 to £4 10s. a week for a single
person (which still left them well below the Government's poverty
line unless they had other means) in October 1967, and there were

similar increases for widows, dependent relatives, the sick and the unemployed. These were the only real beneficiaries from Mr James Callaghan's April Budget, which had proclaimed that 'sterling was riding high', that the economy was 'on course' and that the Government's considered policy was now 'steady as she goes'. Otherwise it effected the minimum of change in any direction.

By June, when the details of the extra pensions were announced, it was already clear that these confident predictions were well off target. The balance of payments, after achieving an unexpected surplus for the last quarter of 1966, following the July pay freeze, had taken a sharp nosedive during the 'period of severe restraint' and was now running at a deficit rate even more adverse than that which the Wilson government had inherited in 1964. It was becoming clear, at least in the inner recesses of Whitehall, that the severest dose of deflation since the war had had virtually no effect in strengthening the crisis-torn foundations of the $2·80 pound. From now on devaluation, which had been declared on every official occasion for the past three years to be unthinkable, ineffectual, ungentlemanly and irrelevant, became increasingly likely, not to say inescapable. But meanwhile the farce had to be prolonged by all the usual histrionic devices which are apparently inseparable from any adjustment of the fixed-parity international monetary system.

In fact the ideal moment for such a step had probably already passed. This was not October 1964, when the economy was still overheated by the Conservatives' rather desperate 'break for freedom' boom, nor the crisis month of June 1966, but the spring of 1967, when the country's industrial capacity was significantly underemployed—Hoover, for instance, reckoned at that time that they could cut at least £4 off the price of a washing-machine if they had been able to run their production lines at full speed—and the move could have been engineered from a position of real, if somewhat temporary, strength. Foreign funds, which had poured out of London the previous summer, were now pouring back. Some £463 million was used to pay off central bank credits used to stop the earlier drain, and there was much more in the pipeline, as the world, briefly, overcame its suspicions of sterling and accepted the profit from Britain's (necessarily) high interest rates.

No real attempt, it seems, was made to seize on this uniquely favourable set of circumstances. The Treasury had been specifically forbidden even to think about devaluation; the City and the Bank of England rejected it wholly, as supposedly damaging to Britain's, and particularly London's, financial status; and most newspaper editors and professional economists felt inhibited by the general notion that it was somehow 'disloyal' even to discuss the prevailing exchange value of the pound. Only one backbench MP, Austen Albu, who had been a junior minister in the Department of Economic Affairs, had the temerity to call for devaluation in April, and he was treated as an economic pariah. At the party political conferences in September, only the insignificant Liberals voted to support 'any necessary adjustment' involved in rejecting what one of their members, Christopher Layton, called 'the suffocating inheritance from Britain's Victorian position, the idea that the sterling system as at present constituted and at present exchange rates, is immutable'.

Such voices were lost in the storm of support for the *status quo*. On 20 July, the anniversary of the great 1966 freeze, Mr Edward Heath, leader of the Conservative opposition, went out of his way to advise members of his party not to engage in public discussion of the fateful subject. Already figures were out to show that in the first six months of 1967 the trade deficit—even after a rise in export prices and a small fall in import prices which together were worth £250 million to the balance of payments—was bigger than that recorded for the whole of 1966. Unemployment was at new heights, having virtually doubled from the 1·2 per cent registered a year before. Pressure on sterling, which had started to build up in May, became intense at the time of the Six Day Arab-Israeli War. But on 24 July Mr Callaghan found it expedient to issue another ringing statement of resolution to the House of Commons. 'Those who advocate devaluation', he said, 'are calling for a reduction in the wage levels and the real wage standards of every member of the working class of this country. I just do not want either to devalue our own word or to bring down the standard of life of our own people.' For good measure he added that 'overseas it might upset several foreign currencies and endanger the financial mechanism of the world'. And three days later Mr Wilson himself warned a group of recalcitrant MPs who had produced a pamphlet on the forbidden topic that the Government in its wisdom had rejected their solution because of the danger that it might trigger off a world recession.

The British public, taught by long experience to take such prognostications with a certain amount of salt, busied itself elsewhere. It played sufficient Bingo to give the Mecca organization a profit of £10,000 on each of its nationwide chain of gambling halls. It drank more beer than it had consumed since 1915 (despite a tenfold rise in the average price per pint) and the second highest quantity of spirits since 1920 (surpassed only in the election year 1964). It bought more motor cars (allowing for price changes), paid more tax on its cigarettes (despite smoking rather fewer of them) and enjoyed less in the way of domestic help than in any year for which there are previous records.

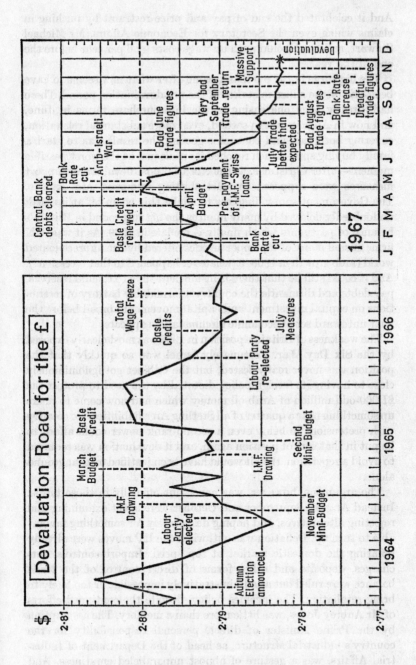

And it celebrated the end of pay and price restraint by pushing in claims which even the Secretary for Economic Affairs, Mr Michael Stewart, reckoned would push up wage costs by 6 per cent before the end of the year.

The big surge in car purchases came after what now seems to have been one of the sillier mistakes of the pre-devaluation period. There had already been one easing of the hire-purchase terms in June, and now in August came a second, even more substantial relaxation, covering both cars and consumer goods. The result was to start a family buying spree which reached its peak just at the worst possible moment—after Christmas, as the essential post-devaluation support measures were supposed to start shifting resources into exports. The Government's unwillingness to choke this boom off at its peak undoubtedly delayed by many months the big turnround in Britain's balance of payments which finally came late in 1969. As it was, UK firms missed many of the opportunities offered by the unprecedented world trade growth in 1968–9 (whatever happened to that recession?). And it could still be that there is insufficient time to rebuild reserves, pay debts and dismantle the country's formidable battery of restrictions on capital investment and capital movement abroad before the next untoward set of economic circumstances appears.

The weakness of Britain's position in 1967 was most clearly exposed by the Six Day War. Fortunately Israel won so quickly that the position was never really tested, but the Cabinet got ignominiously close to having its foreign policy dictated by the need to protect the £1,000-odd million of Arab oil money which had now come to make up something near a quarter of all Sterling Area liabilities. No country with pretensions to being even a second-rank power could afford to be put in that sort of position again, and if devaluation was required to avoid a repetition, then it would have been justified on that ground alone.

The argument, however, was never put officially in those terms. Instead August, September and October were spent examining and rejecting alternatives, and hoping desperately for something favourable to turn up. Deflation was out, when the HP moves were already reflating the domestic market at top speed. Import controls, surcharges, deposits and other forms of direct control of the trade balance were ruled out as administratively impossible or too likely to bring retaliation. The incomes policy, despite the continued efforts of Mr Aubrey Jones, was little more than a memory. The assumption by the Prime Minister of direct, personal responsibility for the country's industrial structure, as head of the Department of Industrial Affairs, was a gesture of almost unparalleled emptiness. And meanwhile, after a slight lift in July, the monthly trade figures grew steadily worse. The deficit was £29 million in August, £67 million in September, and when the October figures were published in mid-November they showed a truly horrendous deterioration to £107 million, topped only by the £153 million ultimately reported (after all the excitement was over) for November itself. Understandably, the Common Market countries, with whom Britain was engaged for most of this year in rather desultory negotiations for membership, decided in October that the time had come to point out that, with or without General de Gaulle, there would be no welcome in Europe until the painful problems of sterling had been cleared up once and for all. It was at this point, as far as can be ascertained, that the Treasury and even the Bank of England realized that devaluation had moved from the 'possible' to the 'probable' side of the filing cabinet.

The last hectic weeks are still too recent and too well documented to be worth retelling in great detail—the Government's 11 November statement that 'the worst is over for the pound'; the extraordinary bungling at Parliamentary Question Time which set off the last two days of foreign-exchange madness; the week-long, six-capital cotillion of bankers and finance ministers before a final figure was agreed; and the memorable statement of Lord Chalfont, a few hours before the final announcement, that 'there is no plan to alter the exchange rate' (a remark which could only be charitably interpreted to mean, as someone said at the time, that his cabinet colleagues were devaluing without a plan, and in a mad, panic rush). The upshot was that at 9.27 p.m. on Saturday, 18 November, a man from Telefis Eireann in Dublin rang up the *Sunday Times* in London to say that he had the Irish Minister of Finance sitting in a studio waiting to react to an event of world-shattering importance and could somebody please tell him what it was going to be. Three minutes later, the pound was devalued, in terms of the dollar, and most other world currencies, as it turned out, by precisely 14·3 per cent.

The Pound in 1970

When the Pound for the moment is worth £1

Britain woke up on 20 November 1967 to start life at $2·40. Effectively she owned not one penny of gold or foreign currency reserves, everything having been pledged several times over in the fight to save the previous parity. Her overseas debts, to central banks, and to the International Monetary Fund, had risen by something in the region of £3,000–£4,000 million during the battle, mostly repayable in the eight years to 1975; and in addition there was a matter of £1,200–£1,500 million which the Bank of England had gambled unsuccessfully on the forward exchange market, on the proposition that it was possible to hold the old rate.

Most of Mr Callaghan's direr nightmares (apart from the one about devaluing the word of a politician) failed to materialize. There was certainly no reduction in the wage levels of every member of the working class. On the contrary, average earnings, seasonally adjusted, went up by some 22 per cent between 1967 and the end of 1969. As prices at the same time rose, on average, by only 13·6 per cent, it could hardly be maintained that the standard of living of the great mass of the population had taken a particularly hard knock either.

For the time, it is true, it did appear that 'the financial mechanism of the world' might have been put into some kind of danger. The first reaction to the devaluation news from Mr Henry Fowler, the secretary of the US Treasury, was that 'the dollar is now in the front line'. And so it proved. The doubts about sterling, which had expressed themselves in a growing unwillingness by banks, merchants and even central governments to hold on to the stuff for any longer than was absolutely necessary for everyday business, now were transferred to the other great world reserve currency. And as the value of the dollar has been fixed, since Roosevelt's key decision in 1933, in terms of gold—at the rate of $35 an ounce—rather than in other currencies, this took the form of a mounting speculative drive to buy gold.

Since 1960 the leading industrial nations had agreed to join Britain, the traditional host to the international gold market, and the US, as the most interested party, in a co-operative device known as 'The Gold Pool' with the object of holding the price within a fraction of the agreed $35 mark. This followed a sudden burst of gold mania which had temporarily pushed the London quotation to around $40, and for eight years everything worked according to plan. Throughout that period, though, the American balance-of-payments deficit, which had provided most of the finance for Europe's post-war recovery, was growing to an extent which the now rich and successful Europeans were no longer prepared to tolerate. France, in particular, had deliberately set out to build up large gold reserves and to cut her dollar dependence to the minimum. And the week after Britain's devaluation she screwed up the pressure for dollar devaluation—

which of course has to take the form of an increase in the official world price of gold—by revealing that six months before she had withdrawn all support from the operations of the Gold Pool.

During the last quarter of 1967, it cost the remaining pool members some $1,400 million worth of gold reserves to keep the $35 price intact. The market remained relatively calm throughout the first two months of 1968, but then in March the lid blew off. Frenzied buying on the London, Zurich and Paris markets made it impossible to control the price any longer. The world's finance ministers and officials performed one of their ritual dashes to Washington, the Gold Pool was suspended, and the international gold trade was severed, in one of those 'temporary compromises' which so often turn out to be permanent, into two distinct parts—the 'official' end, where gold still continues to circulate from central bank to central bank at a fixed $35 an ounce, and the 'free' market for hoarders, speculators, jewellers and gold-leaf-hammerers, where it can theoretically cost whatever the supply and demand situation dictates. And that, so far as dollar devaluation is concerned, has so far been that.

Ending the gold rush, however, merely switched the spotlight back to the pound. The immediate post-devaluation sequence—ineffectual support measures, ministerial attempts to make the exercise look both planned and painless, a not very credible package of government spending cuts, a savage-seeming budget from the new Chancellor, Mr Roy Jenkins, which somehow failed to slow down consumer spending, and a dreadful balance-of-payments result for the first six months—all served to sap the confidence of the remaining overseas holders of sterling. Even the 'old commonwealth' members of the Sterling Area—particularly Australia, which for the first time in her history had chosen not to follow Britain in a currency change— showed a growing unwillingness to keep all their eggs in the Bank of England's still leaky-looking basket. Heavy conversions of official and unofficial balances into dollars and other currencies, like the very strong West German deutschmark, started once more to put a heavy strain on the pound. By September the rate had dropped near to the new, low support level of $2·38, and only yet another international co-operative heave—this time in the form of $2,000 million worth of credits, arranged through the world's central bankers meeting in Basle, to be used to guarantee official sterling balances against any further devaluation—held it even there. It is still unclear whether this is a step towards the ultimate sharing out of Britain's reserve currency responsibilities among, for example, the other big European powers; or whether it is merely a device for tiding the Sterling Area concept over a bad patch, waiting for Britain's renewed financial strength to make it a going concern again.

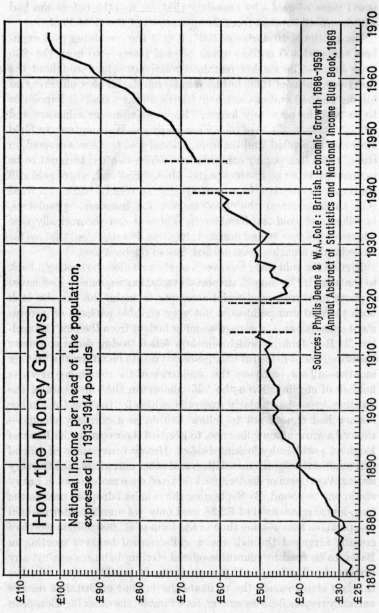

How the Money Grows

National Income per head of the population,
expressed in 1913–1914 pounds

Sources: Phyllis Deane & W.A.Cole : British Economic Growth 1688–1959
Annual Abstract of Statistics and National Income Blue Book, 1969

The renewed strength was still some way from making its unequi-
vocal appearance. For as soon as the Basle crisis was over, there came
a new twist in the monetary plot. The French franc, badly weakened
by the big, inflationary wage settlements which followed the students'
and workers' riots in May 1968, was beginning to look badly overvalued beside the increasingly solid deutschmark. West Germany's
success in consistently holding inflation below the levels tolerated by
other people paid off in the form of ever increasing export competi-
tiveness, and all the international traders and finance houses, which
had previously been hedging their commitments in pounds and
dollars, now started framing their policy on the assumption that the
franc would have to be devalued and the mark revalued—probably
in such a way as to reduce the gap between them by around 20 per
cent.

In the end this was more or less what happened. But the process
of cut and thrust, all mixed up with French pride, the eclipse and
departure of de Gaulle, and the convolutions of a bitterly fought
German election, took almost a year, from the dramatic but inconclusive Bonn meeting of November 1968, to the final fixing of an
increased, and for a period, floating German rate in October 1969.

Almost throughout this period the pound, as one of the still-
vulnerable currencies, felt the wind of every shake and shudder in the
Paris–Bonn duel, and it passed almost without notice at first, that
the long-delayed benefits of devaluation were actually coming
through into the economic statistics. Early in September it was
announced that the balance of payments for the second quarter of
1969 had moved into surplus. The discovery that, for complicated
technical reasons, export figures had been significantly under-
estimated over a longish period put another £10 million a year on the
plus side of the trading account, reinforcing a goodish rise in overseas
sales altogether, and an even bigger post-devaluation jump in the
'invisible' receipts from banking, insurance, shipping and overseas
investments, all helped to push the net balance further into the
black. At the time of writing, Britain's payments on current and
long-term capital account have been running a surplus for the past
nine months at a rate equal to an annual £600 million (though this
may already be crumbling). The pound, prior to the June election,
had spent a whole four months above its $2·40 parity level without
benefit of official support, and could claim, at least for this so far
brief period, to be among the strongest currencies in an ever-shifting
world. The eminently respectable and responsible London *Financial
Times* has already written one leading article solemnly explaining
why an immediate revaluation is not essential.

That, then, is where the whirligigs of time have lately landed the international trading pound. The external position is at any rate strong enough to allow British citizens to take abroad more or less what they like, rather than the £50 a year which has been a symbol of the country's financial humiliation since the summer of 1966. And the course of other people's inflation has been such as to preserve, so far, a large part of the net competitive advantage gained by the lowered 1967 exchange rate. The net effect of devaluation, after allowing for all the small adjustments like dropping the rebate of indirect taxes and the extra cost of imported raw materials, was to make British exports approximately 7 per cent cheaper in overseas market (or alternatively 7 per cent more profitable for things like whisky, where demand does not significantly respond to price changes). By the end of the third quarter of 1969, according to the Treasury's December Monthly Economic Assessment, export prices were still between 4 and 5 per cent cheaper, in dollar terms, than they had been two years before, while almost all Britain's main competitors were appreciably dearer. Unit manufacturing costs, which had risen twice as fast as Germany's over the whole period 1954–67 (though Germany had accelerated a lot in the second half) were now running level pegging with all the big industrial countries in sterling terms, and a good deal lower than any of them in dollar terms, especially after the highly favourable franc–deutschmark adjustment.

But what about the pound actually located in people's pockets? Whatever international improvement there has been, it has certainly not translated itself very noticeably to the domestic scene. Although Mr Wilson's famous phrase, quoted at the head of the last chapter, was technically accurate enough—contrary to popular mythology, the pound did not buy 14·3 per cent less groceries, or fewer totalisator tickets on Monday, 21 November 1967, than it had on Saturday, 19 November—it could hardly stretch to cover the following twelve or twenty-four months. By November 1968 the retail price index had risen 5·5 per cent—well above the 3 per cent average for the first years of the Labour government—and 1969 put a further 5·4 per cent on top of that. By early 1970 the rate had accelerated to nearly 8 per cent. All the Merrett & Monk equations showing how much a working man—let alone a working director—needs to give himself a genuine pay increase are now at least twice as forbidding. With 5 per cent inflation a man with the average industrial wage of £24 a week now needs an annual increase of at least 6 per cent just to preserve his current living standard after paying his taxes. To get a 2 per cent uplift in real terms would take almost a 9 per cent rise, which is more or less in line with the current crop of big-union claims. The senior executive, at around £8,000, needs virtually 10 per cent to stay ahead of the game. The £13,000 a year main board member finds himself wistfully calculating just how far short of the necessary 17 per cent he is actually going to fall when the company accountants do their sums. Meanwhile, almost unprecedentedly, stagnation and inflation go together hand in hand.

That is the treadmill which the new government is going to have to slow down. Otherwise it is hard to see Britain hanging on to her hard-won gains of the last two years. And the onset of decimalization next February, which is bound to give at least some small, fortuitous (not to say gratuitous) twist to the price spiral is not likely to be any particular help, either.

The signs of the monetary times are everywhere, if you keep your eyes open, and we might as well close with a note on the economic significance of that well-known social phenomenon, the Boy Scout Movement. In the 1900s, when it started, and the 15s. cost of the uniform was an effective barrier to keep out the children of everyone below the skilled artisan and the middle-class clerk, it was laid down that in order to become a First Class Scout a boy had to be able to read and write and—at a time when sweets could be had for four ounces a penny—to have personally earned the sum of 6d. to put into his savings bank.

By the spring of 1970, however, circumstances had slightly changed. The Scouts at Taunton, in Somerset, sent out a circular letter to the people of the town announcing regretfully that they had been forced to discontinue the twenty-year-old festival known as 'Bob a Job Week' in which they were in the habit of performing any task offered to them for a flat rate of 1s. a time. From henceforth the event was to be rechristened, non-committally, Scout Job Week, and each job was expected to be paid for at a 'reasonable rate'. As the District Commissioner, Mr Ian Chalmers, said in his covering note: 'We would ask those who take advantage of the service we offer to remember that the value of the bob is very much less than when we began.' And as the bob goes, so goes the pound.

Main Sources and Books for Further Reading

General

ASHWORTH, William: *An Economic History of England, 1870–1939.*

BURNETT, John: *A History of the Cost of Living.*

BURNETT, John: *Plenty & Want.*

CLAPHAM, J. H.: *An Economic History of Modern Britain.*

COLE, G. D. H. & POSTGATE, Raymond: *The Common People, 1746–1946.*

DEANE, Phyllis & COLE, W. A.: *British Economic Growth, 1688–1959.*

FRIEDMAN, Milton & SCHWARTZ, Anna J.: *A Monetary History of the United States, 1867–1960.*

LANDES, David: *The Unbound Prometheus: Technological Change, 1750 to the Present Day.*

MATHIAS, Peter: *The First Industrial Nation.*

MITCHELL, B. R. & DEANE, Phyllis: *Abstract of British Historical Statistics.*

PEACOCK, Alan T. & WISEMAN, Jack: *The Growth of Public Expenditure in the United Kingdom.*

PHELPS-BROWN, E. H. & BROWNE, Margaret: *A Century of Pay.*

SAYERS, R. S.: *A History of Economic Change in England, 1880–1939.*

Theory of Money

BLOOMFIELD, Arthur I.: *Short-Term Capital Movements under the Pre-1914 Gold Standard.*

BRESCIANI-TURRONI, Constantino: *The Economics of Inflation* (Germany 1914–23).

CROOME, Honor: *Introduction to Money.*

CROWTHER, Geoffrey: *An Outline of Money.*

FETTER, Frank Whitson: *The Development of British Monetary Orthodoxy, 1797–1875.*

FRIEDMAN, Milton: *The Optimum Quantity of Money.*

HARROD, Roy: *Money.*

HIRSCH, Fred: *Money International.*

KEYNES, John Maynard: *The General Theory of Employment, Interest and Money.*

Q

KEYNES, John Maynard: *A Treatise on Money*.
LINDERT, Peter H.: *Key Currencies and Gold, 1900–1913*.
MORGAN, E. Victor: *A History of Money*.

Prelude

FEAVERYEAR, Sir Albert: *The Pound Sterling*.
FETTER, Frank Whitson: *The Development of British Monetary Orthodoxy, 1797–1875*.
LOYN, H. R.: *Anglo-Saxon England*.
MACKENZIE, A. D.: *The Printing of the Bank of England Note*.
SMITH, Adam: *Wealth of Nations*.
STENTON, Dorothy Mary: *The Early Middle Ages*.
WHITELOCK, Dorothy: *The Beginnings of English Society*.

Victorian England

ALDBURGHAM, Alison: *Shops & Shopping, 1800–1914*.
ALTICK, Richard D.: *The English Common Reader*.
ARCH, Joseph: *Autobiography*.
BAGEHOT, Walter: *Lombard Street*.
BOOTH, Charles: *Life and Labour of the People in London*.
BRIGGS, Asa: *Victorian Cities*.
BRUCE, Maurice: *The Coming of the Welfare State*.
CHAMBERS, J. D.: *The Workshop of the World: 1820–1880*.
CHAMBERS, J. D. & MINGAY, G. E.: *The Agricultural Revolution, 1750–1880*.
COLEMAN, O. C.: *Courtaulds, An Economic & Social History*.
COURT, W. H. B. (Ed.): *British Economic History 1870–1914: Commentary and Documents*.
FRIED, Albert & ELTMAN, Richard M. (Ed.): *Charles Booth's London*.
HALL, A. R. (Ed.): *The Export of Capital from Britain, 1870–1814*.
HOBSBAWM, E. J.: *Industry & Empire*.
HOBSBAWM, E. J.: *Labouring Men*.
HOBSON, J. A.: *Gold, Prices and Wages*.
INGLIS, K. S.: *Churches and the Working Classes in Victorian England*.
JENKS, Leland: *The Migration of British Capital to 1875*.
KELLETT, J. R.: *The Impact of Railways on Victorian Cities*.
LAYTON, W. T.: *An Introduction to the Study of Prices*.
LYND, Helen Merrett: *England in the Eighteen-Eighties*.
MANN, Tom: *Memoirs*.
MARSHALL, Alfred: *Principles of Economics*.
Morgan Grenfell, 1838–1954 (anon: privately printed).
MORRIS, James: *Pax Britannica*.

SAUL, S. B.: *The Myth of the Great Depression, 1873–1896.*
SAYERS, R. S.: *Gilletts in the London Money Market, 1867–1967.*
THOMPSON, F. M. L.: *English Landed Society in the Nineteenth Century.*
YOUNG, G. M.: *Victorian England.*

Early Twentieth Century

BASSETT, R.: *Nineteen Thirty-One.*
BEALES, L. & LAMBERT, R. S. (Ed.): *Memoirs of the Unemployed.*
BELL, Lady: *At the Works.*
BOWLEY, A. L. & HOGG, M. A.: *Has Poverty Diminished?*
BROCKWAY, A. F.: *Hungry England.*
CLARKE, Stephen V. O.: *Central Bank Co-operation, 1924–31.*
DANGERFIELD, George: *The Strange Death of Liberal England.*
DEARLE, M. B. E.: *The Cost of Living* (1926).
HARROD, Roy: *Life of John Maynard Keynes.*
JOHNSON, Paul Barton: *Land Fit For Heroes.*
JONES, David C.: *The Cost of Living for a Sample of Middle-Class Families* (1928).
KEYNES, J. M.: *Essays in Persuasion.*
LEITH-ROSS, Sir Frederick: *Money Talks.*
MOGGRIDGE, D. E.: *The Return to Gold, 1925.*
MOWAT, C. L.: *Britain Between the Wars.*
ORWELL, George: *The Road to Wigan Pier.*
OWEN, A. D. K.: *Survey of the Standard of Living in Sheffield.*
PHELPS BROWN, E. J.: *The Growth of British Industrial Relations.*
POLLARD, Sidney: *The Development of the British Economy, 1914–67.*
RICHARDSON, H. W.: *Economic Recovery in Britain, 1932–39.*
ROUTH, Guy: *Occupation and Pay in Britain, 1906–1960.*
ROWNTREE, B. Seebohm: *Poverty, A Study of Town Life* (1901).
ROWNTREE, B. Seebohm: *Poverty & Progress* (1941).
TODD, J. A.: *The Study of Prices* (1931).

Post-1945

ATKINSON, A. B.: *Poverty in Britain and the Reform of Social Security.*
BEVERIDGE, Lord: *Full Employment in a Free Society.*
BRITTAN, Samuel: *Steering the Economy.*
CARTTER, Allan Murray: *Redistribution of Incomes in Post-War Britain.*
CLARKE, Colin: *The Cost of Living* (1957).
COOPER, Richard N.: *The Economics of Interdependence.*
DOW, J. C. R.: *The Management of the British Economy, 1945–60.*

GARDNER, Richard N.: *Sterling-Dollar Diplomacy*.
GREGG, Pauline: *The Welfare State*.
HARROD, Roy: *A Policy Against Inflation*.
HUTCHISON, T. W.: *Economics and Economic Policy in Britain, 1946–66*.
MERRETT, A. J. & MONK, D. A. G.: *Inflation, Taxation and Executive Remuneration*.
ORGANISATION FOR EUROPEAN ECONOMIC CO-OPERATION: *The Problem of Rising Prices*.
ROWNTREE, B. Seebohm & LAVERS, G. R.: *Poverty & the Welfare State*.
SEERS, Dudley: *Changes in the Cost of Living Since 1938*.
SELDON, Arthur (Ed.): *Not Unanimous*.
SISSONS, Michael & FRENCH, Philip: *The Age of Austerity*.
STURMEY, S. G.: *Income and Economic Welfare*.
TITMUSS, Richard: *Income Distribution and Social Change*.
WALTERS, A. A.: *Money in Boom and Slump*.
WORSWICK, G. D. N. & ADY, P. H.: *The British Economy 1945–50*.
WORSWICK, G. D. N. & ADY, P. H.: *The British Economy in the 1950s*.
WYNN, Margaret: *Family Policy*.

Index